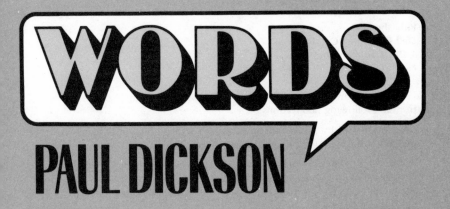

WORDS

PAUL DICKSON

A Connoisseur's Collection of
Old and New, Weird and Wonderful,
Useful and Outlandish Words

Illustrated (in part) by Paul Dickson

A DELL TRADE PAPERBACK

A DELL TRADE PAPERBACK

Published by
Dell Publishing Co., Inc.
1 Dag Hammarskjold Plaza
New York, New York 10017

Grateful acknowledgment is made for permission to reprint excerpts
from the following publications:

CALL MY BLUFF by Frank Muir and Patrick Campbell. Reprinted by
permission of the publisher, Methuen London Ltd. and Frank Muir.

OUNCE DICE TRICE by Alastair Reid, drawings by Ben Shahn.
© 1958 by Alastair Reid and Ben Shahn. By permission of Little,
Brown and Company in association with the Atlantic Monthly Press.

BURGESS UNABRIDGED by Gelett Burgess. Reprinted by
permission of Roland P. Carreker, Jr., and Miriam J. Carreker.

Dell ® TM 681510, Dell Publishing Co., Inc.

ISBN: 0-440-59260-7

Reprinted by arrangement with Delacorte Press
Printed in the United States of America

First Dell Trade Paperback printing—August 1983

PHOTO CREDITS

NASA: pages 13 (LEM), 83 (Talaria), 173 (Galactic Ghoul), 201 (Scarp), and 314
    (Afterbody)
U.S. Navy: pages 26 (Sneeze guard), 315 (Bollard), 316 (Davit), and 317 (Fluke)
Maritime Administration: pages 317 (Fishybacking) and 319 (Oilberg)
U.S. Forest Service: page 130 (Peavey)
Department of Energy: page 336 (Waldo)
Stars & Stripes: page 73 (Neckar)
U.S. Army: pages 12 (Jeep), 104 (Ground zero), 188 (Camofleur), 214 (Pidgin), 229
    (Punk [Army]), and 318 (Combat emplacement evacuator)
Bureau of the Census: page 18 (UNIVAC)

To my mother, Isabelle C. Dickson,
*who first taught me there was no
such thing as "mere words"*

CONTENTS

CONTENTS

To be a collector of language is an innocent occupation. The snatchers and hoarders of birds' eggs and of flowers first create a scarcity, then hunt down the rareties (or, even worse, hire others to go marauding for them) and finally exterminate the beauty which they crave. . . . To hunt words is to do no trespass.

—**Ivor Brown,**
from *A Word in Your Ear,*
a book in which he also termed
the English vocabulary
"the El Dorado of collectors"

INTRODUCTION

I am a word collector. I approach my collecting with a zeal that borders on the compulsive.

I confess that in the name of collecting I have labored through the pages of the driest scholarly publications to come up with the odd gem like *nutation,* which is the wobble in the earth's axis caused by the pull of the moon.

I candidly admit that I have spent time that could have been used increasing the GNP compiling totally useless but altogether satisfying collections including 315 phobias and 74 gums (from *alk gum* through *zapota gum*). I have just started a nut list because so many of the names for nuts are just that: *guru nut, vomit nut, hiccup nut,* and *canary nut* for starters.

I must report that in my hunt for words I have dug deeply into the trash barrels at the post office looking for odd catalogs that have been thrown away by people coming in to pick up their mail. If I had been too proud to dig in the trash, I would never have found the tool catalogs that enabled me to realize there is really no such thing as a plain pair of pliers but scores of differently named pliers, including nine that

Paul Dickson/1

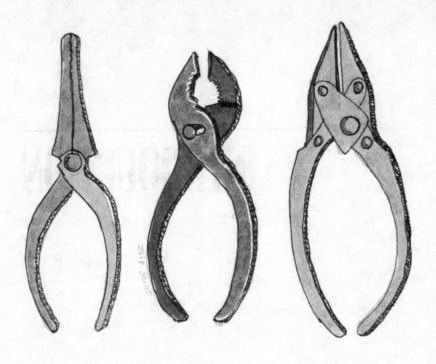

begin with the letter *L* (*lineman's side pliers, lock ring pliers, long-handle diagonal cutting pliers, long-nose pliers, long-nose side cutting pliers, long-nose tip cutting pliers, long-reach needle nose pliers, long-reach short-nose duckbill pliers,* and *looping pliers*).

I confess that the slightest nudge will set me off in a new direction. When I saw a sign in the window of a costume and novelty shop that proclaimed "Yes, We Have Warts!" (presumably the kind you glue on), it got me to respond, "Yes, but what kind of warts?" With the help of my *Dictionary of Dermatological Words, Terms and Phrases,* I learned that one can grow an *acuminate wart, anatomic wart, common wart, digitate wart, fig wart, filiform wart, flat wart, mosaic wart, necrogenic wart, para-ungual wart, periungual wart, plane wart, plantar wart, prosector's wart, senile wart, subungual wart, venereal wart,* or a *vulgar wart.*

Speaking of highly specialized dictionaries, I have become obsessed with them. My hoard now includes such works as *The Dictionary of Paper, The Dictionary of Gambling, The Glossary of Meteorology,* and

The Dictionary of Magic. I have three dictionaries of CB radio slang and am on the track of a second logging dictionary.

Besides odd dictionaries and words, I am forced to admit that I have accumulated verbal and written oddities of every description—talk show euphemisms for death ("She was just coming into her own when she left us"), punny names for places that cut and dress hair (Hair Today, Lunatic Fringe, Rape of the Lock, Delilah), and newspaper head-lines of parochial school football victories (Sacred Heart Slams Our Lady of Mercy, 38–6). I even have a small but prized collection of dictionary entries that lead you nowhere (one not very old dictionary tells one that *halicore* is a noun meaning *the dugong*).

I also admit to using up other people's time in my endless quest for collector's items. I have imposed myself on Army colonels, bartenders, and antique dealers in the hope of coming up with a great military acronym, drinking term, or name for an obscure piece of furniture. I always talk with people who sit next to me on airplanes, in the shame-less hope that I might be able to exploit them for a few professional terms. (This is how I found that half a computer *byte* is a *nibble.*) I have actually gone as far as to wangle an interview with Frederick C. Mish, the editorial director of the G. & C. Merriam Company, to nail down the answer to such important questions as whether or not *angry* and *hungry* are the only English words that end in *-gry*. (The answer is on page 194.) My visit to the Merriam Company, in Springfield, Massachu-setts, also enabled me to see its files, which contain 13 million citations on the use of individual English words. Quite simply, it is the greatest English word collection in the world.

Finally, I confess that I am not only a word collector but also a word exhibitionist who has long schemed to display parts of his collection. What follow are 52 separate museum-style displays containing ele-ments of the overall collection. I hope not only that you enjoy them, but that you get hooked in the process.

Paul Dickson/3

ACRONYMS

—An Assembly of Antic Abbreviations—

Although they existed before World War II, they have proliferated in the period from 1940 to the present. Even the name for them is modern, having been coined under federal auspices during the war. The term acronym (from *akros,* meaning tip, plus *onym,* name) was first introduced to scholars in a 1943 issue of *American Notes and Queries,* which traced it to Bell Telephone Laboratories, which had created the word as a title for a pamphlet to be used to keep workers abreast of the latest initialized titles for weapons systems and agencies.

Acronyms are best described as pronounceable formations made by combining the initial letters or syllables of a string of words. Two classic examples are SCUBA (Self-Contained Underwater Breathing Apparatus) and RADAR (Radio Detection And Ranging). These two have reached the highest status an acronym can reach: becoming so widely accepted that they are treated as regular words. Both scuba and radar are now commonly written in lower case.

Beyond the pure acronym there are two significant variations. The first is the initialism, which is a straightforward combination of letters rattled off as letters (ACLU, NFL, COD, etc.). The second is the port-

Paul Dickson/5

manteau or telescope word, which is a blend of two or more words in which the roots are generally recognizable. The U.S. Navy loves portmanteaus: NAVFORKOR (NAVal FORces, KORea) and BUPERS (BUreau of PERSonnel) are two of many.

For the word collector, acronyms offer a fertile and fascinating area. For one thing, new ones are being created daily. The Gale Research Co. of Detroit, which publishes the *Acronyms, Initialisms, and Abbreviations Dictionary* (AIAD), put out its first edition in 1960 with 12,000 entries. The seventh edition contains 211,000 entries, and the eighth edition due out in late 1982 will easily break the quarter-million mark.

I have collected acronyms for more than ten years. These are my favorites:

ABBA. Swedish pop group whose name is an acronym made up from the first names of the members of the group: Agnetha, Benny, Bjorn and Anni-frid.

ABRACADABRA. The name of a pioneering listing of 400 "space-age" abbreviations first published by the Raytheon Company in the early 1960s when a collection of 400 was sizable. ABRACADABRA stood for ABbreviations and Related ACronyms Associated with Defense, Astronautics, Business and RAdio-electronics.

ABSCAM. The famed code name for the FBI foray into the murky realm of congressional ethics. Early stories said the name stood for AraB SCAM, which disturbed some Arab-Americans. The FBI claimed it stood for "Abdul Enterprises," which was the name of the front group for the operation.

ACNE. Action Committee for Narcotics Education.

ACORN. ACronym-ORiented Nut.

ACRONYM. Allied Citizens Representing Other New York Minorities.

ADCOMSUBORDCOMPHIBSPAC. For a long time the longest acronym in captivity. It was, for instance, the longest of 45,000 entries in the 1965 edition of the *Acronyms, Initialisms, and Abbreviations Dictionary.* It is from the U.S. Navy and stands for "Administrative Command, Amphibious Forces, Pacific Fleet Subordinate Command." It has still not been bettered in English, although if it ever is, the new champion will probably come from the Navy, which seems to have a special penchant for long acronyms. Another Navy creation: COMSERFORSOPACSUBCOM for Commander, Service Force, South Pacific Subordinate Command.

According to the *1981 Guinness Book of World Records,* the

longest acronym is a 56-letter monster from the Soviet Union describing a scientific laboratory.

ALOHA. Aboriginal Lands Of Hawaiian Ancestry, the name of an effort to compensate aboriginal residents for lands taken from them in the nineteenth century.

ALTAIR. A third-generation acronym from the Pentagon that contains two earlier acronyms: ARPA (for Advanced Research Projects Agency) Long-range Tracking And Instrumentation RADAR (RAdio Detection And Ranging). Such acronyms embedded within other acronyms have been termed *tour de force acronyms* by Kenneth H. Bacon in an article on the subject in *The Wall Street Journal.* Bacon used the Army's SCAMPERS as an example: Standard Corps Army MACOM (for Major Army Command) PERsonnel System.

APPALLING. The creation of the late Theodore M. Bernstein, *New York Times* editor and expert on English usage, for Acronym Production, Particularly At Lavish Level, Is No Good.

APPLE. Advanced Propulsion Payload Effects. NASA.

ARISTOTLE. Annual Review and Information Symposium on the Technology Of Training and LEarning, an Air Force formulation. ARISTOTLE is but one of a number of classic acronyms. Among others, PLATO (Programmed Logic for Automated Training Operation), ADONIS (Automatic Digital ON-line Instrument System), SOCRATES (System for Organizing Content to Review And Teach Educational Subjects), and CASSANDRA (Chromatogram Automatic Soaking, Scanning ANd Digital Recording Apparatus).

BEDOC. Beds Occupied. Army.

BESS. The official acronym for no less than three NASA satellites: Biological Experiment Scientific Satellite; Biomedical Experiment Scientific Satellite; and Biomedical Experiment Support Satellite. The confusion this must generate may be incalculable.

BICYEA. Top-of-the-line ice cream from Bresler's. The name is an acronym for Best Ice Cream You Ever Ate. It is pronounced byeche-ya.

BIRD. One of many examples of what happens to the names of prestigious international organizations when their names are (1) translated and (2) acronymized. BIRD stands for *Banque Internationale pour la Réconstruction et le Dévelopement,* or the International Bank for Reconstruction and Development.

BIRDDOG. Basic Investigation of Remotely Detectable Deposits of Oil and Gas, U.S. Geological Survey experimental satellite project.

BOGSAAT. Acronym cynically applied to the preferred technique of high-level decision making in America. It stands for a Bunch Of Guys Sitting Around A Table.

BOLTOP. Better On Lips Than On Paper. It is one thing to write SWAK on the back of a sealed envelope, but if you really mean business, write SWAK—BOLTOP!

BOMFOG. Brotherhood Of Man, Fatherhood Of God. Term that journalists have attached to the pious, homily-ridden blather of politicians. It is often referred to as *bomfoggery*. Garry Wills traced the origin of the term in a column in *The Washington Star*. He said it dates back to a time when Nelson Rockefeller was on the campaign trail. "When Nelson was winding up a campaign speech, he liked to orchestrate the coda around 'the Brotherhood of Man Under the Fatherhood of God' and that phrase was a signal to accompanying journalists to sidle back toward the campaign bus."

BURP. BackUp Rate of Pitch, a NASA term for a type of spacecraft motion.

BUSWREC. Ban Unsafe Schoolbuses Which Regularly Endanger Children.

BX. According to NASA Reference Publication 1059, "Space Transportation System and Associated Payloads: Glossary, Acronyms and Abbreviations," published in January 1981, BX stands for box. What's more, FLG stands for flag and FLP for flap. One is hard-pressed to think of a situation in which an abbreviation that saves only one letter actually saves time and causes less confusion. The Army uses BX to refer to Base eXchange—an updated version of the old PX, which stood for Post eXchange.

Cabal. There is a legend that this word is an acronym for the names Clifford-Ashley-Buckingham-Arlington-Lauderdale, who were conspiratorially inclined cabinet members in the court of Charles II. It actually derives from the Hebrew *cabala* ("full of hidden mystery") but makes a nice story anyhow.

CAUTION. Citizens Against Unnecessary Tax Increases and Other Nonsense, a group formed in St. Louis in the early 1970s to oppose a large bond issue.

CHAMPION. Compatible Hardware And Milestone Program for Integrating Organizational Needs. Air Force.

CHASE. Cut Holes And Sink 'Em, a Navy Ammunition Disposal System.

CHRIST. Christians Heeding Righteousness Instead of Satanic Tyranny, a conservative religious organization.

CLAM. Chemical Low-Altitude Missile. Air Force.

COBOL. Common Business Oriented Language. A disproportionate number of names for computer programs, like COBOL, are acronyms or portmanteaus. For instance, FORTRAN is a compression of FORmula TRANslation, and JOVIAL stands for Joules Own Version International Algebraic Language. SNO-BOL stands for StriNg Oriented symBOlic Language, a language used in manipulating strings of symbols.

COED. Computer Operated Electronic Display.

COLA. Cost Of Living Adjustment.

COYOTE. Call Off Your Old Tired Ethics.

CROC. The Committee for the Recognition of Obnoxious Commercials, an ad hoc group that provides toilet bowl-shaped awards to reluctant Madison Avenue winners.

CRUD. Chalk River Unidentified Deposit. From the U.S. Nuclear Regulatory Commission's *Handbook of Acronyms and Initialisms*.

DACOR. An IBM product—DAta CORrection system—that had to be renamed when the acronym for its first name was figured out. It was originally called the Forward Error-Control Electronics System. Then there is the probably apocryphal story that Tiffany's once refused to inscribe the silver collection plates of the First Unitarian Church of Kennebunkport with initials.

DASTARD. Destroyer Anti-Submarine Transportable ARray Detector.

DIED. Department of Industrial and Economic Development (of Ohio). Now defunct.

DIMPLE. Deuterlum Moderated Pile Low Energy reactor, a British nuclear reactor.

DISCO. Defense Industrial Security Clearance Office.

DUA. Acronym that shows how acronyms have even created confusion on the other side of the moon. During the Apollo 12 mission while astronauts were making their seventh lunar revolution, there was some minor trouble in the spacecraft with an emergency light. Controllers in Houston diagnosed the problem and said,

> "We think we've figured it out, your DUA was off."
> After a few seconds of silence, the response from Apollo 12 was, "What is a DUA?"
> "Digital Uplink Assembly," replied Houston.

EGADS. The word created for the signal used to destroy a missile in flight: Electronic Ground Automatic Destruct System.

EIS. Environmental Impact Statement. This is the kind of acronym that bureaucrats and members of Congress use every day and expect the rest of us to understand. A few years ago a Massachusetts congressman proclaimed in a headline in a newsletter to constituents, "Air Force to do EIS on PAVE PAWS." PAVE PAWS is an Air Force radar system that stands for Precision Acquisition of Vehicle Entry-Phased Array Warning System. It is pronounced ice which makes it all the more confusing.

FADD. Fight Against Dictating Designers, one of several groups that sprang up to protest changes in fashion in the early 1970s. Another group whose sole purpose was to fight the turn from mini to midi was GAMS, for Girls/Guys Against More Skirt.

FAGTRANS. First Available Government TRANSportation, term used in military transportation orders.

FASGROLIA. The FASt GROwing Language of Initialisms and Acronyms, term created by *Time* in 1966 to describe the phenomenon.

FIDO. Freaks, Irregulars, Defects, Oddities; coin collector's term for a minting error.

FROG. Free-Rocket Over Ground, a U.S. designation for a Soviet missile system. (Author's note: When I first heard this acronym, I was a reporter covering military appropriations hearings in the late 1960s. Until I was told what FROG stood for, I was stunned by what seemed to be undue congressional and military alarm over small Russian amphibious animals.)

FUBAR. One of a series of military acronyms for things that are less than 100 percent perfect. FUBAR, which stands for Fouled-Up Beyond All Recognition (in the cleaner of two explanations), dates back to World War II. See also FUBB, FUMTU, JANFU, NABU, SAPFU, SUSFU, TARFU, and TUIFU. Snafu is the granddaddy of them all.

FUBB. Fouled-Up Beyond Belief.

FUMTU. Fouled-Up More Than Usual.

GASSAR. General Atomic Standard Safety Analysis Report. Nuclear Regulatory Commission.

GLCM/SLCM. These respectively stand for Ground-Launched Cruise Missile and Sea-Launched Cruise Missile and have been much discussed in Congress in recent years. They are pronounced GLICK-em and SLICK-em.

GOO. Get Oil Out, the name of the citizens' group formed in California after an oil slick appeared off Santa Barbara in 1969. GOO was such an appropriate and memorable acronym that it may have helped gain prominence for the group.

GOOBS. Going Out Of Business Sale. This acronym is used by a group of Washington, D.C.–area consumer groups that act as watchdogs over stores that are regularly going out of business.

GWIBIT. Guild of Washington Incompetent Bureaucratic Idea Throat-cutters. The term was coined in 1943 by Representative Karl E. Mundt, who explained at the time, "A gwibitizer is not to be confused with a kibitzer; the latter merely stands on the sidelines and watches while the former sits in the path of progress and trips those who traverse it."

HADES. Hypersonic Air Data Entry System.

HAIR. High Accuracy Instrumentation Radar.

HAL. A crypto-acronym from the film *2001: A Space Odyssey*. The demonic computer HAL of that film reveals his true identity when each letter of the acronym is advanced one letter to IBM.

HAWK. Homing All-the-Way Killer, an aptly named missile. HIP in the context of this weapon stands for HAWK Improvement Program.

HINT. Puckish TV news talk for Happy Idiot News Talk. HINT takes place, for instance, when the weatherperson is thanked for providing a nice weekend. "I'll see what I can dish out for the next few days," is the common humble reply.

HUT. Television business term for "Households Using Television." This sets up situations in which neighborhoods are described in terms of their "HUT percentages."

IGOR. Intercept Ground Optical Recorder. NASA.

INFANT. Iroquois Night Fighter And Night Tracker system, Vietnam-era weapons system produced for the Army by the Hughes Aircraft Co. Martial acronyms like INFANT and BAMBI (Ballistic Anti-Missile Boost Intercept) are among many innocuous or innocent-sounding names for fearsome realities. These fly in the face of Winston Churchill's admonition that things military should have military names and that he would never send British troops off to fight in something called Operation Begonia or the like.

IRAN. Inspection and Repair As Necessary. NASA.

JANFU. Joint Army-Navy Foul-Up. World War II. Not to be confused with JAAFU (Joint Anglo-American Foul-Up) or JACFU (Joint American-Chinese Foul-Up).

Jeep. Name derived from GP for General Purpose, which was the vehicle's original designation. Jeeps are now being phased out by the

Army, which will replace them with High Mobility Multipurpose Wheeled Vehicles, words that do not lend themselves to an easy nickname.

JOOM. Junior Observers Of Meteorology. During World War II, JOOMs were trained to replace Weather Bureau men who had gone to war. The JOOMs were just one of a number of wartime four-letter personnel including British FANYs (First Aid Nursing Yeomanry), WAVES (Women Accepted for Voluntary Emergency Service), and WASPs (Women's Auxiliary Service Platoon, an American unit in the Panama Canal Zone).

JUMPS. Joint Uniform Military Pay System.

KISS. Keep It Simple Stupid. Used when things are getting too complex.

LANTIRN. Low Altitude Navigation Targeting InfraRed system for Night. Air Force.

LEM. NASA's Lunar Excursion Module. This was the original name for the moon landing craft which was abruptly changed to LM for Lunar Module. *Time* reported in its February 14, 1969 issue, ''On the theory that Lunar Excursion Module (LEM) was too frivolous a name

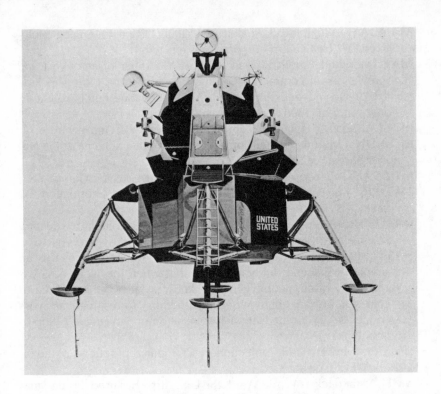

for the moon landing craft, NASA gravely renamed it Lunar Module, thus reducing the friendly LEM to the now unpronounceable LM."

Lox. Liquid oxygen. Gaseous oxygen, on the other hand, is gox.

MA. One of the 50 two-letter state abbreviations that the Postal Service has been pushing since 1963, when it began putting them on postmarks. MA is one of seven of these designations that begin with *M* —MA, MD, MI, MN, MO, MS, and MT. MA stands for Massachusetts but is easy to confuse with Maine and Maryland. No less confusing is AK, which stands for Alaska but could just as easily represent Arkansas, and CO, which is Colorado's code, not Connecticut's. Few people have mastered the two-letter system, which was, after all, designed for "machine readability." A growing underground is quietly subverting the system by writing out names like Ohio and Iowa and using old-fashioned abbreviations like Mass. and Penn. for what have officially become MA and PA.

MAD. Mutual Assured Destruction, a concept of nuclear planning.

MADDAM. Multiplexed Analog to Digital, Digital to Analog Multiplexed, a Coast Guard computer system term.

MAP. Modified American Plan. One of a number of acronyms and abbreviations in common use in the travel industry. Others include FIT (Foreign Independent Travel), APEX (Advance Purchase EXcursion), and B&B (Bed and Breakfast).

MECCA. Master Electrical Common Connector Assembly. NASA.

MOBIDIC. MOBIle DIgital Computer, a computer scheme at the National Bureau of Standards.

MUDPAC. Melbourne University Dual-Package Analog Computer.

MUDPIE. Museum and University Data Processing Information Exchange.

NABU. Non-Adjusting Ball-Up, contemporary addition to military screw-up acronyms of the FUBAR school.

NASA. The National Aeronautics and Space Administration. It is an example of a successful acronym in that when the word NASA is spoken or written, people generally know what is being referred to —that is, if they are not members of either the North American Swiss Alliance (NASA) or the National Association of Synagogue Administrators (NASA).

NECCO. New England Confectionery COmpany, producers of the famous NECCO wafers.

NMI. As far back as World War I, the U.S. Army has used this designation, which stands for No Middle Initial, to complete the names of servicemen. NMI, in effect, became the middle name of great numbers of Americans.

NOSE. National Odd Shoe Exchange.

NW-NW. No Work-No Woo. This was the slogan adopted by women workers at the Albina shipyards in Portland, Oregon, during World War II. According to the *Reader's Digest* of January 1944, "They agreed not to date men who were absent from work."

OAO. One And Only. Used at the U.S. Naval Academy for one's sweetheart.

OTE. OverTaken by Events. An abbreviation that has begun cropping up with regularity in Washington in recent years and applied to such things as reports and budget requests: "If we don't get that report done, we may be OTE."

ONO. Or Nearest Offer. Often used in British classified ads.

PAUSE. People Against Unconstitutional Sex Education. PAUSE is part of a galaxy of morally upright groups that also includes MOMS (Mothers for Moral Stability) and POPS (People Opposed to Pornography in Schools).

PAW. People for the American Way, a recently formed group to offset the influence of the new religious right wing. A good acronym for punny headlines: "TV Ads Give the Moral Majority PAWs," for instance, from *The Washington Post.*

PAWOB. Passenger Arriving WithOut Baggage. Airlinese for a human whose bags have been mislaid or misdirected en route.

PAWS. Phased Array Warning System. Air Force.

PITS. Payload Integration Test Set. NASA.

POGO. Polar Orbit Geophysical Observatory, a NASA satellite.

POLF. Parents Of Large Families. POLF was used during the period of the national "War on Poverty."

POME. Prisoner Of Mother England. According to the seventh edition of the *Acronyms, Initialisms, and Abbreviations Dictionary,* this term was originally used in the nineteenth century to describe a convict in an Australian penal colony and then developed into "pom" or "pommie" as a nickname for any Australian. "A second theory," says the *AIAD,* "maintains that the nickname is short for 'pomegranate,' a red fruit, and refers to the sunburn that fair-skinned Englishmen quickly acquire upon arrival in Australia."

Posh. Ultra-smart, luxurious. Although *Webster's Third* says that its origin is unknown, several British authors claim it to be an acronym for "port out, starboard home." Norman Moss explains in his book *What's the Difference? A British/American Dictionary:* "On the ships taking Britain's imperial officials and their families to the Far East, the most sought after and most expensive cabins were on the port side of the ship on the way out and the starboard side on the way home, because these were the ones most shielded from the strong sun." Frederick C. Mish, editorial director of the G. & C. Merriam Company, says that his company will continue to list it as a word of unknown origin until someone comes up with something more substantial than an anecdote.

POT. Portable Outdoor Toilet. Army.

POTUS. For the President Of The United States. According to *The Wall Street Journal,* this acronym was a favorite of Lyndon Johnson's but displeased Richard Nixon who preferred to be called "the President" and did away with POTUS. It was also used during the Kennedy Administration.

POWER. A federal writing course. Producing Organized Writing and Effective Reviewing.

PRAM. Productivity, Reliability, Availability and Maintainability office. Air Force.

QANTAS. For Queensland And Northern Territories Air Service. This proves the fact that one of the few ways to get around the *u*-follows-*q* rule is through an acronym.

RALPH. Reduction and Acquisition of Lunar Pulse Heights. NASA.

REPULSE. An FBI acronym–code name for an effort to counter attempts by Soviet KGB agents to link the name of J. Edgar Hoover with that of a Johnson Administration aide arrested on a morals charge in 1964. REPULSE stood for Russian Efforts to Publish Unsavory Love Secrets of Edgar.

ROSE. Rising Observational Sounding Equipment (which by any other name . . . ?).

RUNCIBLE. Originally a nonsense word created by Edward Lear, but now a no-nonsense acronym in computerdom standing for Revised Unified New Computer with Its Basic Language Extended.

SAHAND. Society Against "Have A Nice Day."

SANTA. Souvenir And Novelty Trade Association.

SAP. Society for Applied Spectroscopy.

SAPFU. Surpassing All Previous Foul-Ups.

SAPT. Special Assistant to the President for Telecommunications, during the Johnson Administration.

SATIRE. Semi-Automatic Technical Information REtrieval.

SCOPE. One of many examples of identical acronyms that read out differently depending on whether you are talking about a computer system or a program to rehabilitate former prisoners. Some of the SCOPEs: System for the Coordination Of Peripheral Equipment; Service Center Of Private Enterprise; Senior Citizens' Opportunities for Personal Enrichment; Supportive Council On Preventive Effort; Summer Community Organization and Political Education program; State Commission On Public Education; Scripps Cooperative Oceanic Productivity Experiment; and Select Council On Post-high-school Education.

SEE. Stop Everything Environmentalists. Derisive term with no official standing.

SINS. Situational Inertial Navigation System. Navy.

SLOB. Satellite Low Orbit Bombardment.

SMEAR. Span/Mission Evaluation Action Request. NASA.

SMOOSA. Save Maine's Only Official State Animal, a Maine group attempting to end the annual moose season.

Snafu. Situation normal: all fouled-up. This Army acronym, which goes back at least to World War II, has long ago achieved lowercase status. It now is listed as an adjective, a verb, and a noun in *The Random House Dictionary of the English Language.*

SOW. Statement Of Work. Common military usage.

SSSH! The Michigan-based Society for Silent Snowmobiles Here!

SOS. Many have claimed that this distress call is an acronym for Save Our Ship. Not so. It is simply three easily remembered and transmitted letters in Morse code.

ST. WAPNIACL. Prior to 1947, schoolchildren had only to recall the name of this saint and they would know not only the names of the government departments but the order in which they were created:

State 1789	Navy 1789
Treasury 1789	Interior 1849
War 1789	Agriculture 1862
Attorney General 1789	Commerce 1903
Post Office 1789	Labor 1913

This came to an end when War and Navy were consolidated in 1947.

SUNFED. Special United Nations Fund for Economic Development.

SUSFU. Situation Unchanged; Still Fouled-Up.

SWAG. Scientific Wild-Assed Guess. Good for bluffing, as in "I used the SWAG methodology."

SWAMI. Standing-Wave Area Motion Indicator.

TARFU. Things Are Really Fouled-Up.

3-H. The late Hubert H. Humphrey, as abbreviated by certain tabloids. "3-H Mourns RFK" was one headline using the abbreviation.

TUIFU. The Ultimate In Foul-Ups.

UNIVAC. UNIVersal Automatic Computer. The name of the world's first commercial computer, delivered to the Bureau of the Census in 1951.

UTTAS. Utility Tactical Transport Aircraft System, a helicopter that is pronounced yew-tahs.

VAMP. One of the earliest recorded acronyms, if not the earliest. VAMP, rediscovered by William and Mary Morris, dates back to the mid-nineteenth century, when it was used in fire-fighting circles for Voluntary Association of Master Pumpers. Prior to the Morrises' revelation, it had been broadly concluded that the earliest English acronym was ANZAC, a World War I designation for the Australian and New Zealand Army Corps.

WAFFLE. Wide Angle Fixed Field Locating Equipment.

WAMPUM. Wage And Manpower Process Utilizing Machines. This is one of many acronyms that have been used in recent years at the Bureau of Indian Affairs.

WANAP. WAshington National AirPort, as stated on military travel orders.

WASP. Wyoming Atomic Simulation Project.

WATSUP. The Wessex Association for The Study of Unexplained Phenomena, a group of British UFO spotters.

WBFP. Recent addition to the classified real estate advertising vocabulary. It stands for WoodBurning FirePlace.

WHAM. Cynical acronym used by U.S. troops during the war in Vietnam for "Winning the Hearts And Minds of the people."

WONG. Weight On Nose Gear. NASA.

WUMP. White, Urban, Middle class, Protestant.

ZEBRA. Zero Energy Breeder Reactor Assembly. British nuclear project.

ZIP. The Zip in Zip Code stands for Zone Improvement Plan.

2

ALIMENTARY WORDS

—A Hearty Ration of Terminology from Either Side of the Kitchen Door—

Acetarious. Applied to those plants that are used in salads.

Albedo. The white, pithy inner peel of citrus fruits.

Alliaceous. Having the definite aroma of garlic.

Analeptic. Word for a diet that is restorative or promotes good health.

Bain marie. Double boiler; two pots.

Bard. To cover meat with strips of bacon.

Basin. The dimple at the bottom of an apple.

Batrachivorous. Frog-eating. Along with *arachnivorous* (spider-eating) and *xylivorous* (wood-eating), one of the more obscure of the -vorous words in the language.

Beestings. The first milk taken from a cow after giving birth to a calf. It is especially rich.

Bench tolerance. Baker's term for the property of dough that allows it to ferment at a rate slow enough to prevent overfermentation while it is being made up into bread, buns, or whatever, on the bench.

Biggin. In a coffeepot, the perforated basket that contains the grounds.

Bletting. The spotted appearance of very ripe fruit when decomposition has begun.

Bobeche. A circular wax-catcher that fits over a candle. It is pronounced bowbesh.

Brackle. To break bread or cake or crumble into pieces.

Bromatology. A treatise or essay on food, a study of food.

Bullition. Act or state of boiling.

Burette. An oil and vinegar cruet.

Butterboat. A small gravy boat used for melted butter.

Cafetorium. A large room common to industrial and military installations that combines the functions of a cafeteria and an auditorium.

Carapace. The upper shell of lobsters, crabs, crayfish, and turtles.

Celtuce. Celery-lettuce. A lettuce with an edible stalk that tastes like a lettuce and celery combination.

Cepivorous. Onion-eating.

Chela. The large claw of a lobster or crab.

Chex. Imperfect but usable eggs sold at a reduced price. Chex are commonly eggs that are cracked but have membranes that are intact.

Clementine. The hybrid produced from an orange and a tangerine.

Cockle. Valentine candy in the shape of a heart with a small message on it like "Love Ya" or "Snookums."

Coll. Stew produced from odds and ends, originally a hobo term.

Coral. Lobster ovaries, which turn a bright coral when cooked.

Crumber. Miniature carpet-sweeper for removing crumbs from a table.

Cutlet bat. A bat or mallet used to pound cutlets or other meat before cooking them.

Daffle. An oven mop.

Deaconing. The practice of putting the best-looking food on top, such as putting the most attractive fruit on the top of a basket.

Dragées. Marginally edible silver balls used to decorate baked goods. Pronounced dra-zhees.

Dredge. To coat or sprinkle a piece of food with a dry ingredient such as flour, sugar, or crumbs. Not to be confused with dusting, which is coating pans or work surfaces with flour, starch, or some other dry substance.

Dredger. Device used by bakers to dredge sugar on your doughnuts.

Eggfoam. Lightly beaten egg used to coat food before it is fried.

Épergne. A series of bowls attached to an ornamental metal stem. Pronounced ip-urn.

Eupeptic. Having good digestion. The opposite of dyspeptic.

Farctate. Full; stuffed. A farctated diner is one who could not eat another morsel.

Farinaceous. Mealy.

Fletcherize. To chew thoroughly and specifically—30 chews to the mouthful. From American nutritionist Horace Fletcher, who advocated the practice.

Flipper. One of three specific terms for a deviant can of food. The three are *flipper, springer,* and *sweller.* The U.S. Navy, which uses a lot of canned goods, gives these three official definitions:

> **Flipper**—A can of food that bulges at one end, indicating food spoilage. If pressed, the bulge may "flip" to the opposite end. Can and contents should be discarded.
>
> **Springer**—A marked bulging of a food can at one or both ends. Improper exhausting of air from the can before sealing, or bacterial or chemical growth may cause swelling and spoilage.
>
> **Sweller**—A can of food having both ends bulging as a result of spoilage. Swellers should be discarded, except molasses, in which this condition is normal in a warm climate.

Franconia. Browned, as whole potatoes are browned with a roast.

Frill. Paper decoration on the bone end of a chop.

Frizzle. The process of cooking in fat until crisp and curled at the edges.

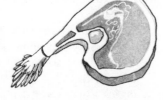

Funistrada. A "nonsense" food name created by the U.S. armed forces for use in preference surveys along with 375 real foods. The idea was to use *funistrada* and two other nonsense names as a control to see if those taking the poll were paying attention. In a 1974 survey *funistrada* ranked relatively high: above such things as eggplant, instant coffee, apricot pie, harvard beets, canned lima beans, grilled bologna, and cranberry juice. The other two nonsense names used in these surveys are *buttered ermal* and *braised trake,* neither of which rank as high as *funistrada.*

Gastrology. The science of keeping oneself well and happily fed.

Gemel. A fused set of cruets for oil and vinegar with divergent spouts.

Hachoir. A crescent-shaped chopping knife with two handles used with a circular bowl into which it fits. It is also called a *mezzaluna,* which is Italian for half-moon.

 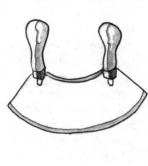

Kissingcrust. Crust formed where one loaf touches another in the oven.

Limequat. Lime/kumquat hybrid.

Limivorous. Mud-eating. Here is an old word that has not been used very often; however, with the advent of mud-wrestling as a bar sport it may be ready to come into its own.

Mandoline. Vegetable slicer with an adjustable blade. The vegetable is rubbed up and down the mandoline.

Mother. A slime of yeast and bacteria that forms on fermenting liquids that is used to get cider to turn into vinegar. Sediment in vinegar is also called mother.

Nidorous. Resembling the smell or taste of roasted fat.

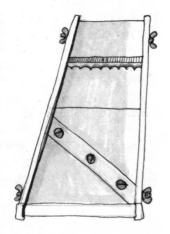

Nubbin. A small or imperfect ear of corn.

O'Brien. A style of preparing sautéed vegetables with pimentos and diced green peppers.

Oligophagous. Eating only a limited number of specific foods.

Papillote. Frilly paper hat used to decorate the end of a cutlet or other bone. Pronounced pappy-lote.

Piggin. A wooden tub having a handle shaped by continuing one of the staves above the rim. Today small piggins are often found in restaurants as butter holders.

Pipkin. A tiny pan for melting butter.

Plumcot. Plum/apricot hybrid.

Pobbies. Small pieces of bread that have been squashed together with milk and fed to birds and baby animals.

Poltophagy. The prolonged chewing of food, in which the food is reduced to a semiliquid state.

Prosage. Vegetarian sausage made of pure vegetable protein.

Ramekin. A small individual casserole.

Rasher. One thin slice of bacon.

Rimmer. Implement for ornamenting the edge of a piecrust.

Roasting jack. Device for turning a roasting spit.

Roux. A mixture of flour and fat used in cooking as a thickening agent. Rhymes with blue.

Runcible spoon. A three-pronged fork, curved like a spoon, that is usually used for serving. Runcible is a nonsense word coined by Edward Lear. Originally Lear variously applied the word to spoons, hats, cats, and geese.

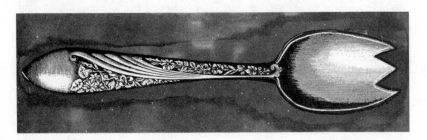

Runnels. Runways that appear on platters to catch juices.

Rutmus. Mixture of mashed potatoes and turnip with hot butter sauce.

Scotch hands. Two wooden handles used for shaping balls of butter.

Semese. Half-eaten.

Skirt. The technical term in the ice cream business for the little extra globule of ice cream that appears at the base of a scoop of ice cream on a cone. Certain ice cream scoopers have been advertised for their ability to avoid "overserving and wasteful skirt."

Sneeze guard. The clear plastic or glass shield that hovers over salad bars, cafeteria lines, and the like.

Sugar spots. The name for the brown flecks that appear on banana skins.

Tiffin. Midmorning snack or luncheon.

Tomalley. The "green stuff" of cooked lobster. It is the liver of the creature, and to many it is a great delicacy. "[It] is the quintessence of the creature and the nearest we mortals can come to the ambrosia of the Greek gods" is what writer Robert P. Tristram Coffin wrote in a typical tomalley testimonial.

Tomato shark. Implement used in peeling and removing stems from tomatoes.

Turophile. Cheese fancier. A coinage of Clifton Fadiman's.

Veganism. Extreme vegetarianism. A vegan excludes dairy products as well as meat.

Wham. Meatless ham made of textured soy.

Whye. Cross of wheat and rye.

Yingling. Candy made of peanuts, butterscotch chips, and Chinese noodles. The mix is boiled and formed into a small haystack.

Zarf. Holder for a handleless coffee cup. Contemporary zarfs are made of plastic.

Zester. A small rake-like tool used to shave the top layer of skin from an orange or lemon. These shavings are used to flavor such things as sauces and icings.

ANIMAL TALK

—Words from the Other Species—

Aculeate. Equipped with a sting (adj.), or an insect with a sting (noun).
Anoestrum. Period between the "heats" of animals.
Baculum. Small bone in the penis of certain mammals.
Barbel. A slender tusk-like appendage that appears on the lips of certain fish.

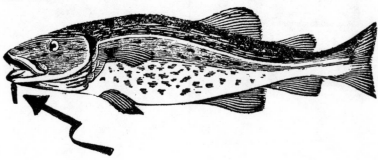

Byssus. The "beard" that mollusks use to attach themselves to rocks and other objects. Rhymes with vices.

Calks. The projections at the ends of horseshoes that help horses keep their footing.

Carapace. The upper body-shell of tortoises, lobsters, crabs, and other crustaceans.

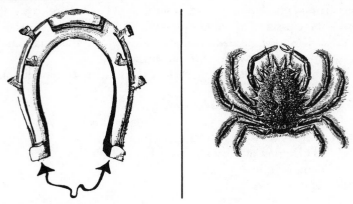

Corvine. Crow-like; pertaining to a crow.

Croches. The small knobs on the antlers of deer and other similarly antlered animals.

Cygnet. A young swan.

Dew-claw. The little claw behind a dog's foot; the false hoof of a deer.

Dewlap. The loose skin that hangs from the neck of an ox or cow.

Dowcet. A testicle of a deer or rabbit.

Dzo. Animal created by crossing a cow and a yak.

Eft. The name for a newt during the period of its life when it lives on land.

Ephemeromorph. Biologist's term for forms of life that are so low they cannot be classified as either animal or vegetable.

Epizootic. Describing a disease that is widespread in animals, as opposed to epidemics, which are human.

Flews. The large upper lips of certain dogs, such as bloodhounds, which hang down pendulously.

Fornix. The upper shell of an oyster.

Furcula. The clavicular bone of a bird; the wishbone.

Gablocks. Spurs used by fighting cocks.

Geep. The offspring of a sheep and a goat, also called a *shoat.*

Grilse. Young salmon.

Gruntle. The snout of a pig.

Hinnable. Able to neigh or whinny.

Hinny. The offspring of a horse and a she-ass.

Implumous. Without feathers.

Joey. A baby kangaroo.

Jumart. The offspring of a cow and donkey.

Labtebricole. Living in holes.

Mordacity. Likely to bite, a biting quality.

Nasicornous. Having the horn on the nose.

Nide. A single hatching of pheasants.

Nuddle. To rub or push with the nose; to press close to the ground with the nose, as an animal does.

Pannage. Pig food. This term is more commonly used in Britain than America.

Petulcous. Butting like a ram. Overly aggressive.

Ranarium. A frog farm.

Scut. A very short tail, such as that of a hare.

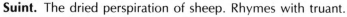

Suint. The dried perspiration of sheep. Rhymes with truant.

Tantony. The smallest pig in a litter.

Trocar. Tool inserted into a bull or cow to relieve intense gas pressure that sometimes results from eating too much clover. In a recently

revealed letter that Harry Truman sent an old friend in 1951, the former president said he wished he could apply a trocar to the "stuffed shirts" in government. "You know what happens when you stick one of them into an old bull that's clovered. The report is loud and the wind whistles—but the bull usually comes down to size and recovers."

Ungual. Pertaining to or having a nail, hoof, or claw.

Wattle. The fleshy growth on the neck or face of the turkey and other fowl. Also known as a *snood.*

Weanel. A newly weaned animal.

Wether. A castrated male sheep.

Yakalo. An animal that is half yak and half buffalo.

Zebrula. The product of the union of a horse and zebra.
Zum. A cross between a yak and a cow.

4

ANTONYMS

—An Aggregation of
Rare Counter Terms—

Often one form of an English word is much more popular than its opposite. Here are some of the more unusual antonyms I have collected.

Adiabolist. To the devil what an atheist is to God.

Amitular. Auntly actions and qualities. Created by Bergen Evans to rectify a "reprehensible omission" of the English language, which has never had a counterpart for *avuncular,* which refers to uncle-ish behavior.

Antapology. The reply to an apology; saying "That's all right" after someone has apologized for stepping on your foot.

Ante-jentacular. Before breakfast, as opposed to the more commonly heard *post-prandial* (after dinner).

Autonym. A writer's own name; the opposite of pseudonym.

Cacophemism. Using a harsh or cruel expression where a milder one would be proper; the opposite of euphemism. Some would argue that a *dysphemism* is another opposite—albeit in the other direction—of euphemism. Using a disparaging or belittling term to describe something that deserves more is a dysphemism. It is, for instance, dysphemistic to speak of a mansion as a shack or a BMW as a jalopy.

Ciplinarian. One who teaches disorder. The opposite of disciplinarian.

Clairaudient. Able to hear things not actually present in the same manner that a clairvoyant is able to see things not actually present. A *clairsentient* is able to perceive sensations not actually present.

Cuckquean. A female cuckold.

Dystopia. The opposite of a Utopia, such as the state imagined in George Orwell's *1984* or the film *Rollerball*. *Anti-utopia* is another term used to describe this state.

Gruntle. To put in a good humor. It is the positive opposite of disgruntle and is seldom used, for the simple reason that it sounds like a bad-humored word. A marvelous collection of "Words Rarely Used in Their Positive Form," from Advertent (giving attention—the flip of inadvertent) to Wieldy (strong; manageable—not unwieldy), appears in *The Book of Lists #2* by the Wallace family.

Illth. The opposite of wealth.

Marcidity. The state of great leanness. Obesity's opposite extreme.

Merman. The male counterpart of the mermaid.

Misandry. Female hatred of males. A rare word for the female equivalent of misogyny.

Monoglot. Unlike the polyglot or the person who is bilingual, the monoglot speaks only one language.

Nescience. Ignorance—a far cry from prescience.

Nullibicity. The ubiquitousness of ubiquitousness as a word leads to the question of its opposite. Nullibicity is the state of being nowhere. *Nullibiety* means the same thing.

Paravail. The opposite of paramount.

Pedipulate. Manipulation by foot.

Pessimal. Optimal's opposite.

Philogynist. A lover of women; the misogynist's opposite number.

Sannup. Squaw's husband; married male Indian.

Sedentes. Those who remain in one place; the opposite of migrants. Prounced said-en-tays.

Spintry. Male whore.

Tarassis. Male equivalent of hysteria. *Hysteria,* which borrows from the Greek for uterus (the same borrowing used in hysterectomy), is the female form of tarassis.

Ubiety. Thereness; being in a place; the opposite of absence.

Urning. A word for a male homosexual. The equivalent of lesbian, which exclusively refers to a female homosexual. An extremely rare word, which was reintroduced in Theodore M. Bernstein's *Dos, Don'ts & Maybes of English Usage.* He hunted the term down in reaction to the common belief that there was no English word for exclusively male homosexuality. The word is pronounced oorning and the practice is *urningism.*

Another possibility is *comasculation,* which appears in Josefa Heifetz Byrne's collection of words, *Mrs. Byrne's Dictionary,* and is defined as "homosexuality between men."

BLUFF WORDS

—A Swarm of Stumpers—

Call My Bluff is the name of the long-popular British television game show that pits two teams of three against each other. A word is given to team A along with its proper definition. Team A then presents the true definition along with two outlandish fabrications to team B, whose job is to sort out the right definition. B is then given a word, and the team with the most successful record at the end of the show wins. The only rule that must be kept in mind is that one of the three definitions given must be true.

To give an example of how it works, here is how the word *bonze* was handled by the mainstays of the show, Frank Muir and Patrick Campbell, which is quoted from their book, *Call My Bluff:*

a) *"Bonze"* is a rather secret trade-word still used in the world of bootmaking, especially among the high-class gentlemen's bootmakers in St. James. A bonze is the tracing made of the outline of a customer's foot from which, of course, the "last" is cut. At one particular bootmaker's they still have the bonzes of Lord Nelson and Disraeli, and of at least one duke of whom it is said in the trade that he had "a bonze like a boat."

b) *"Bonze"* is derived from the Portuguese word *"Bonzo,"* and is an impolite but not necessarily offensive name for a Japanese clergyman. You might wonder why the Portuguese, who live a very very long way away from the possibility of seeing even a Japanese layman, would feel the need for an impolite word for a Japanese cleric, but they do, and it's "bonze." It's also impossible to understand why some English dogs are called Bonzo, but they are.

c) *"Bonze"* was a game resembling ninepins which was prohibited-by-statute, during the fifteenth and sixteenth centuries, on the grounds that it was knocking over too many public figures. It wasn't played in a pub or bowling alley, but out-of-doors, where there was more room for power-play bonzing: i.e., bashing hell out of ninepins painted to look like the government of the day.

The correct answer is *b.*

Let us now move on to a collection of real words and their real definitions that are ideally suited to *Call My Bluff* and other recreational wordplay.

Acinaceous. Consisting of or full of kernels.
Anomphalous. Without a navel. Medieval paintings of Adam and Eve often showed the couple anomphalously.
Apricate. To bask in the sun; to sunbathe.
Asitia. Lack of appetite; dislike of food.
Aspergillum. Rod or brush used for sprinkling holy water.

Bagasse. Sugarcane refuse.
Bandoline. A hairdressing made from quinces.
Banghy. Porter's shoulder yoke in India. Also, *bangy.*
Bastinado. That form of torture in which the tortured is beaten on the soles of his feet with a stick or rod.

Bottomry. A loan to equip or repair a ship.

Burke. To kill by suffocating with your hand or a wet plaster. Named after a William Burke who with an accomplice killed 15 people in this manner and sold their bodies to medical students for dissection. The method was employed because it left no telltale marks of violence. (Burke was hanged in 1829 in Edinburgh.) The word is also used figuratively in the sense of stifling or smothering an investigation or other proceeding.

Capoletti. Triangular-shaped ravioli.

Cenotaph. A tombstone in memory of someone buried somewhere else at some other time.

Circumforaneous. Wandering from house to house.

Chiliomb. The sacrifice of 1,000 animals.

Chryselephantine. Made of gold and ivory.

Coruscate. To give off glitter or sparkles of light; to be brilliantly witty.

Cratch. A crib for corn and other grain, which is raised off the ground to protect its contents from water, rodents, and other hazards.

Cromlech. Prehistoric table-like monument made by placing a flat rock on top of two vertical rocks or a circle of rocks. Pronounced chrome-leck.

Danegeld. Public blackmail. A danegeld was occasionally levied to pay off the Danes who invaded England in the days before William the Conqueror.

Eellogofusciouhipoppokunurious. Very good; very fine.

Eriff. A two-year-old canary.

Errhine. Made to be snuffed into the nose.

Exigent. Urgent; needing immediate attention. A good word to use on packages and letters, since everybody else writes *rush* or *urgent*.

Fenks. Whale blubber refuse; rotten blubber. At one time used as manure in farming.

Fescue. A small stick used by teachers to point to specific letters or numbers.

Flabellum. A large fan carried by attendants to the Pope; or, a fan used to keep flies away from the Communion wine.

Futtocks. The upright curved ribs of a ship coming up from the keel.

Gadroon. A small-scale, ruffle-like ornamentation used on furniture and silver as a decorative edging.

Ganch. To execute by impaling on hooks.

Gelogenic. Tending to produce laughter.

Helminthous. Infested with worms.

Hippocaust. The burning of a horse in sacrifice.

Ichor. In mythology, the fluid that ran instead of blood in the veins of the gods.

Ignivomous. Vomiting fire.

Paul Dickson/39

Impavid. Without fear.

Izzard. Ancient term for the letter *z*.

Jargoon. A second-rate zircon.

Keckle. To preserve from chafing by covering with canvas, tape, or whatever. A cable is sometimes keckled with rope. Primarily a nautical term.

Kex. Dried hemlock. It is an antiquated word that has come back into its own with the advent of Scrabble.

Kheda. An enclosure for capturing wild elephants.

Mansuetude. Tameness; sweetness of temper.

Meniscus. The curved upper surface of liquid in a tube.

Mesothesis. That which is put in the middle to serve as a balance, or compromise, to opposing principles.

Mulm. The organic sediment that gathers at the bottom of an aquarium.

Musnud. The cushioned throne of an Indian prince.

Myocide. An agent that kills mold.

Nigroglobulate. To blackball.

Noria. An apparatus for raising water, made up of buckets attached to a wheel.

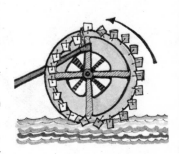

Nummamorous. Money loving.

Ogygian. Incomparably ancient, antediluvian. Pronounced oh-gigi-ann.

Ormolu. Bronze or brass that has been gilded.

Podsnappery. Self-satisfied philistinism. From the character Podsnap in Dickens's *Our Mutual Friend*.

Ptarmic. That which causes sneezing.

Pushkin. A strainer hung on a barrel faucet to catch and strain cider, vinegar, or whatever.

Quisquillous. Made of rubbish.

Rammish. Strongly scented.

Roorback. A false report circulated to damage the reputation of a political candidate. The term dates back to 1844 when two New York State newspapers published extracts from a book, *Roorback's Tour Through the Western and Southern States* by Baron von Roorback, which contained libelous material about presidential candidate James K. Polk. Among other things, he was accused of being involved in the slave trade. The book and its author were both nonexistent.

Rundle. Another word for a ladder rung. A completely superfluous word since rung rings so true.

Sanguisugent. Bloodsucking.

Saponify. To convert to soap.

Scissel. The strip of metal from which the blanks for coins have been cut. Rhymes with missile.

Scree. A pile of debris at the base of a cliff.

Sectile. Capable of being cut easily with a knife.

Silurian. Terribly old. The Silurian is part of the Paleozoic era. Mark Twain used the word to indicate doddering old age.

Sjambok. Whip made from rhinoceros or hippopotamus leather.

Spraints. The droppings of an otter.

Stummel. The shank and bowl of a wooden pipe—that is, all save the stem.

Ucalegon. A neighbor whose house is on fire.

Urbacity. Excessive or foolish pride in one's city.

Withy. Flexible and tough.

Yclept. Denoting called or named. It is the past participle of the archaic verb *clepe*. Pronounced ee-klept.

Ylem. The primordial stuff from which the various elements of matter were formed—neutrons, protons, etc. Pronounced eye-lem.

BODY ENGLISH

—Words for Things
You Can't Run Away From—

Aconal. Relating to the elbow. An archaic term with a host of possible modern applications ranging from mass transportation to pro basketball.

Acronyx. Ingrown nail.

Albuginea. The white of the eye.

Aspectabund. Of a pleasantly changing countenance.

Axilla. The armpit.

Blype. A piece of skin that peels off after a sunburn.

Buccula. Double chin.

Canthus. The point at either end of each eye where the upper and lower lids meet.

Carminative. Relating to farting; that which induces gas.

Cerumen. Earwax.

Chaetophorous. Bristle-bearing; in need of a shave.

Cilia. An eyelash.

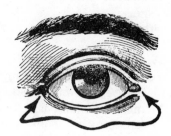

Circadian. Having to do with bodily cycles, such as those that are interrupted by jet air travel.

Columella. The fleshy part of nose, just above the lip, that separates the nostrils.

Dolichopodous. Having long feet.

Dorsum. The back part of the tongue.

Embrasure. The space between your teeth.

Exungulation. Paring the nails.

Frenulum. The thin muscle under the tongue.

Furfuration. The falling of dandruff from the scalp, or other situations in which dead skin falls in small particles.

Gelasin. A dimple in the cheek that appears when one smiles.

Geromorphism. Looking older than one's real age.

Gnathion. The tip of the chin.

Gonion. Either end of the lower jaw, the part just under the ear.

Hallux. Big toe.

Hirci. Armpit hair.

Hircinous. With a goat-like odor.

Horripilation. Shuddering sensation, as one feels when his "hair stands on end"; gooseflesh.

Lentiginous. Heavily freckled.

Lunula. The white crescent-shaped part of the fingernail at the base of the nail.

Macrotous. Large-eared.

Melanotrichous. Having black hair.

Noop. The sharp point of the elbow. An old word, native to Scotland.

Olecranon. The "funny" bone; the projecting bone of the elbow.

Opisthenar. The back of your hand.

Oscitancy. The act of yawning.

Ozostomia. Evil-smelling breath.

Pandiculation. A stretching and yawning, as people are likely to do just before or after sleeping.

Papuliferous. Pimply.

Patrician. One of many named beards. The Patrician is a very long, very full, almost rectangular beard like the kind that adorns the Smith Brothers on the cough drop box. A beard-trimming chart, published by W. W. Bode of San Francisco around 1888, names no less than 15 distinct styles including the Dundreary, the Vidette, and the San Diego.

Paxwax. The neck tendon—properly, the nuchal ligament.

Philosity. The degree of body hair.

Philtrum. The indentation in the middle of the upper lip just below the nose. This word's rarity was underscored by an editorial that appeared in *The Washington Star* in late 1969, which expressed distress that "there is still no satisfactory term in English to describe . . . the indentation in the center of the human upper lip." One of the paper's readers set the record straight.

Plook. Scottish word for a nasty boil or pimple.

Podobromhidrosis. Smelly feet.

Popliteal. Pertaining to the hollow area at the back of the knee.

Pronasale. The tip of the nose.

Pseudosmia. False smell-perception.

Purlicue. The space between the index finger and the extended thumb.

Pygia. A pain in the rump.

Racklettes. The little lines on the wrist.

Sciapodous. Having very large feet.

Sexdigitism. The state of having six fingers or six toes on a hand or a foot.

Simity. The state of being pug-nosed.

Snoach. The breath through the nose.

Steatopygic. Having excessively fat buttocks; bottom-heavy.

Sternutation. Sneezing.

Tragus. The fleshy bump on your ear between the face and the ear cavity.

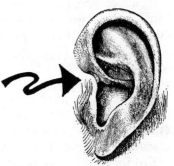

Ulotrichous. Having woolly hair.

Uvula. The thing that hangs down from the back of the mouth (which children invariably think is a tonsil).

Vellus. Short, downy hairs found on the face, not beard hairs.

Vomer. The slender bone separating the nostrils.

BRITISH WORDS

—A Volley of
Transatlantic Differences—

This collection of lesser-known examples of British English was, in part, inspired by a series of quotations:

"Yet another foreign language—that of America."
—George Bernard Shaw

"We and the Americans have much in common, but there is always the language barrier."
—Oscar Wilde

"We are divided by a common language."
—Winston Churchill

"The chief editor of the *Oxford English Dictionary,* Robert Burchfield, said recently that in 200 years or so Americans and Britons would be unintelligible to one another and not be able to converse without a translator."
**—*The New York Times,* Editorial,
July 31, 1981**

Paul Dickson/45

Affiliation order. A paternity suit.

Anorak. A parka.

Anti-bounce clip. Shock absorber.

Arterial road. Main road.

Articulated lorry. Tractor-trailer truck.

Aubergine. Eggplant.

Balaam. Fillers; items used to fill newspaper space.

Bed sitter. Studio apartment.

Beetroot. Beet.

Big dipper. Roller coaster.

Boffin. A scientist or technologist.

Bombing. Actors in England say a play is bombing if it is doing very well.

Boot-to-bonnet. Bumper-to-bumper.

Boudoir biscuits. Ladyfingers.

Bradshaw. Timetable.

Brainstorm. Sudden madness.

Brake-van. Caboose. It is also called a *guard's van.* In England a caboose is the kitchen on the deck of a ship.

Brothel-creepers. Men's shoes with thick crepe soles.

Bumf. Paperwork. This commonly used term of the British bureaucracy comes from the World War II slang word for toilet paper, *bumfodder.*

C-3. 4-F.

Capsicum. Green or bell pepper.

Casual ward. Flophouse.

Cause-list. A trial calendar.

Charabanc. Long-distance sight-seeing bus.

Chicory. Endive.

Chucker-out. Bouncer.

Cleg. Horsefly.

Clever biscuit. Noel Coward's translation of "smart cookie" into English.

Codswallop. Nonsense.

Corf. A creel, a container for fish.

Cornet. Ice cream cone.

Cos. Romaine.

Counterfoil. Check stub.

Courgettes. Zucchini squash.

Crisps. Potato chips. British *chips,* on the other hand, are French fries.

Cubby. Glove compartment.

Cuffuffle. Slang for a dither; agitated.

Cutting. A newspaper clipping.

De-bag. To take someone's pants off as a joke.

Dixie. Iron pot.

Doggo. To be in hiding, to lay low.

Dogsbody. A person who will do the odd jobs that nobody else wants to do.

Drawing pins. Thumbtacks.

Dual carriageway. Divided highway.

Endive. Chicory.

Erk. The lowest rank in the Navy or Air Force.

Face flannel. Washcloth.

Fanlight. Transom.

Fanny. The female pudenda.

Fish slice. Spatula or pancake turner.

Fixings. Hardware.

Fleck. Lint. On the other hand, *lint* in England means surgical dressing.

Flex. Electric cord.

Flyover. Overpass.

Fully found. All expenses paid.

Fusby. Fat and squat.

Gash. Spare parts or leftover parts that can serve as spares.

Gaudy. A university or college reunion dinner.

Gazump. To raise the price of something after someone has agreed to buy it. According to Norman Moss in his *What's the Difference? A British/American Dictionary,* "It comes from an archaic colloquial term 'gazumph,' to swindle, which in turn comes from the Yiddish."

Geezer. Hot-water heater.

Geyser. Hot-water heater.

Go-down. A warehouse when used as a noun.

Gooseberry. The fifth wheel at a party or other gathering.

Grabbe. To grope for.

Grotty. Inferior or shabby. Stems from *grotesque.*

Guggle. Gurgle.

Hairgrips. Bobby pins.

Hayter. A rotary mower. This began as a trade name but has since become the word for any such mower.

Hessian. Burlap.

Hoarding. A billboard.

Interval. Intermission.

Jacket potato. Baked potato.

Jollop. Gobble.

Kerb. Curb.

Kirby grips. Bobby pins. They are also known as *hair-slides*.

Ladder. A run in a stocking.

Layabout. Hobo or bum.

Lay-by. Roadside rest area.

Li-lo. Air mattress. Originally a brand name but increasingly being used for all air mattresses.

Lido. A public swimming pool. A municipal swimming pool is often called a *corporation swimming-bath.*

Locum. One doctor covering for another; a clergyman's temporary replacement.

Loose chippings. Gravel.

Mercer. A silk dealer; a shop dealing in expensive fabrics.

Motorway. Turnpike.

Multiple shops. Chain store.

Mutes. Professional pallbearers.

Nappy. A diaper.

Navvy. Construction worker.

Nissen hut. Quonset hut.

Noughts and crosses. Ticktacktoe.

Outdoings. Expenses (as in household expenses) and overhead (as in business overhead).

Pedestal. Toilet bowl.

Pelmet. Curtain valance.

Pillar box. Mailbox.

Pimp. Small bundles of kindling wood.

Pip. Annoy or make angry: "He gives me the pip."

Pip. To beat by a small margin.

Plait. Braid, as both a noun and the verb *to braid.*

Planning permission. Building permit.

Plimsolls. Sneakers.

Plough. The Big Dipper, a.k.a. the *Great Bear.*

Ponce. Pimp, both noun and verb.

Press stud. Snap fastener.

Putty. British nautical slang for muddy bottom.

Road diversion. Detour.

Roneo. To mimeograph or duplicate.

Run-away. A drain.

Shave hook. Paint scraper.

Skew-wiff. Cockeyed.

Slut's wool. A marvelous piece of British slang for dust balls or "dust bunnies."

Small ad. Want ad.

Stumer. A bad check.

Surgery. A doctor's office or the collection of patients in the office. To say that a doctor has a large surgery is to say he has an office full of patients.

Suspenders. A garter belt. (What Americans call suspenders are called braces in England.)

Terjubilee. Sesquicentenary; 150 years. A proper jubilee is 50 years.

Tick (someone) off. To reprimand.

Tiddler. A minnow.

Turn-ups. Trouser cuffs.

Twee. Self-consciously, or overbearingly, cute.

Undercut. Tenderloin.

Verge. The grassy strip at the edge of a highway.

Wellies. Galoshes.

Whitlow. Infected fingernail.

Winklepickers. Pointed shoes.

Zizz. A snooze or nap.

BURGESSISMS

—A Treasury of Rare Coinages
from an American Original—

Gelett Burgess (1866–1951) was an American humorist who loved tours-de-force. One of his favorites was minting words. He coined *bromide* (for a platitudinous bore) and *blurb* (a self-serving book announcement or testimonial), both of which have become part of the language. In 1914 he published *Burgess Unabridged: A New Dictionary of Words You Have Always Needed,* which contained scores of elaborately defined and illustrated words of his own manufacture. Today this brilliant work is largely forgotten and can only be found on the shelves of a few very large libraries. This is an outrage as it contains one major contribution to the language after another. In order to spark a Burgess revival, here are 40-odd annotated examples.

Agowilt. *n.* 1. Sickening terror, sudden unnecessary fear. 2. The passage of the heart past the epiglottis, going up.
   (The fear that comes the minute after you have thrown a burnt match in a wastebasket, the terror that comes after an unexpected elevator jerk, and the startle that comes when your foot reaches for the extra step that isn't there in the darkness are all examples sup-

plied by Burgess. Since this phenomenon was named, the automobile has brought with it countless new instances, ranging from the "Oh no! I've locked the keys in the car" agowilt to the sudden fear, which occurs when you have driven halfway to a vacation spot, that you have forgotten to turn the oven off.)

Allibosh. *n.* A glaringly obvious falsehood; something not meant to be actually believed; a picturesque overstatement.

(From seed catalogs to circus posters, Burgess found allibosh all around him, including "verbal alliboshes" too numerous to mention: "No, I don't think you're a bit too fat, you are just nice and plump.")

Bimp. *n.* A disappointment, a futile rage. *v.* To cut, neglect, or forsake.

(Burgess elaborates: "Did you get that raise in your salary on New Year's Day, or did you get bimped? Were you forgotten on Christmas? Did you draw to a flush and fail to fill? You got bimped. Did you find you had no cash in your pocket when it came time to pay the waiter? Did that firm cancel its order? Bimps!")

Bleesh. *n.* 1. An unpleasant picture; vulgar or obscene art. 2. An offensive comic-supplement form of humor. *a.* Revolting, disgusting, coarse.

Cowcat. *n.* 1. A person whose main function is to occupy space. An insignificant or negligible personality. 2. A guest who contributes nothing to the success of an affair; one invited to fill up, or from a sense of duty. 3. An innocent bystander.

Diabob. *n.* 1. An object of amateur art; anything improbably decorated; handpainted. 2. Any decoration or article of furniture manufactured between 1870 and 1890.

(Burgess had his eye on the hammered brasswork, tortured wood, hand-decorated linen, and tooled leather of his time. The most diabobical of today's goods are those colorful paintings on black velvet that are sold by the side of the road and invariably feature the Last Supper, the New York skyline, or Elvis in concert.)

Digmix. *n.* 1. An unpleasant, uncomfortable, or dirty occupation. 2. A disagreeable or unwelcome duty. *v.* To engage in a necessary but painful task.

(Burgess supplied many examples of the digmix, including dishwashing, fish cleaning, getting a divorce, and taking a child to the dentist.)

Drillig. *n.* A tiresome lingerer; a button-holer.

("The Ancient Mariner was a drillig," according to Burgess, along with many golfers, door-to-door book salesmen, and banquet speakers who note the late hour, promise a few short words, and then drone on for more than an hour.)

Drilligate. *v.* 1. To detain a person when he wants to go to work or get away. 2. To talk unceasingly at an inconvenient time.

Eegot. *n.* A fair-weather friend; one who is overfriendly with a winner. A success-worshiper.

Fidgeltick. *n.* 1. Food that is a bore to eat; anything requiring painstaking and ill-requited effort. 2. A taciturn person, one from whom it is hard to get information.

(Pistachios and artichokes are Burgess's prime examples of edible fidgelticks, while a human type would be a railroad official from whom you were trying to get information after an accident.)

Fud. *n.* 1. In a state of déshabille, or confusion. 2. A mess, or half-done job.

(Remarkably, Burgess created this word years before the invention of pastel-colored plastic hair curlers and the late-twentieth-century custom of proudly wearing them to shopping malls.)

Gefoojet. *n.* 1. An unnecessary thing; an article seldom used. 2. A tool; something one ought to throw away, and doesn't. 3. The god of unnecessary things.

Gixlet. *n.* 1. One who has more heart than brains. 2. An inveterate host; an irresistible entertainer.

(Among other things, a gixlet buys you a drink when you don't want one, pays your fare, and apologizes when he steps on your foot. "The Gixlet, in short," concludes Burgess, "is the joyous, friendly dog, that leaps with muddy paws upon your clean, white trousers.")

Gixlety. *a.* Brutal kindness; misguided hospitality; an overdose of welcome.

Gloogo. *n.* 1. A devoted adherent of a person, place or thing. 2. A married person in love with his or her spouse after the first year. 3. Anything that can be depended on. *a.* Loyal, constant. Foolishly faithful without pay.

Goig. *n.* A suspected person; one whom we distrust instinctively; an unfounded bias; an inexplainable aversion.

Gowyop. *n.* 1. A state of perplexity, wherein familiar persons or things seem strange. 2. A person in an unfamiliar guise.

(Gowyops commonly occur when we run into someone who used to have a beard or has gained 128 pounds since we last saw them.)

Gubble. *n.* 1. A murmuring of many voices. 2. Society chatter. *v.* To indulge in meaningless conversation.

("It's like some huge, slimy reptile, with a hundred mouths," he adds, "all murmuring.")

Gubblego. *n.* A crowded reception, a talking contest.

Hygog. *n.* 1. An unsatisfied desire. 2. An anxious suspense.

("Did you ever wait for a sneeze that wouldn't come?" Burgess asks. "It is a hygog.")

Hygogical. *a.* Unattainable; next to impossible.

Igmoil. *n.* 1. A quarrel over money matters; a sordid dispute. 2. The driving of a hard bargain; a petty lawsuit.

("To lose a friend through an igmoil is the most sordid tragedy of life.")

Impkin. *n.* A superhuman pet; a human offspring masquerading in the form of a beast; an animal that is given overabundant care.

(Burgess adds, "Impkins are canine and feline, but their parents are usually asinine.")

Jirriwig. *n.* 1. A superficial traveler. 2. The Philistine abroad. 3. A bromide in search of himself. *v.* To travel with one's eyes shut. To destroy opportunity.

Jujasm. *n.* 1. A much-needed relief; a long-desired satisfaction. 2. An expansion of sudden joy.

(The first warm day of spring, the moment a baby stops crying in the middle of the night, and a hot drink after a sleigh ride are all jujasmic commonplaces.)

Kripsle. *n.* A worrying physical sensation, an invisible annoyance absorbing one's attention.

(Kripsles abound, with two of the commonest examples being the emerging of a hole in one's sock and the real or imagined looseness of a tooth. Since this term was coined, millions have been made as Madison Avenue has exploited our fear of kripsles, especially those relating to odor. Burgess also gave us *kripsly,* an adverb that is magnificently displayed and understood in the sentence "Walking on spilt sugar is kripsly.")

Looblum. *n.* 1. A pleasant thing that is bad for one; rich, but dangerous, food. 2. A flatterer; flattery.

(Burgess's looblum list includes cigars, green apples, morning cocktails, cocaine, black coffee at night, and hot mince pie.)

Mooble. *n.* 1. A mildly amusing affair; a moderate success. 2. A person or thing over whom it is difficult to be enthusiastic.

(Burgess's further explanation: "The Samoans have a word which means, 'A-party-is-approaching-which-contains-neither-a-clever-man-nor-a-pretty-woman.' It's a mooble. Dancing with your own wife is a mooble—a fairly good play, a dinner-party where the menu makes up for the dramatis personae—moobles!")

Nodge. *n.* 1. The only one of its kind or set. 2. A person who doesn't "fit in"; a Martian.

(Like so many of these words, this one has immediate application. Odd socks, single gloves, and the person who shows up at a natural-food potluck in a tuxedo carrying a bag of Moon Pies will never again lack for a generic name in my mind.)

Nulkin. *n.* 1. The core or inside history of any occurrence. A true but secret explanation. 2. Facts known, but not told.

("Why is a book popular? Publishers strive in vain to discover the literary nulkin.")

Oofle. *n.* 1. A person whose name you cannot remember. 2. A state of forgetfulness regarding a friend or thing. *v.* To try to find out a person's name without asking. 2. To talk to an unknown person without introducing him to a nearby friend.

(This word is remarkable for two reasons. First, that it was not coined before 1914, and second, that once coined, such a useful word has been all but forgotten—*oofled!*)

Paloodle. *n.* One who gives unnecessary or undesired information. 2. Uncalled-for advice. 3. A recital of obvious details. *v.* To give the above; to assume omniscience.

Pawdle. *n.* 1. One who is vicariously famous, rich or influential. 2. A person of mediocre ability, raised to undeserved prominence. *v.* To wear another's clothes.

(Where was this word when we needed it? O Donald Nixon, O Billygate!)

Rowtch. *n.* One who has elaborate gastronomic technique. *v.* 1. To accomplish strange maneuvers over food by means of a knife and fork. 2. To eat audibly or with excessive unction.

(One could compile an encyclopedia of rowtching techniques, starting with some of the examples that Burgess identified—vegecide, for instance, which is the refined habit of cutting well-cooked vegetables with a knife and fork when a fork will do—and continuing to more recent developments. The modern salad bar alone provides a host of examples including the fabled "crouton drop," which is the ability to drop a full ladle of croutons on top of a salad plate that has already been loaded to the point where it would appear to be impossible to add anything more.)

Spillix. *n.* 1. Undeserved good luck; accidental success. 2. A luck stroke beyond one's normal ability.

(Spillix allows you to overhear a fascinating conversation, find money on the street, win a lottery, or score a hole in one.)

Tintiddle. *n.* 1. An imaginary conversation. 2. A witty retort, thought of too late, a mental postscript.

Udney. *n.* 1. A beloved bore; one who loves you but does not understand you; a fond but stupid relative. 2. An old friend whom you have outgrown.

(Burgess clearly understood and had compassion for udnies, having written of them, "You go to them in your troubles and you forget them in your pleasures. You hate to write to them, but manage to scrawl hasty and vapid notes.")

Voip. *n.* Food that gives no gastronomic pleasure; any provender that is filling, but tasteless. *v.* To eat hurriedly, without tasting.

("Every morning," explained Burgess, "millions of Americans go forth sustained for work, but cheated out of the pleasures of a real repast—they have merely fed on voip." To think that he identified voip decades before the introduction of synthetic eggs, engineered tomatoes, hamburger extenders, imitation potato chips, vending-machine pastry, and innumerable dry breakfast cereals.)

Wog. *n.* Food on the face; unconscious adornment of the person.

(A Burgess word that is pure genius. Once one has heard this word,

Paul Dickson/55

it is practically impossible to see someone with spinach or whatever on their face and not think "wog." Unfortunately, for a number of years this word was used in Britain as ugly pejorative slang for a nonwhite male. [It has been said to be an acronym for "wily Oriental gentleman."] One hopes that the Burgessism dominates. An indication that it may is that *The New York Times* columnist Russell Baker devoted his whole column of August 30, 1981, to various wogs—egg wogs, oily lettuce wogs, fish wogs—and what to do about them.)

Wox. *n.* A state of placid enjoyment; sluggish satisfaction.

("After your long tramp in the rain, after your bath and hot dinner, you sit by the fire in a wox.")

Yamnoy. *n.* 1. A bulky, unmanageable object; an unwieldy or slippery parcel. 2. Something you don't know how to carry. *v.* 1. To inflict with much luggage. 2. To carry many parcels at once.

Yowf. *n.* 1. One whose importance exceeds his merit. A rich or influential fool. 2. Stupidness, combined with authority.

("You find the yowf sitting at the Captain's table on shipboard; and at the speaker's dais at banquets. He is top-heavy with importance, and soggy with self-esteem.")

9

CURSES

—A Pack of Proposed Profanities—

Swearing is no longer worth a damn. Its effects have been subverted by forces ranging from the R-rated movie to the Nixon White House tapes. What is called for is a fresh start with a whole new set of obscenities and nasty epithets to work with. Admittedly, the words in my collection —old ones, new ones, and new applications of existing words—are not yet that shocking, but all that has to happen is for this book to get banned from a small-town library and we are in business.

Amplexus. The rutting of frogs and toads. Because of both the sound of the word and its meaning, amplexus deserves better than to be hidden away in the pages of unabridged dictionaries. It is a fine expletive: AMPLEXUS!

Asterisk. Stephen Leacock once suggested that this was a fine word for swearing. " 'Asterisk!' shouted the pirate," wrote Leacock. " 'I'll make it two asterisks,' snarled the other, 'and throw in a dash.' "

The written asterisk symbol also has a certain power. Burges Johnson in the introduction to his *Lost Art of Profanity* quotes from an opinion by Judge Hammond of the Supreme Judicial Court of Massachusetts:

The Watch and Ward Society of Boston years ago brought charges against a certain magazine for printing obscene matter, and my old friend the late Kendall Banning was forced to defend the publication. He felt sure that he could make a case, and during the train ride to Boston he had a sudden idea, and began jotting down such nursery rhymes as he could recall. Then he crossed out significant words and substituted asterisks. In court he asked permission to read these rhymes. They later appeared in a privately printed brochure which aroused delight or horror, according to the state of the reader's mind. A mere sampling will serve here:

> A dillar, a dollar
> A ten-o'clock scholar,
> What makes you *** so soon?
> You used to *** at ten o'clock,
> But now you *** at noon.

> Jack and Jill went up the hill
>   To *******
> Jack fell down and broke his ***
>   And Jill came tumbling after.

Johnson goes on to report that the courtroom broke out in laughter and that Banning made his point.

Auxospore. One of many all-purpose swearwords created by Gelett Burgess, the master of word creation. Auxospore appears in a passage from Burgess's *Find the Woman,* which was published in 1911. In the passage a truck driver, who has gotten in the way of a parade organized by a society to ban profanity, is addressed by the angry Dr. Hopbottom, who is the head of the society:

The doctor shook his fist again and started in earnest. His voice began with calmness and deliberation, but soon rose high—it swept forth in a majestic declamation full of all sorts of forte, staccato and crescendo effects to the noble climax.

"See here, you slack-salted transubstantiated interdigital germarium, you rantipole sacrosciatic rock-barnacle you, if you give me any of your caprantipolene paragastrular megalopteric jacitation, I'll make a lamellibranchiate gymnomixine parabolic lepidopteroid out of you! What diacritical right has a binominal oxypendactile advoutrous holoblastic rhizopod like you got with your trinoctial ustilaginous Westphalian holocaust blocking up the teleostean way for, anyway! If you give me any more of your lunarian, snortomaniac hyperbolic pylorectomy, I'll skive you into a megalopteric diatomeriferous auxospore! You queasy Zoroastrian son of a helicopteric hypotrachelium, you, shut your logarithmic epicycloidal mouth! You let this monopolitan macrocosmic helciform procession go by and wait right here in the anagological street. And no more of your hedonistic primordial supervirescence, you rectangular quillet-eating, vice-presidential amoeboid, either!"

Bigsix. For years publishers and broadcasters have spoken of "the big six" to refer collectively to the words piss, fart, shit, fuck, cock, and cunt. Why not shout "Bigsix" as collective verbal shorthand for the full half dozen? Or call someone "a bigsixing s.o.b."

Bombschmutt. Writer Sherry Suib Cohen introduced this word in an article on four-letter words in *Westchester* magazine. It was created by a student in one of her creative-writing classes who said, "I don't think sex and elimination are obscene. What's obscene to me is war. I think 'bombschmutt!' would be a marvelous curse."

Bumbledicking. Word used to great effect in Preston Jones's play *The Oldest Living Graduate.*

Cacademoid. Insult word for academics created by Reinhold Aman, editor of *Maledicta, the International Journal of Verbal Aggression.* It is a blend of caca, the childish word for feces, and academic. According to *Time,* Aman created the word to describe those who did not appreciate the work he was doing.

Coprolite. A fossilized turd. John Ciardi, for one, believes that this word should be brought into general use because there are so many coprolites among us.

Culch. An old Maine expletive used in the sense of "Rubbish!" "Bull!" or "Bullshit!" Ripe for revival.

Curpin. An old term for chicken rump that could easily be applied metaphorically.

Dicknailing. Epithet used by Rufus Sanders, the pseudonym of Lloyd Barto, in his column for the *Montgomery Advertiser* that ran in the 1880s and 1890s. "Squire Rogers jumped on him with a ring-tail, dicknailing reply" is a line from one of his columns. He also pioneered the use of the word *flugens,* as in "It was cold as the flugens that day."

Eesle. In Boontling, the invented language of the early settlers of California's Anderson Valley, *eesle* was the word for asshole. It was used both in the pejorative and as a greeting ("You old eesle") in the same way that one would say, "How are you doing, you old bastard?"

Feague. Defined in Francis Grose's 1785 *Classical Dictionary of the Vulgar Tongue* as ". . . to put ginger up a horse's fundament, to make him lively and carry his tail well; it is said, a forfeit is incurred by any horse dealer's servant who shall show a horse without first feagueing him. Used figuratively for encouraging or spiriting one up." *Magnificent word!*

Fico. From Samuel Johnson's dictionary, "An act of contempt done with the fingers, expressing a fig for you."

Foutra. A old word of deep contempt. Used, for instance, by Shakespeare: "A foutra for the world and worldlings base." (*Henry IV,* Part II.)

Fugh. (Pronounced foo.) An old exclamation of disgust. It looks stronger written than it sounds when said.

Fumet. Deer dung. Pronounced foo-mitt.

Gardyloo. An archaic warning cry that was made when waste water was tossed out the window. Gardyloo was the English corruption of the French *"Gardez de l'eau,"* for "Watch out for the water."

Golter-yeded gawpsheet. Old English insult recorded in Elizabeth Mary Wright's *Rustic Speech and Folklore.* Its original meaning has been lost, but it has a marvelous ring to it.

Hagbadek. One of five new swearwords created by Burges Johnson in his *Lost Art of Profanity,* which is based on the assertion that *b*'s, *d*'s, *g*'s, *h*'s, and *k*'s have the greatest objurgatory value. The other four: "Bodkogh!" "Khigbod!" "Dakadigbeg!" and "Godbekho!"

Immerd. To cover with dung.

Infandous. Too odious to be spoken or written.

Jobjam. An all-purpose curse word created by Booth Tarkington, who sometimes used it with "dobdab." In one novel one of his characters tells someone "to go to the jobjam dobdab bastinadoed Hellespont helm!"

Kodak. In *The Lost Art of Profanity,* Burges Johnson suggested that kodak was an excellent swearword that George Eastman wasted on a gadget. Other wasted swearwords on Johnson's list: "Kleenex!" "O Hemorrhoids!" "Gestalt!" and "Lydia Pinkham!"

Lewdster. A lecher; one given to illegal pleasures. A lewder than lewd word that goes back to Samuel Johnson's work.

Malaga. Alexandre Dumas introduced this swearword in his *Vicomte de Bragelonne*. The essayist Alfred George Gardiner later wrote of *Malaga:* "It is a good swearword. It has the advantage of meaning nothing and that is precisely what a swearword should mean. It should be sound and fury, signifying nothing. It should be incoherent, irrational, a little crazy like the passion which evokes it."

Mundungus. This very old word was first used to describe dung or odorous garbage, but later came to be used most commonly to describe vile-smelling tobacco. It begs to be sworn with.

Odsplut. A very old British oath that is believed to be a minced version of "God's blood."

Pissabed. Samuel Johnson included this term in his dictionary as "A yellow flower growing in the grass." It would also seem to be a good term of rage, more to the point than, say, calling someone a bastard.

Pornogenitone. Son of a harlot. From the Greek.

Pox and Piles. Common curse of the Middle Ages.

Pricklouse. An archaic term of contempt for a tailor that could be brought back for general contempt.

Riggafrutch. A new expletive that had its debut in Bill Sherk's *Brave New Words*. It was coined by Bob Krueger, a Toronto music teacher.

Slutch. A blend of slut and bitch.

Swyve. Chaucer's copulatory verb.

Taffy. Time was when people would say taffy when they encountered hot air, making it the Pollyannaish equivalent of B.S. It is innocuous in the extreme . . . so innocuous, in fact, that it has a certain shock value to it that makes it a good swearword.

Ted. To spread manure.

Tetragrammaton. A four-letter word.

Tunket. Old New England word for hell (as in "As sure as tunket . . ."). It comes from Tophet, an Old Testament name for the place where human sacrifice was made by fire.

Umslopogus. This is the name of a Zulu chief in an H. Rider Haggard novel, which Burges Johnson felt should have been used instead as a swearword.

Uzzard. A rare gem of a word unearthed by Ivor Brown, British word-hunter *extraordinaire*. An uzzard is a third-generation bastard; a bastard by a bastard out of a bastard.

Waxyquez. All-purpose swearword composed of the five letters—
q, w, x, y and *z*—that have been banned from the Esperanto alphabet.
Should fill a need, as Esperanto is short on swearwords, especially
those made from taboo letters. Created by the author.

Worms in your marrow! A curse used by William Blake.

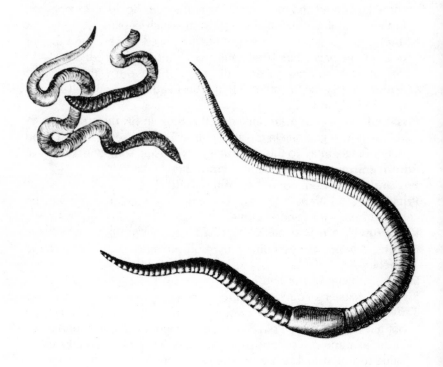

DECORATIVE WORDS

—An Array from Art and Architecture—

Abbozzo. A preliminary sketch; rough.

Afterimage. Experiencing a sensation of color after the stimulus has been removed. Positive afterimage occurs when one can still see a bright image after the eyes have been closed. Negative afterimage occurs when one looks at a blank area after seeing intense color and sees the complementary color to the original.

Arris fillet. A triangular piece of wood or other material used to raise the covering of a roof against a chimney or wall so as to throw off the rain.

Ashlar. Term used to distinguish square-cut, carefully laid masonry from masonry that uses rough, odd-shaped stones. The latter is called *rubble* masonry.

Autotelic. A work that creates its own reason for being, as opposed to a work that is didactic.

Boast. To dress or shape a stone. The outward face of the stones used in churches are usually boasted.

Bocage. Supporting, ornamental background for a ceramic figure.

Breastsummer. A large horizontal beam supporting an exterior wall over an opening such as a large window.

Brunneous. Dark brown. Brunneous is one of a number of marvelous color words. Some other fine examples:

> **Caesious.** Pale blue-green. Pronounced see-zee-ous.
>
> **Castaneous.** Chestnut-colored
>
> **Cesious.** Blue-gray.
>
> **Eau-de-nil.** Light green; literally, the water of the Nile. Pronounced ode-a-nil.
>
> **Ferruginous.** Iron rust–colored.
>
> **Festucine.** A straw-color between green and yellow.
>
> **Filemot.** The color of a dead leaf.
>
> **Glaucous.** Green with a bluish-gray tinge.
>
> **Modena.** Deep purple.
>
> **Pavonine.** Having the iridescence of a peacock's tail.
>
> **Phenicious.** Red with a slight mixture of gray.
>
> **Puniceous.** Bright or purplish red.
>
> **Subfusc.** Dusky; dingy.
>
> **Taupe.** Mole-colored. Rhymes with rope.

Contrapposto. The opposing twist between masses. Commonly used to describe the contrast between the directions of shoulders and hips in the human figure.

Corbiesteps. Steps forming the end of a gable in a masonry building. They are also known as *crowsteps* and *corbelsteps.*

Craquelure. The web of hairline cracks common to old oil paintings. Pronounced crack-lure.

Crenellate. To notch a building, such as the squared notch in the battlement of a fort or castle.

Cribble. To decorate wood or metal by making small dots or punctures on the surface.

Dentils. In classical architecture, a decorative row resembling teeth.

Écorché. The name for the skinned or flayed anatomical figure used by artists to study muscles.

Empaquetage. Work of art consisting of a tightly wrapped object ranging up to and including buildings. A form of conceptual art.

Engobe. In pottery, a decoration made by applying liquid clay to the body of the object being made.

Fenestration. The pattern or scheme of a building's windows. *Defenestration,* on the other hand, is the act of throwing a person or an object out of a window.

Fillister. The groove on the outer edge of a windowpane into which the glass is fitted.

Grimthorpe. To do a rotten job of restoration. From Lord Grimthorpe, who at the end of the last century attempted the restoration of St. Albans' abbey in Hertfordshire, England.

Halation. The quality of light that makes the light-colored area of a painting seem larger than a dark one even though they are the same size.

Hob. The projecting corner of a fireplace. *Hobnob* comes from the sociable habit of sitting around the hob while drinking.

Imbrication. The decorative effect of overlapped edges, such as found on roof tiles and fish scales.

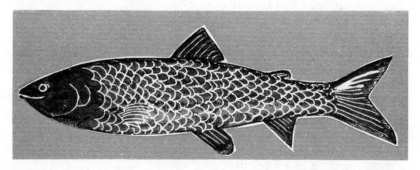

Impasto. Layers of pigment in a painting; a thick and paste-like application of paint.

Inglenook. A chimney corner; a corner by the fire.

Interfenestral. Between windows.

Kibosh. Adding cement or plaster to a sculptured or wooden form. From this comes the old expression "to put the kibosh on," meaning to change in shape or form.

Loggia. An arcade or passageway open on one side. Present in classical architecture as well as motels.

Mahlstick. A stick with a knob at one end that is held across the face of a painting as a rest for the artist's hand. It is often used in painting fine detail.

Maquette. A room in miniature.

Muntin. Narrow wood separations between panes of glass in windows, bookcase doors, etc. Also known as *muttins* and *mutts*. Some people also call them *mullions;* yet there are those who go on to claim that a *mullion* is a vertical separation while a *muntin* can go in any direction (vertical, horizontal, diagonal).

Nogging. Material (brick, cloth, cement, etc.) used to pack the wall crevices of a wooden or log house.

Noodle. To overwork a painting or other work of art by adding too much detail, redefining, and "correcting." It is a critical term commonly applied to a work that lacks vigor.

Nosing. The part of a stair step that projects over the riser.

Oda. A room in a harem.

Oubliette. Dungeon that can only be gotten in and out of through a ceiling trapdoor. Pronounced ou-blee-et.

Patinate. To produce an artificial appearance of age on wood or metal.

Perron. A landing and staircase outside of a building, leading from the first floor.

Plinth. The base of a column or pedestal, usually square.

Putto. It means small boy and is applied in art to the many cherubs that appear in Renaissance painting. The plural is *putti.* Pronounced poo-toe and poo-tea.

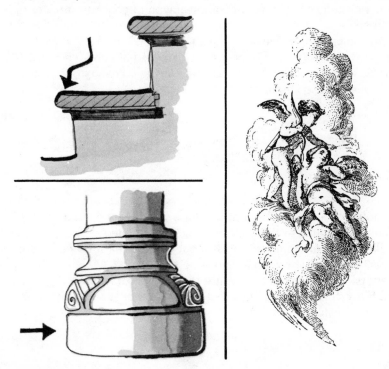

Pyrography. The art of woodburning.

Quadriga. A sculpture of a chariot drawn by four horses, often seen atop a monument.

Rived. Wood that has been split, not sawed. Old houses often have riven timbers or panels. Rhymes with tithed.

Sfumato. The blending of colors through indistinguishable gradations: very smooth transition.

Skintle. To build unevenly with bricks in order to produce a quaint or picturesque effect.

Slaister. To paint or color in an ill and vulgar manner. Even with the advent of punk and new wave, slaister has been relegated to the limbo of a crossword-puzzle word. Ivor Brown, a fan of the word, has written that it ". . . gives a rich and odious suggestion of bad, greasy makeup and of lips crudely incarnadined."

Spall. Construction term for the disintegration of concrete surfaces or corners.

Stipple. In painting, achieving a color tone by making many small dots.

Stomp. A cigar-sized roll of gray paper, pointed at either end, that is used by artists to blend or soften the effects of charcoal or pastels. Sometimes called a *stump*.

Toe-hole. An indented area at the base of a counter, such as that commonly found at the bottom of kitchen counters.

Tortillon. A small stomp (see also) about the size of a small pencil and usually pointed at only one end.

Weepers. Holes built into masonry to allow for drainage.

Zoophoric column. A column that either bears or supports the figure of an animal.

DICKSONARY

—Some 45 Words Created by the Author in Response to Being Placed in the Last Quarter of the Twentieth Century—

Anthonize. To give the public what the public does not want. Named for the Anthony dollar coin that looked and felt like two-bits. The government is a prominent anthonizer (the nine-digit zip, the new two-dollar bill, etc.), but private industry also contributes (Billy Beer, nonmelting ice cream, Nehru jackets, etc.).

Barristrate. Willfully depicting the human condition in terms of lechery, greed, and buffoonery. Derives from Chuck Barris, who has given us *The Gong Show, The Newlywed Game,* and *Three's a Crowd.*

Baskinrobbinsitus. That sudden pain one gets in the sinuses when one eats ice cream too fast.

Baudinize. To promote a book, film, or other property with excessive zeal. Named for Robert Baudin, the disgruntled, publicity-seeking author who in 1979 flew over Manhattan threatening to fly his plane into the window of the company that published his autobiography.

Beepoop. To create a serious situation through a feeble attempt at humor. Term suggested by the flap that ensued when Governor Lee Dreyfus of Wisconsin told the 1980 State Honey Queen that he and his wife call honey "bee poop." This, of course, occasioned passionate protests from the Wisconsin Beekeepers Association, the Wisconsin Honey Producers Association, and others.

BeLee. To commit modest, harmless fraud for those willing to be exploited. Named for the many Bruce Lees who appeared after the actor's death: Bruce Lai, Bruce Li, Lee Bruce, etc. BeLee rhymes with melee.

Bibliorts. Things other than bookmarks used by people to mark a place in a book—ticket stubs, laundry lists, etc. From *biblio-,* the Greek prefix for book, and *orts,* an old, little-used term for scraps.

Boxecrate. To desecrate an area with your standard flat, square, determinedly dull glass and concrete office buildings and apartments.

Btubore. A person who never seems to stop talking about how energy-efficient they have become. Recent woodstove converts are often the worst btubores. The term comes from BTU, the British thermal unit and is pronounced bit-too-bore.

Bureaugance. A blend word of bureaucrat + arrogance formed to cover that particular level of determined arrogance that is common to Senate aides, postal authorities, IRS functionaries, and the pandas at the National Zoo.

Centicipation. Something that has fallen far below that which had been anticipated; a 99 percent failure. The metric prefix *centi-* (for one-hundredth) is used in commemoration of American metric conversion, thus far a perfect example of centicipation.

Comchoutword. Word or words that appear on printed tapes generated by the new computerized check-out machines. The words are generally shortened, so that one occasionally finds unnerving or odd items on the tape. Writing in *The Washington Post,* Ellen Ficklin told of her surprise at finding that she had bought cannibalistic-sounding MAN SOUP MIX (actually a package of Manischewitz soup makings). Comchoutwords are hidden within the bars of these things:

Cosellian. The highest level of smug self-certainty, as in "Cosellian cocksuredness." Inspired by an evening of watching *Monday Night Football* with the sound turned on. Common Cosellian statements include: "As I have repeatedly stated and is being proven here tonight"; "The conclusive proof of what you have been hearing from me all along"; and "As————confided to me before the game."

Elegate. To attempt to elevate something minor into a major scandal. To seize upon something as a Watergate-like incident when it is nothing of the sort—"Billygate," for instance.

Fabricist. A person who discriminates based on the fabric and/or the clothing of others. Liberals who feel that they harbor no prejudices will often toss off lines like "It was horrible! Half the men in the room were wearing polyester leisure suits and one of them was wearing—are you ready for this?—white socks and a white belt."

Frugalflaunt. Conspicuous *non*consumption; to flaunt one's frugality. Putting your compost heap in the front yard is frugalflaunting, as is going to a sumptuous buffet and taking only bean sprouts and parsley. A frugalflaunt *(n.)* is a person who says he wants a Cuisinart but is holding off until they come out with a solar-powered model.

Glenhaven. A name that is so innocuous or trite that you find it difficult to recall. Cedar crest, plaza central, long ridge, and harbor view are all glenhavens.

Gnusman/Gnuswoman. The ruthless, compulsive punster. So called because one of these would take a small child to the zoo on the off chance that the child will ask, "What's a gnu?" and he or she would be able to reply, "Not much. What's a gnu with you?" Times and fashions change, but this type is a constant. A manual on the art of conversation published in London in 1867 contains this description, which sounds just like the gnusperson down the block: "You see by his manner that he does not take the least interest in what you are saying, but is on the watch for anything that suggests a pun or verbal quirk, with which he ruthlessly interrupts you, even although you may be at the most telling or interesting part of your story, and forthwith bursts into a roar of laughter as if he had really said something excessively clever."

Hojonate. A one word compression of a multiworded name for a company, product, or service. From Hojo, which is the hojonate of Howard Johnson. Citgo, Memco, Arco, and Nabisco are common hojonates. Also a verb, *to hojonate,* which is to compress for commercial purposes.

Hrusk. To advance the cause of mediocrity. From the name of Senator Roman Hruska of Nebraska who defended Nixon Supreme Court nominee Clement Haynesworth. Hruska answered those who argued that Haynesworth was mediocre with the point that there are many mediocre people in America deserving representation by a mediocre Supreme Court justice.

Inflatuate. *n.* A blend word from *inflation* and *infatuate,* the inflatuate is a person with a seeming inability to talk of anything but prices and their rise. Although the times may be largely responsible for bringing this economic Hyde out of many a mild-mannered Jekyll, it does not make their behavior any less infuriating.

Internacast. To bring internal matters to the attention of outsiders. The staffs at certain hotels and restaurants are expert internacasters who tell you the manager's policy on overtime, how the busboys never clear station #6, and that the cashier has fallen arches because she has to stand all the time.

Konvenience. A convenience that can only be reached by car, hence much less a convenience. For reasons unclear, many konveniences often feature forced *k*'s in their signs: Kwik-stop, Kash 'n Karry, etc.

Loxocration. The process of saying something nasty to a person in such a way that the person is bewildered. For instance, using the rare word *rebarative* for repulsive or the obscure *foraminated* for bored. Loxocration is an effective means of venting one's spleen without getting punched in the nose.

McWord. An awkwardly pretentious mix of languages or traditions— Miss Piggy's use of *moi,* the name of Wayne Newton's mansion (Casa Shenandoah), and Scots-Irish–surnamed food (McMuffin, McChicken, etc.).

Miragones. Short-lived advertising and marketing miracles—fabrics with *celaperm,* razor blades with *diridium,* deodorant with *lumium,* and so forth. Miragones can be found only in the pages of old magazines.

Mxyzptlk. A person with a particularly difficult name to pronounce. Mxyzptlk is one of Superman's multitude of archenemies. An example of a Mxyzptlkian character was Joe Btfsplk, who used to appear in Al Capp's "Li'l Abner."

Neckar. To test or try something in such a way as to invite disaster: "He neckared the brakes on his new Ford by racing up close to a brick wall and then slamming down on the pedal at the last moment." The term comes from a river of the same name in West Germany, where the prime example of modern neckaring took place in 1979. The U.S. Army helped German authorities test a new bridge spanning the river by driving 34 of its heaviest fully manned M60 tanks onto the structure. It sagged but did not collapse.

Nork. A product that looks especially appealing in its original context —an ad, a catalog, a hotel gift shop—but that loses all appeal very shortly after you get it. Norks are especially common at Christmas and include such items as automatic wine-bottle decorkers, cute hors d'oeuvres sticks, towels with clever inscriptions, and multipurpose electronic gizmos commonly advertised in airline inflight magazines. Most norks are mail-order items.

Othodgeous. A sleazy, down-at-the-heels ambience; sleazy-cozy. Word derives from (and was coined at) the O. T. Hodge Chili Parlor at 814 Pine Street, St. Louis. It is a quintessentially othodgeous place. It is pronounced oath-odge-ous.

Peiaster. *v.* To inadvertently create confusion; to bestir the bureaucracy without meaning to. Another eponym, this one for Ernest Peia of Morris Plains, New Jersey, who by following an old family tradition of naming sons after the father created great confusion at the Social Security Administration. By 1980, when the Associated Press reported on the 66-year-old man's dilemma, Peia had been issued three different Social Security numbers. Pronounced pea-astor.

Peru. Offending unintentionally; bothering B, who is innocent, in an attempt to get to A. A classic peru took place during the Iranian hostage period when *The Washington Post* went out to tweak Iran

Paul Dickson/73

in an editorial entitled "Is Iran Welshing?" The editorial presumably rolled off the backs of the Iranians but infuriated people of Welsh descent in the Washington area.

Peru can be used as both a noun and verb (to peru someone or something, or a peru was committed). The name of the South American nation is used as it is entirely innocent in this matter.

Pibble. A name or a term written to look like what it says, such as:

The inspiration for this word came from a letter from Sara Gump of Savannah, who insisted that she was unable to come up with a proper name for such words, which are commonly used in advertising. I immediately decided to call them pibbles as I had been long concerned with the fact that there was no *pibble* in English.

Prflop. P. R. effort that falls on its face. In June 1981 a classic case took place when a New York public relations firm sent *The Wall Street Journal* three loaves of a new 100 percent natural whole wheat bread. Because they lacked preservatives, two arrived covered with mold. Great publicity for preservatives.

Productese. Designer conversation; talk in which product names are forced for reasons of status. Sample: "Don't spill your Perrier, you might get lime on your Top Siders!"

Punburn. The pain that comes with a pun that has not been expressed. For instance, a friend calls to say that he is in the hospital and has fallen in love with the woman who has been attending him there. You get off the phone and punburn ensues as you realize you should have said, "You mean to say, you took a turn for the nurse."

Punstore. The very specific kind of place—now in proliferation—that uses a cute or atrocious pun to announce itself. It is particularly common to new places that cut or dress hair (Rape of the Lock, Headmaster, Lunatic Fringe) and maternity shops (Heir Apparent,

Great Expectations). Frank Mankiewicz has looked at the trend and asked, "Will banks succumb? . . . the Bread Box?"

Redfox. *v.* To regulate in an excessive and foolish manner; to use regulation in such a manner that the worst fears of the antiregulators are realized. Named for Red Fox denims manufactured by a Mr. Charles Henson of Georgia. After making these pants for close to 30 years, Henson was told by the Federal Trade Commission that he could no longer use the name because they were not made with the fur of red fox.

Smirkword. A word or phrase that you can never again think of in the same light after learning of an earlier or alternative meaning. Cleveland, for instance, is a name that has had an entirely new ring to it after I discovered that it was once common slang for the female pudendum. Another example is flux, a Victorian euphemism for diarrhea. The leading smirkword in contemporary speech is nitty-gritty. According to John Train in his *Remarkable Words,* this was, "originally, black slang for the inner end of vagina."

Sullivan. *v.* To initiate a reform that results in a reinforcement of that which was being reformed. Named for New York State Assemblyman Peter M. Sullivan, who proposed and had enacted a law requiring that all consumer contracts be written in plain English. When the lawyers had finished with the language of his law it came out, in Sullivan's words, ". . . long, complex and downright fuzzy."

Tikitacky. South Seas kitsch; that particular Polynesian look featured in souvenir shops that relies heavily on gaudy plastic flowers, faces carved from coconut shells, and the heads of ancient gods cut from lava-textured plastic.

Translute. Translate + convolute; more than a bad translation, but rather one with a complete change of meaning. A classic translution took place in 1977 when President Carter's statement to the Polish people, "I wish to learn your opinions and understand your desires for the future," was given as "I desire the Poles carnally."

Woeperson. Although we can all think of things that have changed for the worse over the years, the woeperson sees everything in terms of decline, decadence, and desperation. Even a 21-year-old woeperson feels that everything was better when he was younger. One of the cruelest things you can do to a woeperson—equivalent to telling a hypochondriac how well he is looking—is to tell one that your last conversation got you to thinking about all the things that have improved.

Paul Dickson/75

Word word. There are situations in which it is necessary to repeat a word in order to make sure someone knows what you are talking about. For instance, you might be asked, "Are you talking about an American Indian or an Indian Indian?" or "Oh, you're talking about grass grass. I thought you were talking about grass."

From what I have been able to determine, there is no word for this phenomenon, and "word word" seemed to be a logical name to give it.

Zisterous. Relating to reform that will be of greatest benefit to the reformer. Derives from the name Barry Zister, who, as Connecticut State Consumer Counsel, tried to persuade the phone company to print directories backward from *Z* to *A* every odd year to offset the competitive advantage of coming first—like AAAAAA Diaper Service.

DRESS WORDS

—Terms to Go From Head to Toe—

Aglet. The covering at the end of a shoe-lace.

Aiguillette. An ornamental cord, usually pointed, worn with some military uniforms over the left shoulder. It is worn by military aides to U.S. president and by high-ranking officers.

Airplane-back. The portion of a cuff link that is poked through the cuff holes and then held in place as it is folded out like the wings of an airplane.

Beaver. The movable portion of a suit of armor that protects the mouth and chin.

Biretta. Square cap with projections on top worn by Catholic ecclesiastics.

Bottu. Indian forehead-marking used to indicate caste. Rhymes with tattoo.

Brassard. A badge worn on the arm; an armband such as the Military Police wear (with the initials MP on it).

Clock. Decoration on the side of stockings or socks, also known as a *quirk*.

Five-eighths length. In the trade, the name of a garment that reaches halfway between the hips and knees.

Forre. Handkerchief bordering.

BRASSARD

Fourchettes. Strips running along the sides of glove fingers that serve to connect the front and the back of the glove. Pronounced four-shet.

Furbelow. Gathered ruffles and festoonery embellishing a woman's dress.

Fustanella. Short white skirt worn by men in Greece on certain ceremonial occasions.

Gibus. Collapsible opera hat that can be flattened when not in use. From the nineteenth-century Parisian hatter of the same name who invented it. Pronounced ji-boo.

Gigot. A leg-of-mutton sleeve that is extremely full at the shoulder and narrows at the elbow.

Gimme caps. The popular one-size-fits-all baseball-style caps bearing the embroidered logo of John Deere, International Harvester, or whatever. According to *Newsweek,* the term originated when farmers would say to tractor salesmen, "Gimme one of them caps."

Godet. A triangular piece of fabric added to a garment to give it extra fullness.

Goose. Tailor's long-handled pressing iron.

Habille. The dress of a strip-tease artist at the beginning of the act.

Hand. Garment industry term for the feel of a fabric.

Hauberk. Medieval metal tunic.

Paul Dickson/79

Havelock. Cloth hanging down from the back of a soldier's hat as protection against the sun.

Kaffiyeh. Arab headdress made from a folded piece of cloth of the type worn by Yasir Arafat. Pronounced ka-fee-ya.

Keeper. The loop located next to the buckle on a belt. It keeps the end of the belt in place.

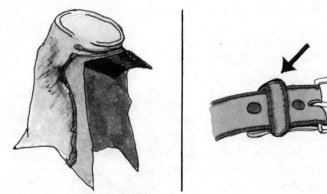

Kiltie. The extended shoe tongue, usually fringed, that folds over and covers the laces. These are common on golf shoes and are sometimes called a *kiltie tongue*.

Klompen. Dutch wooden shoes. If they were carved in France or Canada, they would be called *sabots*.

Lifeline. On a necktie, this is the thread that holds the lining in place and runs from one end to the other. A good lifeline has a tied loop of extra thread at both ends to permit extra give.

Loft. Term used to describe the springiness of wool as it comes back to shape after being crumpled.

Loup. A half-mask.

Maddy. A madras middy.

Mappula. Name for the handkerchief which was used to signal the start of the action in Roman games.

Monokini. Woman's swimsuit consisting of the bottom half only.

Muckender. An old, much franker, word for handkerchief.

Nerd pack. In some circles, the name for those shirt-pocket plastic pouches for holding pens and pencils.

Pannier. A woman's overskirt gathered bustle-like on each side of her body. The term comes from an earlier meaning: pairs of baskets hanging over the sides of mules or packhorses.

Petasus. Broad-brimmed hat of the ancient world; also the winged model worn by Mercury, messenger of the gods.

Phonytail. Artificial hair in the style of a ponytail, used by *Seventeen* in the 1950s and 1960s.

Paul Dickson/81

Pickelhaube. The classic Prussian spiked helmet.

Placket. The opening, containing a zipper or other fastening device, that enables one to get in and out of slacks or a skirt.

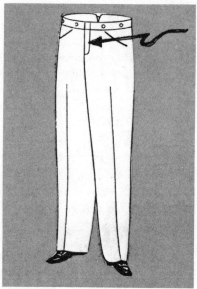

Presser foot. The flat, foot-like piece of metal at the business end of the sewing machine arm. It sits next to the needle and keeps the fabric flat and in place.

Psyche. Mirror in an adjustable frame that reflects a person at full length.

Romal. A whip made from a horse's bridle reins when they are tied together. A Western term from the Spanish *ramal,* a branch road or ramification.

Rowel. The wheel of a spur. The vocabulary of the old West included a number of words and phrases for specific rowels, such as the sunset or sunburst rowel, which was one with many points.

Size lining. Retail talk for grouping merchandise by size, as opposed to *price lining,* which refers to grouping items by their price range.

Skigs. Shoe-business word for a slow-moving item.

Snood. A hairnet often attached to the back of a hat to hold the hair in place. In her *Fashion Dictionary,* Mary Brooks Picken reports that a snood was originally a "Fillet formerly worn around the head by young women in Scotland and considered an emblem of chastity."

Soutache. The narrow braid trimming commonly used to border men's pajamas and bathrobes.

Sporran. A leather pouch, usually covered with fur and ornamented, that hangs in front of a Scottish kilt. It was originally intended to serve as a pocket for the day's ration.

Swacket. Fashion industry term for a sweater that buttons like a jacket.

Talaria. The sandals with wings worn by Mercury.

Tapadero. Toe-fender for Western stirrups. Often shortened to taps. It derives from the Spanish verb *tapar,* to close or cover.

Toe cap. The material covering the toe of the shoe.

Paul Dickson/83

Togate. Wearing or dressed in a toga.
Vamp. The upper part of a shoe.
Wamus. The frontiersman's fringed hunting shirt, usually made of buckskin.
Wase. The circular headcovering or pad used by porters when carrying loads on their heads. A straw pad.

13

DRINKING WORDS

—A Jeroboam of Terms for the Bibulous—

Aerometer. Instrument used for measuring specific gravity, which is the difference between the weight of a beverage and a similar amount of water. In England the excise tax on beer is based on specific gravity.

Agrafes. The cage that holds a champagne cork in place. Believe it or not, there is actually a second word for this same thing, which is a *coiffe*. Both are French words. Agrafes is pronounced a-graph.

Alegar. Vinegar made from ale or beer.

Barm. The froth on beer. Sometimes called *fob*.

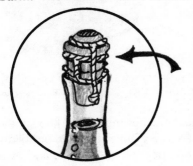

Paul Dickson/85

Beer comb. A special spatula used to scoop foam from the tops of beer glasses and mugs.

Beeswing. Filmy tartar scales that form in some wines after a long period of storage. So called because they look like the wings of bees.

BIB. Short for Bottled in Bond.

Billet. The thumbpiece on the lid of a stein or tankard.

Binned. Term for bottles stored in tiers.

Bottle stink. The term for an unpleasant smell from a wine bottle, which disappears after the bottle is allowed to stand uncorked for a short time. It is a condition not to be confused with terms for permanent harm, such as *corky* (spoiled by a bad cork) or *pricked* (see also).

Bottle ticket. A small plaque hung around the neck of a bottle or decanter with the name of the beverage inside. Often made of silver.

Bouge. The "belly" of a cask, the point where the circumference is the greatest.

Bright. *Racked* (see also) beer as opposed to that with the *lees* (see also) left in.

Brimmer. A glass so full that the liquid touches the brim. Although the liquid has climbed to the brim, there is a slight depression or hollow in the center of the surface. A *bumper,* on the other hand, is a brimmer to which extra drops have been added to fill the hollow to a bump. The difference between a brimmer and a bumper can be demonstrated by floating a cork fragment on the surface. In a brimmer the cork will float to the edge, while it will sit in the middle of a bumper.

Bumper. See *Brimmer.*

Bung hole. The aperture through which beer enters a cask. The bung hole is filled with a *shive.*

Calibogus. A mix of rum and spruce beer.

Capsule. The metal foil or plastic cap that covers the top of a wine bottle, which must be removed before the cork can be removed. Capsules usually carry a logo or trademark.

Comet wine. Wine made during a year in which a major comet appears. Since the comet year of 1811, which was also a great vintage year, there have been those who insist that comet wines are great wines.

Denaturant. A substance added to alcohol to make it unfit for drinking, but without destroying its use for other commercial purposes—hairdressing, for instance.

Départ. The final taste of wine in the mouth. French.

Draff. The spent grains of malt left after the production of whiskey.

Dunder. The dregs left after the distillation of rum. In some rum-making processes, dunder from one run is added to the next for added flavor.

Elongated. When applied to wine, it means that water has been added. If this seems too euphemistic, consider the French term for elongated, *mouillage.*

Épluchage. The process of picking over the grapes to eliminate bad ones. French.

Feints. The last liquid from a still.

Ferruginous. When speaking of beer, this term refers to a taste like water with high iron content. Like wine tasting, beer tasting has its own set of terms, which include *austere, beery* (typical of beer), *brackish, bright, clean, dank, flabby, skunky, swampy,* and *tinny.*

Fliers. White, fluffy particles that float in white wines. Fliers are most likely to appear when the wine is transported from a warm to a colder climate.

Fob. Brewer's term for beer froth. Sometimes called *barm.*

Foreshots. The first liquid to come out of a still.

Gaugers. Revenue officers who measure contents.

Gyle. A quantity of beer brewed at one time; a brewing. Beer kegs carry a stenciled gyle number to indicate which brewing it came from.

Hogen-mogen. Said of strong booze; an exclamation and a description.

Jirble. To pour out a drink unsteadily.

Katzenjammer. A cat's whining, literally, but most often applied to a hangover.

Lees. The dregs of wine or beer.

Legs. Streaks that run down the side of a glass after wine has been swirled in it. Wine with pronounced streaks is said to have "good legs."

Mini-pétillance. Slight sparkle or crackle in a wine.

Muddler. The technical name for a swizzle stick, sometimes called a *mosser.*

Muselage. Muzzling champagne corks by the addition of the traditional tin cap. French.

Must. The unfermented, freshly pressed grape juice used for wine making.

Nebuchadnezzar. The largest champagne bottle size, capable of holding 104 glasses. It is larger than the 83-glass *Balthazar,* 62-glass *Salmanazar,* 41-glass *Methuselah,* 31-glass *Rehoboam,* 21-glass *Jeroboam,* and 10-glass *magnum.* Your standard *bottle* holds a mere five glasses. Putting all this into bottles, we have:

Magnum	=	2 bottles	Jeroboam	=	4 bottles
Rehoboam	=	6 bottles	Methuselah	=	8 bottles
Salmanazar	=	12 bottles	Balthazar	=	16 bottles
		Nebuchadnezzar	=	20 bottles	

Nip. One sixth of a quartern (a 5-oz. measure).

Noggin. A quarter of a pint.

Oast. A kiln for drying hops.

Oenology. The art and science of wine making. Pronounced e-nol-ogy.

Peated. Scotch taster's term for the degree to which a particular Scotch has a smoky or peaty character. A Scotch may be "well peated," "lightly peated," etc.

Perry. Pear cider made along the same lines as apple cider.

Plonk. Cheap, ordinary table wine. British slang.

Pomace. The substance remaining after the juice has been extracted from apples, grapes, or whatever. Pomace is often used as animal food.

Pony. Half a jigger, three quarters of a shot, an ounce.

Potheen. Irish name for illegally distilled whiskey.

Pricked. Of wine that has turned to vinegar. The term may be an anglicization of the French *piqué,* which refers to a wine that has become or is becoming vinegary.

Punt. The concave area at the bottom of certain wine bottles. It allegedly gives strength to the bottle and is not there to give the false impression of extra quantity.

Racked. Wine or beer that has been separated from its *lees.*

Shebeen. Illegal Irish drinking den.

Shive. A circular wooden plug that is hammered into the hole in a cask after it has been filled.

Shuked. Said of wine casks that have been taken apart, with the staves bundled for ease of transport.

Sling. Synonym for cocktail, as in Singapore Sling.

Soda back. Current bar talk for soda on the side.

Spile. A small peg that fits into a hole in the *shive* (see also) of a cask.

Stillion. A stand for a beer keg or wine cask.

Tastevin. The small silver saucer that is used for wine tasting. Tastevins are often hung around the neck of a wine steward by a chain as a symbol of authority.

Ullage. What is not in a cask or bottle; that which is left after evaporation, leakage, or use.

Ullaged. Said of a bottle or cask, part of whose contents have spilled, been consumed, or evaporated.

Vallinch. Long glass tube used for taking samples from casks.

V.S.O. Initialism associated with cognac for Very Special Old. *V.S.O.P.* stands for Very Special Old Pale, and *V.V.S.O.P.* stands for the same thing except that an extra Very is thrown in for good measure.

Weeper. A wine bottle that is leaking through its cork.

Well succeeded. Said of wines that have fulfilled the expectation of their vintage.

Wine cradle. Basket used to serve wine at a slant.

Working. Continuing fermentation. Overdevelopment.

Worm. The business end of a corkscrew.

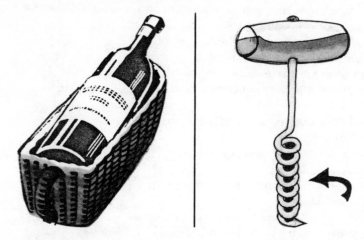

Worn. Term for wine that has been too long in the bottle or spirits that have been too long in the cask.

XXXX. Originally, X stood for the number of times a liquor had been distilled, so that XXXX stood for the strongest and purist. Later it came to mean simply the strength of a liquor or beer. Today the system is in disuse.

Zymurgy. The branch of industrial chemistry that deals with fermentation, distillation, and wine making.

ECRETSAY ONGUESTAY

—From Arague to the Vague Specific, the Art of Covert Talk—

When I was a kid, my aunt and my mother were able to converse fluently in a secret language that, I was later to learn, is called *Turkey Irish*. I could not understand a word of it. This used to drive me crazy, especially around Christmas when they would openly but secretly jabber on about impending surprises. I am now in the process of becoming fluent in Turkey Irish so that my children will not be deprived of the confounding beauties of a secret tongue.

Arague. Language in which *arag* is introduced before vowels. Praragimaragararagily faragound aragin aragenglaragand.

Back slang. This is primarily a British habit by which slang is created by spelling words backward. *Ecilop* is slang for police. Iona and Peter Opie, in their *Lore and Language of Schoolchildren,* report that it is common to boys in certain trades ". . . where it is spoken to ensure that the customer shall not understand what is being said ('*E*vig reh *e*mos de*l*o garcs de*n*e'—'Give her some old scrag end')."

Boontling. A contraction of Boonville Lingo, Boontling is a language that was created by the early residents of upper Anderson Valley in

Mendocino County, California. In his book, *Boontling: An American Lingo,* Charles C. Adams termed it ". . . a deliberately contrived jargon which was spoken extensively between 1880 and 1920." Writing about it in *The Christian Science Monitor,* Raymond A. Lajoie said, "When spoken, it sounds like English that is not quite understandable, like a kind of double-double talk. . . . When written, it looks like someone used a typewriter with his fingers crossed."

One of the reasons the language was created was to allow adults to gossip without fear of their children or outsiders understanding. As a result, Adams reports, approximately 15 percent of the language was made up of "nonch harpins"—objectionable talk. A few "nonch harpins":

> **Burlap:** To have sexual intercourse, sometimes *burl.* Other words for the same act: *Bow* and *geech.*
> **Keeboarp:** Premature male orgasm.
> **Dreef:** Interrupted coitus.
> **Squirrel ribby:** An erect penis.
> **Moldunes:** Breasts.
> **Afe:** A fart.

Carving verbs. In Elizabethan England there existed a special vocabulary for the table that included specific verbs for carving various game, fish, and poultry. In his dictionary, *Words, Facts and Phrases,* Eliezer Edwards writes, ". . . persons using the wrong term were looked upon with some pity and contempt." Here is a collection of those verbs, gathered from a variety of sources:

Allay a Pheasant	Lift a Swan
Barb a Lobster	Mince a Plover
Break a Hare	Rear a Goose
Chine a Salmon	Sauce a Capon
Culpon a Trout	Scull a Tench
Disfigure a Peacock	Side a Haddock
Dismember a Hen	Splat a Pike
Display a Quail	Splay a Bream
Fin a Chevin	Spoil a Hen
Fract a Chicken	String a Lamprey
Frush a Chub	Tame a Crab
Gobbet a Trout	Thigh a Pigeon

Thigh a Woodcock | Unbrace a Mallard
Trench a Sturgeon | Unjoint a Bittern
Transon an Eel | Unlace a Coney
Tusk a Barbel | Unlatch a Curlew

Wing a Partridge

CARVING.

VERYBODY should know how to carve. Parents should instruct their children in this necessary art, and on given occasions practically exercise the youngsters in the use of the "big" knife and fork.

Ladies ought especially to make carving a study ; at their own houses they grace the table, and should be enabled to perform the task allotted to them with sufficient skill to prevent remark, or the calling forth of eager proffers of assistance from good-natured visitors near, who probably would not present any better claim to a neat performance.

Carving presents no difficulties ; it simply requires knowledge. All displays of exertion or violence are in very bad taste ; for, if not proved an evidence of the want of ability on the part of the carver, they present a very strong testimony of the toughness of a joint.

Lightness of hand and dexterity of management are necessary, and can only be acquired by practice. The flakes, which in such fish as salmon and cod are large, should not be broken in serving, for the beauty of the fish is then destroyed, and the appetite for it injured. In addition to the skill in the use of the knife, there is also required another description of knowledge, and that is an acquaintance with the best part of the joint, fowl or fish being carved. Thus in a haunch of venison the fat, which is a favorite, must be served with each slice ; in the shoulder of mutton there are some delicate cuts in the under part. The breast and wings are the best part of a fowl, and the trail of a woodcock on a toast is the choicest part of the bird. In fish a part of the roe, melt or liver should accompany the piece of fish served. The list, however, is too numerous to mention here ; and, indeed, the knowledge can only be acquired by experience. In large establishments the gross dishes are carved at the buffet by the butler, but in middle society they are placed upon the table. In the following directions, accompanied by diagrams, we have endeavored to be as explict as possible ; but while they will prove as landmarks to the uninitiated, he will find that practice alone will enable him to carve with skill and facility.

Part of a Sirloin of Beef.—There are two modes of

helping this joint : either by carving long thin slices from 3 to 4, and assisting a portion of the marrowy fat, which is found underneath the ribs, to each person ; or by cutting thicker slices in the direction 1 to 2. When sent to the table the joint should be laid down on the dish with the surface 2 uppermost.

An Aitch-Bone of Beef.—This is a simple joint to carve, but the slices from it must be cut quite even, and of a very moderate thickness. When the joint is boiled, before cutting to serve, remove a slice from the whole of the upper part of sufficient thickness, say a quarter of an inch, in order to ar-

AITCH-BONE.

rive at the juicy part of the meat at once. Carve from 1 to 2 ; let the slices be moderately thin—not too thin ; help fat with the lean in one piece, and give a little additional fat which you will find below 3 ; the solid fat is at 1, and must be cut in slices horizontally. The round of beef is carved in the same manner.

Ham.—It is served as placed in the engraving, and should come to the table ornamented. Carve from A to B, cutting thin slices slantingly, to give a wedge-like appearance. Those

HAM.

who prefer can carve the hock at D, in the same direction as from A to B, then carve from D to C, in thin slices, as indicated in the diagram.

The Sirloin of Beef.—The under part should be first served, and carved as indicated in the engraving, across the

SIRLOIN OF BEEF.

bone. In carving the upper part the same directions should be followed as for the ribs, or in the center, from A to B, and helping the fat from D.

Sucking Pig.—The cook should send a roast pig to table garnished with head and ears. Carve the joints, then divide the ribs, serve with plenty of sauce : should one of the joints be too much, it may be separated : bread sauce and stuffing should accompany it. An ear and the jaw are favorite parts with many people.

Boiled Tongue.—Carve across the tongue, but do not cut through ; keep the slices rather thin, and help the fat from underneath.

Brisket of Beef must be carved in the direction 1 and 2 quite down to the bone, after cutting off the outside, which should be about three-quarters of an inch **thick.**

Ribs of Beef are carved similar to the sirloin, commencing at the thin end of the joint, and cutting long slices, so as to assist fat and lean at the same time.

Round or Buttock of Beef.—Remove the upper surface in the same manner as for an aitch-bone of beef, carve thin horizontal slices of fat and lean, as evenly as possible. It requires a sharp knife and steady hand to carve it well.

Leg of Mutton.—The under or thickest part of the leg should be placed uppermost, and carved in slices moderately thin, from B to C. Many persons have a taste for the knuckle,

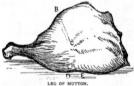

LEG OF MUTTON.

and this question should be asked, and, if preferred, should be assisted. When cold the back of the leg should be placed uppermost, and thus carved ; if the cramp bone is requested, and some persons regard it as a dainty, hold the shank with your left hand, and insert your knife at D, passing it round to E, and you will remove it.

Ribs of Beef.—There are two modes of carving this joint. The first, which is now becoming common, and is easy to an amateur carver, is to cut across the bone commencing in the center, and serving fat from A, as marked in the engraving of the sirloin ; or it should be carved in slices from A to C, commencing either in the center of the joint or at the sides. Occasionally the bones are removed, and the meat formed into a fillet ; it should then be carved as a round of beef.

The Loin of Mutton, if small, should be carved in chops, beginning with the outer chop ; if large, carve slices the whole length. A neat way is to run the knife along the chine bone and under the meat along the ribs : it may then be cut in slices ; and by this process fat and lean are served together. Your knife should be very sharp, and it should be done cleverly.

Neck of Mutton, if the scrag and chine bone are removed, is carved in the direction of the bones.

The **Scrag of Mutton** should be separated from the ribs of the neck, and when roasted the bone assisted with the meat.

Haunch of Mutton is carved as haunch of venison.

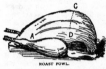

ROAST FOWL.

Roast Fowl.—This operation is a nice and skillful one to perform ; it requires both observation and practice. Insert the knife between the legs and the side, press back the leg with the blade of the knife, and the joint will disclose itself : if young, it will part, but at best, if judiciously managed, will require but a nick where the joints unite. Remove your wing from D to B, cut through and lay it back as with the leg, separating the joint with the edge of your knife, remove the merrythought and neck bones next : this you will accomplish by inserting the knife and forcing it under the bones : raise it, and it will readily separate from the breast. You will divide the breast from the body by cutting through the small ribs down to the vent, turn the back uppermost, now put your knife into about the center between the neck and rump, raise the lower part firmly yet gently, it will easily separate ; turn the neck or rump from you, take off the side bones and the fowl is carved.

In separating the thigh from the drumstick, you must insert the knife exactly at the joint, as we have indicated in the engraving ; this, however, will be found to require practice, for the joint must be accurately hit, or else much difficulty will be experienced in getting the parts asunder. There is no difference in carving roast and boiled fowls, if full grown ; but in a very young fowl when roasted, the breast is served whole. The wings and breast are in the highest favor, but the leg of a young fowl is an excellent part. Capons, when very fine and roasted, should have slices carved from the breast.

Geese.—Follow with your knife the lines marked in the engraving, A to B, and cut slices, then remove the wing, and if the party be large, the legs must also be removed, and here the *disjointer* will again prove serviceable. The stuffing, as in the turkey, will be obtained by making an insertion at the apron.

GOOSE.

Guinea Fowl are carved in the same manner.

Quails, Landrail, Wheatears, Larks, and all small birds are served whole.

Grouse and Plover are carved as partridges.

Snipe and Woodcock are divided into two parts ; the trail being served on a toast.

Fish should never be carved with steel ; assisting requires more care than knowledge ; the principal caution is to avoid breaking the flakes. In carving a piece of salmon as here engraved, cut thin slices, as from A to B, and help with it pieces of the belly in the direction marked from C to D. The best flavored is the upper or thick part.

MIDDLE CUT OF SALMON.

Haddock.—It is dressed whole, unless unusually large. When sent to the table it is split its whole length, and served one-half the head to the tail of the other part ; it is carved across.

Mackerel should always be sent to table head to tail. Divide the meat from the bone by cutting down the back lengthwise from 1 to 2 : upper part is the best. All small fish, such as herrings, smelts, etc., are served whole.

MACKEREL.

Neck of Veal.—Were you to attempt to carve each chop and serve it, you would not only place a gigantic bit upon the plate of the person you intended to help, but you would waste time, and if the vertebræ had not been jointed by the butcher

NECK OF VEAL.

you would find yourself in the position of the ungraceful carver, being compelled to exercise a degree of strength which should never be suffered to appear ; very possibly, too, assisting gravy in a manner not contemplated by the person unfortunate enough to receive it. Cut diagonally from B to A, and help in slices of moderate thickness ; you can cut from C to D in order to separate the small bones ; divide and serve them, having first inquired if they are desired.

The Breast of Veal.—Separate the ribs from A to B ; these small bones, which are the sweetest and mostly chosen. you will cut them as D D D, and serve. The long ribs are divided as at C C C ; and having ascertained the preference of

Paul Dickson/95

the person, help accordingly. At good tables the scrag is not served, but is found, when properly cooked, a very good stew.

BREAST OF VEAL.

Calf's Head.—There is much more meat to be obtained from a calf's head by carving it one way than another. Carve

CALF'S HEAD.

from A to B, cutting quite down to the bone. At the fleshy part of the neck end you will find the throat sweetbread, which you can help a slice of with the other part ; you will remove the eye with the point of the knife, and divide it in half, helping those to it who profess a preference for it : there are some tasty, gelatinous pieces around it which are palatable. Remove the jaw-bone, and then you will meet with some fine-flavored lean ; the palate, which is under the head, is by some thought a dainty, and should be proffered when carving.

Boiled Turkey is trussed in a different fashion to the

BOILED TURKEY.

roast, but the same directions given for the first apply to the second. The legs in the boiled turkey being drawn into the body may cause some little difficulty at first in their separation, but a little practice will soon surmount it.

Fillet of Veal.—Cut a slice off the whole of the upper

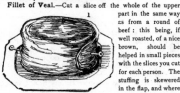

FILLET OF VEAL.

part in the same way as from a round of beef : this being, if well roasted, of a nice brown, should be helped in small pieces with the slices you cut for each person. The stuffing is skewered in the flap, and where the bones come out there is some placed ; help this with the meat, with a piece of the fat.

Loin of Veal.—This joint is sent to table served as a sirloin of beef. Having turned it over, cut out the kidney and the fat, return it to its proper position, and carve it as in the neck of veal, from B to A ; help with it a slice of kidney and fat. The kidney is usually placed upon a dry toast when removed from the joint.

Shoulder of Veal is sent to table with the under part placed uppermost. Help it as a shoulder of mutton, beginning at the knuckle end.

A Shoulder of Mutton.—This is a joint upon which a great diversity of opinion exists, many professing a species of horror at its insipidity, others finding much delicacy of flavor

SHOULDER OF MUTTON.

in certain parts. In good mutton there is no doubt but that, if properly managed, it is an excellent joint, and, if judiciously served, will give satisfaction to all who partake of it. It should be served hot. It is sent to table lying on the dish as shown in the annexed engraving.

Commence carving from A to B, taking out moderately thin slices in the shape of a wedge ; some nice pieces may then be helped from the blade-bone, from C to B, cutting on both sides of the bone. Cut the fat from D, carving it in thin slices. Some of the most delicate parts, however, lie on the under part of the shoulder ; take off thin pieces horizontally from B to C, and from A ; some tender slices are to be met with at D, but they must be cut through as indicated.

The shoulder of mutton is essentially a joint of titbits, and therefore, when carving it, the tastes of those at the table should be consulted. It is a very insipid joint when cold, and should therefore be hashed if sent to table a second time.

Wild Duck and Widgeon.—The breast of these fowls, being the best portion, is carved in slices, which being removed, a glass of old port made hot is poured in, the half of a lemon seasoned with cayenne and salt should then be squeezed in, the slices relaid in their places, and then served the joints being removed the same as in other fowl.

Partridge.—Separate the legs, and then divide the bird into three parts, leaving each leg and wing together. The breast is then divided from the back, and helped whole, the latter being assisted with any of the other parts. When the party consists of gentlemen only, the bird is divided into two by cutting right through from the vent to the neck.

Pigeon.—Like woodcock, these birds are cut in half, through the breast and back, and helped.

Roast Turkey.—Cut long slices from both sides of the breast down to the ribs at the breast-bone. If a large bird the legs may be removed, and the drumsticks taken off. The stuffing may be removed by making an incision in the apron.

Boiled Fowl.—There is but little difference in the mode of carving roast and boiled fowl, and that little lies in the breast of the former being generally served entire—the thigh bone, too, is preferred by many to the wing.

Double Dutch. A secret language in which vowels are pronounced normally but consonants become syllables:

b - bub	k - kuk	s - sus
c - cash	l - lul	t - tut
d - dud	m - mum	v - vuv
f - fuf	n - nun	w - wash
g - gug	p - pup	x - xux
h - hutch	q - quack	y - yub
j - jug	r - rug	z - zub.

It takes practice even to say hello and good-bye—hutchelullulo and gugoodudbubyube. The secret key to Double Dutch was revealed in an article by Dr. James F. Bender in *The New York Times Magazine* of December 31, 1944. Not only did he reveal the secrets of Double Dutch, Opish, Pig, and Turkey Irish (see below), but he asserted that no less than 50 million Americans spoke one or more synthetic tongues.

Eggy-peggy. A primarily British language in which *eg* or *egg* is inserted before each vowel. Nancy Mitford refers to it in her *Love in a Cold Climate:* "Lady Montdore . . . led me to the table and the starlings went on with their chatter about my mother in 'eggy-peggy,' a language I happened to know quite well. 'Egg-is shegg-ee reggealleggy, pegg-oor swegg-eet?' "

Framis. Double-talk for double-talk. Unfortunately, this form of talking does not enjoy the same popularity it did prior to and through World War II. Well done, it is a skillful blend of meaningful and meaningless words that when delivered leads the listener to think he is either hard of hearing or losing his mind. Or to be more to the point: a durnamic verbal juberance with clear mokus, flaysome, and rasorial overtones. In 1943, *Life* magazine carried an article on double-talk by George Frazier that contained some hints for those wishing to master it. The most important:

—Certain sounds work better than others. Some of them are: *oil, urf, erris, eufen, orsin, awn,* and *urma.* You can create a basic vocabulary prefixed by consonants or syllables.

—The best way to start is with short sentences or phrases. Frazier suggested asking a waiter for such unprocurable dishes as:

Steefils on toast	Zilts with sauerkraut
Kerbits and milk	Vimilforty cheese kribbles from Holland.

—Never smile while talking.

—Use enough legitimate words to convince the listener that you are not talking framis.

Jerigonza. Spanish Pig Latin in which the letter *p* is inserted after each vowel, turning *buenos dias* into *bupepnos dipaps*. It was described by a B. Sacto-Hirano in the second edition of *A Pamphlet on the Four Basic Dialects of Pig Latin.*

King Tut. This language is described in Alan Milberg's *Street Games.* Vowels stay the same. A *u* is added to every consonant and then the consonant is repeated. *T* becomes *tut* and *b* becomes *bub.* Double consonants are expressed with the word *square*—*gg* becomes *gug square.* All *y*'s become *yuk.* Nunotut tuthuhatut easusyuk tuto mumasustuterur!

Opish. Pronounced Ah-pish. Vowels remain the same, but *op* is added after each consonant so that, for example, the first three days of the week become: Moponopdopayop, Topuesopdopayop. Wopedopnopesopdopayop. A variation uses *ob.*

Pig Latin. Easiest to use and the most popular of the secret languages, Pig Latin is based on two simple rules: (1) Take the first letter of the word that is to be said, put it at the end of the word, and then add *ay.* (2) Do not invert letters if the word begins with *a, e, i, o,* or *u,* but add *ay* to the end of the word. Itsay eallyray eryvay implesay. A variant form uses *kee* in place of *ay,* which is impleskee ootkee.

Platysyllabic Pig. The name given to a form of Pig Latin in Brig. Gen. Cyclops Stonebone's *Pamphlet on the Four Basic Dialects of Pig Latin.* It divides words into syllables and inserts *iv* (the *iv* of ivory) after the initial consonant. Box becomes bivox. It becomes more complicated with givigivantivic wivords.

(The author of the aforementioned pamphlet was actually William Murray Cheny, who published one of the few scholarly works on Pig Latin in 1953.)

Ruly English. A language invented by Simon M. Newman for the Patent Office in the 1950s in which every word has only one conceptual meaning and each concept has only one word to describe it. It was created to get away from regular "unruly" English in which, for instance, the word "through" has 13 distinct meanings. Ruly features many "between" words, such as *resilrig* to describe a state between resilience and rigidity. Somewhat rigid is *sli resilrig* and very flexible is *sub resilrig.*

Rx. On a doctor's prescription, s.o.s. does not mean that the patient is in distress but that the drug ordered is to be taken "if necessary." Other notations commonly used in doctor/pharmacist communications:

aa	of each	p.c.	after meals
ad lib	as desired	p.r.n.	when required
b.i.n.	twice a night	q.i.d.	4 times a day
c	with	q.s.	as much as required
caps	capsule	q.4 h.	every 4 hours
gm	gram	s	without
gtt	a drop	stat	immediately
o.d.	every day	t.i.d.	3 times a day
o.m.	every morning	t.i.n.	3 times a night

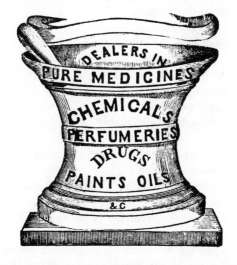

Short-order Code. Although not used as commonly as it once was, short-order cooks, waiters, waitresses, and soda jerks developed an elaborate set of code words and numbers. The words are not impossible to figure out (Adam and Eve on a raft = two poached eggs on toast), but numbers contain no clues to their meaning. Here are the most commonly used numbers:

2½ - Small glass of milk.
5 - Large glass of milk.
13 - White bread; also, the boss is nearby.

Paul Dickson/99

14 - A special order; stand by for something out of the ordinary.

19 - Banana split.

21 - Limeade. (This and other numbers ending in 1 call for a single, 22 is a call for 2 limeades, 23 for three and so forth.)

22 - Customer's check has not been paid.

23 - Scram; leave me alone, I'm working.

30 - The end, the place is closing.

33 Red - Coca-Cola with cherry syrup.

36 - Postum.

41 - This can stand for either a lemonade or a small glass of milk.

48½ - To be fired; someone who has been 48½ed has just been discharged.

51 - Hot chocolate.

55 - Root beer.

55½ - Small root beer.

66 - An empty bowl or glass; dirty dishes.

73 - Best wishes.

81 - Glass of water.

86 - Sold out or unavailable, as in "86 the banana cream pie."

87½ - Look at the beautiful girl out front.

88 - Love and kisses.

95 - There is a customer walking out without paying.

98 - Look out, the assistant manager is near.

99 - Beware, the manager is approaching.

Turkey Irish. A language in which *ab* is inserted before vowels. It is one of the rarest. Dr. James Bender wrote in his 1944 *New York Times Magazine* article that it showed up only in certain communities, such as Yonkers, New York, but would be unheard of a few miles away. Habavabe aba nabicabe dabay.

Tutahash. Like Double Dutch except that the letters *c, h, r, w, x, y,* and *z* are respectively rendered *cus, hash, rur, w, x, yum,* and *zuz.*

Vague Specific. An important concept and term created by Richard B. Gehman in an article in *Collier's* in 1949. It refers to the habit of "referring vaguely to specific persons or things." Gehman gave many examples, including this conversation from under his own roof:

"Here," my wife said, "you can take these."

"Where do you want them?"

"Oh, put them out there somewhere."

"With the others?"

"No," said my wife decisively, "put them with those things behind the others."

FIGHTING WORDS

—A Muster of Military Terminology—

Air support. Bombing. In 1974 an Air Force colonel won a Double-speak Award from the National Council of Teachers of English for his complaint about reporters writing about a U.S. bombing mission: "You always write it's bombing, bomb-ing, bombing. It's not bombing! It's air support."

Balbo. A massive flight formation involv-ing hundreds of aircraft. Named after the Italian general Italo Balbo, who led a mass flight from Italy to the United States and returned in 1933. Balbos are often seen at the ends of movies about World War II.

Balloon goes up, the. Term dating back to the 1950s for a big war, as in "What happens if the balloon goes up?"

Bident. An ancient two-pronged weapon. Less commonly referred to than the three-pronged *trident*.

Bricole. A harness worn by humans for pulling guns or other heavy loads.

Caltrop. Military device used for stopping cavalry and horse-drawn vehicles. It is a small, multipointed piece of iron that always presents at least one sharp spike when thrown on the ground.

City-bargaining. A concept in nuclear war strategy by which a war is controlled after it has begun. Specifically, you "bargain" by knocking out one of your enemy's cities in response to his attack on your country.

Cocarde. The emblem on the wing of a warplane that indicates which country it is from.

Conservatory. Glass-enclosed machine-gun turret common to large World War II–era aircraft.

Derosing. Word formed from acronym for "Date of Estimated Return from OverSEas." To derose is to go home.

DOE reaction. The end; DOE stands for Death of Earth.

Escalation agility. Ease with which one side or the other can escalate in a weapons exchange.

Foo. A mysterious military onlooker. He was described in a British naval magazine in 1946: "Mr. Foo is a mysterious Second World War product, gifted with bitter omniscience and sarcasm."

Fougasse. A land mine that explodes and blows metal and other debris in a predetermined direction.

Fratricide. When one element of a weapon with more than one warhead knocks out one of its brother warheads. Used in conjunction with MIRV (Multiple Independently targeted Reentry Vehicle).

Fugleman. Model soldier; one who stands in front of other soldiers to demonstrate, drill, or whatever.

Furphy. A latrine rumor. A reference to the Furphy Brothers who furnished field latrines to the Australian Army (1890–1916).

Gaffle. The lever used in cocking a crossbow.

Generalissima. A word that apparently exists only in the abstract. The journal *Word Ways* was able to find four generalissimos (Chiang Kai-shek, Franco, Trujillo, and Stalin) but no woman with the corresponding title.

Gigaton. A measure of energy released that is equivalent to a billion tons of TNT.

Ground zero. The point where a nuclear weapon explodes; also the nickname of the small open area at the center of the Pentagon.

Horned scully. An underwater obstacle designed to rip the bottom out of a boat or ship. It consists of long, pointed rails embedded in concrete.

Kopfring. Metal ring welded to the tip of a bomb to reduce its penetration into the ground or water.

Lapidate. To stone.

Machicolation. A floor opening, parapet, or other place from which boiling water, hot lead, rocks, or other objects can be dropped on an enemy. Machicolations are common to castles and fortresses.

Megacorpse. A nuclear-age word for a million dead people.

Meteorskrieg. A super blitzkrieg. The term was coined by American general Stephen O. Fuqua to describe the speed and power of the German drive in France and Belgium in the spring of 1940.

Nth Country Problem. The further proliferation of nuclear weapons. Until France joined the club some years ago, this was known as the 4th Country Problem.

Permissive-link. An element in the workings of a nuclear weapon that must be completed or supplied before the weapon can be armed or fired. The link itself can be anything from a key to a coded radio signal.

Post-attack economy. Fancy Pentagonese for the America that will exist after a nuclear interchange (if there are enough people left to maintain an economy).

Quakers. Quakers or *Quaker guns* are dummy cannon used to deceive the enemy. They were traditionally placed in the portholes of ships or in the gunholes of forts.

Rug rank. A higher ranking officer; those who rate a rug on the floor of their offices.

Sciamachy. Fighting an imaginary enemy; combat with a shadow. Pronounced sigh-a-maky.

Suitcase warfare. A term that drives home the size and portability of new types of weaponry. To quote from the definition of this term that appears in the report of an insurance industry think tank, ''It is conceivable that an object the size of a suitcase, and carried as inconspicuously, could contain any of several substances which could destroy whole structures and even whole cities.''

Surviving spouse. Department of Defense term to replace the words *widow* and *widower*. The official term for what a surviving spouse is given is a *death gratuity,* which sounds like a tip you give an undertaker.

Tacnuk. Tactical nuclear weapon.

Thalassocracy. Rule of the sea; sea power.

"Total Nuclear War." It says under this entry in the Defense Department's *Dictionary of Military and Associated Terms,* "Not to be used. See general war." This squeamishness about total war reaches a peak in the official *Dictionary of United States Army Terms,* which shies away from defining not only *total nuclear war* but also *general war, nuclear war,* and *war.*

Unk-unks. Short for technological unknown unknowns. Used by military planners whose unk-unks usually pertain to what the Soviet military planners are planning.

Uti possidetis. The principle that states that a nation owns the territory it holds at the end of a war. It is pronounced you-tea-possa-detis.

Wargasm. The condition that occurs when all the nuclear and thermonuclear buttons get pushed.

Wild card. The term used to describe a major unforeseen development that could wipe out less dramatic scenarios and projections. A nuclear holocaust, the total downfall of civilization in its present form, a worldwide totalitarian state, and extraterrestrial invasion are all wild cards.

Woompher bomb. Term that emerged in the late 1950s for a technological breakthrough of such magnitude that the country that made it would have a decisive strategic advantage.

Zumbooruk. A small swivel-cannon fired from the back of a camel.

16

FILLERS

—Regional Americanisms and Foreign Words That Fill Major Gaps in Mainstream English—

Absquatulate. To leave hurriedly and stealthily. This is an old Americanism in need of revival.

Ambeer. Tobacco spittle in the Ozarks.

Anti-goddlin'. Uneven, out of whack; southern United States.

Baffona. A woman with a not too unpleasant mustache. Italian.

Brindle. Any dark color that cannot be classified. It is often used in New England to describe the color of a cow or horse.

Catawampously. This word was defined in the "Que Paso?" column of the *Arizona Republic* as "Chest-out, big doggin' bravado as in 'Ol' Red, he stomped catawampously into that there saloon and offered to fight ever'body all at once.'"

Cejijunto. Spanish for a person with one long continuous eyebrow. It is both an adjective and a noun and pronounced ceh-he-hunto.

Crème faussée. French for fake cream. It has so much more style than, say, artificial cream or nondairy creamer.

Culacino. Italian for the mark left on a tablecloth by a wet glass.

Doppelgänger. The apparition of a living person, as opposed to a ghost that is the apparition of a dead one. German.

Dozy. Wood that hasn't been properly seasoned in Maine, according to E. B. White in his essay "Maine Speech."

Ehestandswinkel. German for incipient balding at the temples.

Espantoon. A policeman's nightstick in Baltimore.

Fantods. The fidgets; the willies—a venerable piece of American slang used, among other places, in *Huckleberry Finn:* "They was all nice pictures, I reckon, but I didn't somehow seem to take to them, because if ever I was down a little, they always gave me the fantods."

Het. Past participle of *heat* in northern New England.

Hip-skeltered. Askew, crooked, or irregular in the Ozarks. This is one of a number of fine regional *catawampus* words including *slaunch-wise, skewgee, sky-gogglin', sky-wampus,* and *slantindicular.*

Homme moyen sensuel. Literally, a man of average desires; ordinary man. A wonderful name for an average guy who would like to be called something with a little more zip than average guy.

Huskanawed. An expression used to describe a person who appears as if he had been submitted to the action of an emetic or enema. It derives from the word *huskanawing* used by Virginia Indians to describe an ordeal of initiation to which young males were subjected. Part of the ordeal involved heavy doses of emetics.

Jizzicked. Something so far gone that no repair can fix it. New England.

Jorum. A big drink, especially in New England.

Kippage. State of great excitement, anguish, or passion. It is a Scottish word.

Lagniappe. In Cajun country this is a small present given when a purchase is made, or, more to the point, when a bill is paid. Washington journalist William D. Hickman, originally from East Texas, recalls, "At my grandmother's grocery it was usually bubble gum or a penny Tootsie Roll."

Lagom. Swedish for *just enough.* An American friend who has spent many years in Sweden maintains that *lagom* fills a vacuum in English. It is pronounced lag-ome.

Mulligrubs. A state of temporary depression, an archaic but apt term.

Peeze. To leak in small bubbles; a small leak. From Newfoundland.

Pindling. Small and ill-nourished, such as a pindling chick. The opposite of *thriving* in New England.

Pizzlesprung. Pooped. Kentucky.

Reef. A strong tug. New England.

Schadenfreude. Taking malicious delight in the misfortune of others. German.

Scurryfunge. According to John Gould in *Maine Lingo,* a scurryfunge is a ". . . hasty tidying of the house between the time you see a neighbor coming and the time she knocks on the door."

Shacklety. Ozarkian for a building that is about to fall down.

Sigogglin. Tilted to the right, as, for example, a leaning barn. A tilt to the left is *antisigogglin.*

Slimpsy. Sleazy, cheap, of poor quality. Yankee talk.

Sloomy. Sluggish, spiritless, and dull.

Tunk. A light blow. "That jar lid won't come off unless you tunk it." A word from New England.

Weltschmerz. Sadness over the evils of the world. Pronounced velt-shmairtz.

Whale. To strike vigorously, as in "whaling the bejeezus" out of a fence post. Old Yankee word.

Yuns. Word used in and around Pittsburgh for "you ones"; the long-missing plural of *you* that has always been lacking in the English language.

Zàzzera. Italian for the hair that grows on the back of the neck.

FIZZLERS

—Terms Whose Time
Has Not Yet Come—

There is something fascinating about new words and phrases that are introduced or suggested and then flop. What follows is a modest collection of such flops, including a sampling of proposed nonsexist pronouns that were doomed from the start because they looked and sounded more like Estonian than English.

Americaid. One of a group of 22 words created by the Nixon Administration in 1972 as possible replacements for the word *welfare*. Among other suggestions: *Amerishare, Faircare, Sharefare, Americare, Yourfare, Benefaid,* and *Famfare*.

Autel. An early competitor for the name of a new kind of lodging. The competition was won by *motel*. *Autotel* also lost.

Banana. When Alfred Kahn, President Carter's resourceful inflation fighter, was reprimanded by the White House for using the word *recession,* he substituted the word *banana*.

Cashomat. The first name used for the now ubiquitous electronic tellers attached to American banks.

Chairone. Word for chairperson that was pushed by a number of advocates in the early 1970s. It is a particularly rare word because it was accepted by the editors of *Webster's Third New International Dictionary,* added to the supplement, and then taken out. Words are almost never accepted and then rejected in this manner. According to Frederick C. Mish, editorial director of the G. & C. Merriam Company, "It was simply a case of a word that got a lot of attention, but did not work in the long run. It doesn't sound (chair-one) right and when it is written it looks like an Italian word."

Chirtonsor. In 1924, 3,000 barbers voted to go by this name.

Chunnel. The long-planned, occasionally revived tunnel under the English Channel between England and France. It was first proposed in the middle of the nineteenth century and was last revived as an idea in the 1960s.

Clothing Refresher. A self-descriptive term adopted by the washerwomen of San Francisco in 1849 to upgrade the name of their work. Like so many other attempts to up one's status with a new name, clothing refresher did not take hold. Bartenders are still called that despite an attempt by some members of that profession to become known as *beverage counselors.* Other failures: *guidance worker* for bill collector and *director of pupil personnel* for truant officer.

Co. Word to replace he or she, suggested by writer Mary Orovan. The plural is *cos* and himself and herself become *coself.*

Cost Growth. In 1969 the Pentagon launched an effort, spearheaded by Deputy Secretary of Defense David Packard, to banish the term cost overrun and replace it with cost growth.

Cytherean. The adjective for the planet Venus that was informally agreed upon by space scientists who needed a stand-in for the traditional word, venereal, which had become too closely associated with earthy behavior. The Greek name for Venus, Aphrodite, had become similarly tied to the flesh. Cytherean comes from the name of the island of Cythera, which is where Aphrodite first landed after her birth at sea. Similarly, science fiction writers have tended to use *Venusians* for inhabitants of the planet to avoid the association of the venereal. Venusian may have a future, but Cytherean has bombed.

District Work Period. Term created and officially sanctioned by the House of Representatives in late 1976 to replace what then Speaker "Tip" O'Neill called "an ugly term the press likes to use." The ugly term is "recess," and while congressmen may call it a DWP, everybody else still calls it a recess. The Senate, incidentally, has had no better luck with its official replacement, "nonlegislative period."

E. Neutral stand-in for he and she created by the Broward County Florida schools in response to the federal call for desexed language in school publications. The same people also came up with *Ir,* a neutral personal pronoun for him and her.

Electrolethe. A less jarring name that has been suggested for the electric chair.

Enco. For years the name for various corporate parts of the giant Standard Oil Company of New Jersey. When the company decided to settle on one international trademark, it considered Enco but decided instead on Exxon when it found that "enco" sounded like the Japanese term for "stalled car."

Et. Third-person-singular pronoun which is created from the *e* in *he* and *she* and the *t* in *it.* It was created by Aline Hoffman of Sarnia, Ontario. It appears in Bill Sherk's *Brave New Words.*

Femcee. Female emcee; mistress of ceremonies. The term came into being in the 1950s along with *toastmistress,* which had far greater success than femcee.

Frarority. A collegiate social organization that admits both sexes. Such places are common, but the name is not. Ditto for *freshperson.*

Girlcott. *Time* magazine's term for a woman's boycott circa 1970.

Hesh. Combined "he and she," one of a number of genderless pronouns proposed by Professor Robert Longwell of the University of Northern Colorado. Also proposed by Longwell:

> **Hirm:** "him or her" composite.
> **Hizer:** "his or her" word.
> **-wan:** Sexless suffix. The plural is *-wen*—more than one policewan would be policewen.

Huperson. A short-lived suggestion for a neutral replacement for human.

Jhe. Coinage to use where *he* is customary but not appropriate. This neutral personal pronoun, pronounced gee, was invented by Professor Milton R. Stern of the University of Michigan.

Journey's End. What the *Cincinnati Enquirer* calls its death notices.

Kin-mother. Name adopted in 1942 by the Mother-in-Law Association as a replacement for mother-in-law, which the group felt had acquired a bad reputation. Other replacement names that the MILA had considered: *our-ma* and *motherette.*

Klansperson. Nonsexist title advocated by the Grand Dragon of the Ku

Klux Klan, according to William Lambdin's *Doublespeak Dictionary.*

MUSIC. In 1969 when there was much criticism of the military industrial complex, a group of congressmen tried to get people interested in a new name, MUSIC, for Military University, Union, Science, Industrial Complex. For a while supporters of the new name used lines like "Some critics are out of tune with 'MUSIC' " to get the idea across, but it never caught on.

Newsperson. In his *American Usage and Style: The Consensus,* Roy H. Copperud terms this the "most obnoxious" of the new neuter words as it replaces reporter, which is "as asexual as it can be."

Noctician. A failed attempt to give the night watchman higher status.

Norseperson. A Norseman desexed. Former Carter speech-writer Walter Shapiro told of its use in an article in *The Washington Post:* "In 1977, Carter speech-writers, in a puckish gesture, celebrated the anniversary of Leif Ericsson's discovery of America by referring to him as a 'gallant Norseperson' in an official proclamation. Reportedly Carter . . . was not amused."

Nova. Name of a type of Chevrolet that is now marketed in the Spanish-speaking world as the Caribe. This change was made after sluggish initial sales were traced to the fact that *"No va"* means "does not go" in Spanish.

Per. Stand-in for him and her, derived from *person.* Novelist Marge Piercy used this word in per book *Woman on the Edge of Time.*

Personhole. Term created in 1978 by the Woonsocket, Rhode Island, city council as part of a drive to eliminate supposedly sexist language. It replaced manhole in Woonsocket's official circles.

Pn. Short form of person to replace Mr., Mrs., and Ms. Suggested in the early 1970s by *Everywoman* editor Varda One, who feels we should all be addressed as *Person.* Pn. is pronounced "person" just as Mr. is pronounced "mister."

Product Safety Campaign. Term that General Motors attempted to introduce in 1972 as a replacement for *recall.* A GM press release stated that ". . . customers are being notified about three separate product safety campaigns affecting approximately 6,000 vehicles."

Rockoon. A balloon-launched rocket, an idea from the late 1950s whose time has yet to come.

Sanitarians. One of a number of failed attempts to give the busboy (or girl) an upgraded name. Sanitarian was the suggestion of the Wisconsin Restaurant Association in the late 1950s. At about the same time, the Chicago Restaurant Association plumped for *table-service man.*

Others that have been suggested: *waiter assistant, restaurant porter,* and *service aide.*

Spose. Term suggested by several readers of *Saturday Review* for two people living together. It comes from the oft-asked question " 'Spose they'll ever get married?''

Thon. Third-person genderless pronoun that has been suggested. William Zinsser, in his book *On Writing Well,* wrote, "Maybe I don't speak for the average American, but I very much doubt that thon wants that word in thons language or that thon would use it thonself.''

Timmie. Name derived from the French *intime* and suggested by Mrs. Gordon Corbett of Anchorage, Alaska, in the pages of *Saturday Review.* "Now,'' she wrote, "I can refer to the beloved partners of our children as our own dear Timmies.'' Along with the aforementioned *spose,* other suggestions sent to *Saturday Review* included: *co-vivante, with-live, shackmate,* and *grynnfink,* which was composed from leftover Scrabble letters.

While others strive to create the right word, it would appear that the term with the best chance of survival is *posslq,* a term invented by the Census Bureau. Posslq (pronounced poss-ill-que) is an acronym for "Person of Opposite Sex Sharing Living Quarters.'' The term was made famous by CBS poet-in-residence Charles Osgood, who used it as the subject of a poem that began with the line,

> *There's nothing that I wouldn't do*
> *If you would be my posslq.*

None other than Ann Landers has deemed the word ". . . so simple to pronounce, so non-judgmental and pleasing to the ear.'' She adds that it is easier on parents than "this person I'm living with.''

Waitron. Neutral term suggested for waiter and waitress.

Womure. One of a number of new gender words seriously suggested by Temple University Professor James F. Adams as a substitution for words in which man appears, including *womure* for manure. *Womure* has yet to take off. Neither have *womic* for manic nor *womuscript* for manuscript.

FORMATIONS

—A Sampling of Shapes
and Conditions—

One of the most extensive groups of words in the language are those having to do with the shapes of things. Those on display here are words that captured my fancy and represent less than a tenth of my total "shape" collection.

A logical question that suggests itself is: Who actually uses these words? The answer is that they do get used by specialists in certain areas of science and medicine. Dermatologists, for instance, talk of filiform warts and foliaceous growth.

Acinaciform. Scimitar-shaped.
Acinform. Clustered like grapes.
Actinoid. In the shape of a star.
Aduncous. Bent like a hook.
Aliform. Wing-like.
Ampullaceous. Bottle-shaped; possessing a round body.
Anfractuous. Full of twists and turns.

Anguiform. Snake-shaped. Not to be confused with *anguilliform,* which means eel-shaped.

Arcuate. Bow-shaped.

Auriform. Ear-shaped.

Balanoid. Acorn-shaped.

Belemnoid. Dart-shaped; not to be confused with *beloid* or *belonoid,* which are respectively arrow-shaped and needle-shaped.

Bicaudate. Two-tailed.

Bicipital. Having two heads.

Biomorphic. Free-form. Shaped as a living form. The opposite of geometric.

Boluliform. Sausage-shaped.

Bursiform. Pouch-shaped.

Calathiform. Cup-shaped.

Calceiform. Slipper-shaped—pronounced cal-see-a-form. Not to be confused with *calciform,* which is pebble-shaped.

Campanulate. Bell-shaped.

Carbunculoid. Shaped like a large boil or carbuncle.

Caricous. Fig-like.

Claviform. Club-shaped.

Clithridiate. Keyhole-shaped.

Cordate. Heart-shaped.

Coroniform. In the shape of a crown.

Cristiform. Crest-shaped.

Cucumiform. Cucumber-shaped.

Decussate. X-shaped; intersecting.

Dendriform. Tree-shaped.

Dodecagon. A twelve-sided form.

Dolioform. Barrel-shaped.

Echinoid. Like a sea urchin.

Ensiform. Sword-shaped.

Erose. Uneven and irregular. Rhymes with heroes.

Eruciform. Like a caterpillar.

Esquamate. Without scales.

Evase. Wider at the top; in the shape of a vase.

Falcate. Crescent-shaped.

Favaginous. Like a honeycomb.

Filiform. In the shape of a thread.

Fissilingual. Fork-tongued.

Flabellate. Fan-shaped.

Foliaceous. Leaf-like; leafy.

Forticate. Scissor-like; deeply forked.

Fucoid. Like seaweed.

Fulgurous. Lightning-shaped; charged with lightning.

Furciferous. Fork-shaped.

Fusiform. Spindle-shaped.

Geniculated. Having knee-like joints.

Glabrous. Smooth; bald.

Guttiform. Shaped like a drop.

Hamiform. Hook-shaped.

Harengiform. Herring-shaped.

Hederiform. Shaped like ivy.

Helicoid. Screw-shaped.

Hexagram. In the shape of the Star of David.

Hordeiform. In the shape of a grain of barley. Pronounced hore-dee-form.

Hypsiloid. Like the Greek letter *upsilon;* V-shaped.

Incanous. Covered with soft white hair.

Infundibular. Funnel-shaped.

Janiform. Having two faces, like the Roman god Janus.

Lamelliform. Like a thin plate in form.

Lanceolate. Tapered to a point at either end, as with certain leaves.

Lanuginous. Covered with soft, downy hair.

Latirostrous. Broad-beaked.

Linguiform. Tongue-shaped.

Lunette. Anything shaped like a half-moon.

Mammose. Breast-shaped.

Margaritaceous. Pearl-like.

Marmoreal. Marble-like; cold and white.

Monilliform. Segmented like a string of beads.

Moriform. Mulberry-shaped.

Muriform. Resembling or suggesting the pattern of a brick wall, such as certain cellular tissue.

Napiform. Turnip-shaped.

Nummular. Like a little coin.

Obconic. Pear-shaped.

Obrotund. Round, but squashed down on the top and bottom.

Oriform. Mouth-shaped.

Ostreophagous. Oyster-shaped.

Palmate. Shaped like a human hand.

Pandurate. Fiddle-shaped.

Papilionaceous. Butterfly-shaped.

Paradigitate. Having an equal number of fingers on each hand. It can also be applied to toes.

Pectinate. Comb-like; having teeth like a comb.

Pedimanous. Having feet in the shape of hands, as is true of monkeys.

Pemphigoid. Bubble-shaped, bubble-like.

Penniform. Having the form of a feather. If this would seem to be a word that is not used that often, consider the cases of *bipenniform, demipenniform,* and *semipenniform.* None of these are to be confused with *pinniform,* which means shaped like a pin *or* feather.

Piliform. Thread-shaped.

Pineal. Pineapple-shaped.

Pisiform. Shaped like a pea or peas.

Plataleiform. Spoon-billed.

Plicate. Folded in the manner of a fan.

Pulvinate. Swelling or bulging like a cushion.

Punctiform. Like a point or dot.

Pyriform. Pear-shaped.

Quincunx. An arrangement of five things so that one is in each corner and in the middle of a square. The term is sometimes used to describe the arrangement of plants or shrubs in a garden.

Remiform. Shaped like an oar.

Reniform. Kidney-shaped.

Resofincular. Resembling a wire hanger, a coinage of Lewis Burke Frumkes that first appeared in his 1976 *Harper's* article "A Volley of Words."

Retiform. Net-shaped.

Rhinocerial. Very heavy, as a rhinoceros.

Samariform. In the shape of a winged seed pod.

Scalpriform. Chisel-shaped.

Scaphoid. Boat-shaped.

Sciuroid. Like a squirrel or a squirrel's tail.

Scrotiform. Pouch-shaped.

Scutiform. Shield-shaped.

Selliform. Saddle-shaped.

Sigmoidal. Curved in two directions.

Siliquiform. In the form of a small pod or husk.
Sinorous. Snake-like.
Soleiform. Slipper-shaped.
Sphenoid. Wedge-shaped.
Squaliform. Shark-shaped.
Squamous. Scaly or full of scales.
Stelliform. Star-shaped.
Stirious. Resembling icicles.
Strombuliform. Like a screw or spinning top.
Subulate. Awl-shaped.
Sudiform. Stake-shaped.
Sycosiform. Fig-shaped.
Tauriform. Bull-shaped.
Totipalmate. With fully webbed toes.
Unciform. J-shaped.
Undecagon. An eleven-sided form.
Unifoliate. Having one leaf.
Urceolate. Pitcher-shaped. Pronounced your-sea-a-lit.
Utriform. Like a leather bottle.
Velutinous. Having a soft and velvet-like surface.
Vermiform. Having the shape of a worm.
Verruciform. Wart-shaped.
Virgate. Wand-shaped; long and slender.
Vulviform. V-shaped.
Xiphoid. Sword-shaped.
Zosteriform. Girdle-shaped.
Zygal. H-shaped.
Zygomorphous. Yoke-shaped.

GAME NAMES

—A Leisurely Volley of Terms from Playground and Playing Field—

Ape hanger. Extremely tall handlebar on a bicycle or motorcycle.

Aunt Emma. Croquet term for a man or woman who wastes time and talent playing in a dull and conservative manner.

Baby split. In bowling, a split where either the 2 and 7 pins or the 3 and 10 pins are left standing. Part of a rich collection of terms for bowling splits that includes the *Bedpost* (7 and 10 upright), *Bucket* (leaving 2-4-5-8 or 3-5-6-9), *Cincinnati* (an 8-10 split), *Four Horsemen* (1-2-4-7 or 1-3-6-10), *Half Worcester* (leaving either the 3 and 9 or the 2 and 8 standing), *Lily* (split that leaves 5-7-10 standing), *Sour Apple* (same as Lily), *Spread Eagle* (2-3-4-6-7-10 split), and *Woolworth* (5 and 10 standing). While it is obvious how the Woolworth got its name (5 and 10), the *Kresge* (one name for the 5 and 7 split) is harder to figure out.

Baff. Billiards. To hit the table before hitting the ball. In golf, *baffing* is striking the ground immediately behind the ball.

Baize. Billiards. The green material that covers the table.

Baltimore chop. Baseball. A ball that is hit just in front of the plate and bounces high enough to allow the runner to make it to first.

Besom. The curler's broom, used to aid the curling stone move down the ice. Pronounced bee-zum.

Birling. Logrolling on water. The logger's contest.

Blowout. The proper name for those party table items that unfurl when blown into.

Boondocking. Tiddledywinker's term for sending an opponent's wink or winks far from the cup.

Burger. Skateboarding. A bad bruise or scrape.

Caber. Heavy tree trunk used in the Scottish sport of caber-tossing, which is throwing tree trunks for distance.

Canogganing. Winter activity in which one races downhill in a canoe instead of skis. It ranks with *Husskiing* (in which teams of huskies pull individuals on skis) as the most obscure of the winter sports.

Cat. A draw in ticktacktoe.

Cesta. Jai alai. The player's wicker basket-glove.

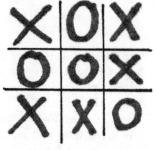

Cleek. The number one iron in golf. Cleek is one of a number of old names for clubs that have been replaced by sternly descriptive standard terms. *Niblick* is the now seldom heard original name for the sand wedge, and the *brassie* was a niblick with its head shod with a brass plate.

Crease. Hockey. The rectangular area in front of the goal that cannot be entered by offensive players without the puck.

Crotch. Handball/Racquetball/Squash. The intersection of two court playing surfaces, such as a wall and the floor.

Cuban fork ball. Baseball. A suspected spitball.

Cup of coffee. Baseball. Short time in the major leagues by a minor league player.

Dormie. Golf. A player who leads by as many holes as are left to play —e.g., a four-stroke lead after the fourteenth hole.

Double Dutch. Name for the jump rope action that takes place when two turners turn two ropes inward in an eggbeater motion.

Dumpers. Sometimes called "dump words," dumpers are special words used to clear one's Scrabble rack when it is burdened with too many vowels. *Idiom, melee, bureau,* and *apogee* are well-known and commonly used dumpers. Advanced dumpers, however, use such words as *oribi, aalii, balata,* and *hoopoe.* One would be hard-pressed to come up with a better dumper than *cooee,* which any 17-pound dictionary will tell you is "a prolonged shrill cry used as a signal by Australian aborigines."

Eeph. Lacrosse. Scooping the ball up off the ground and passing it. Rhymes with beef.

Eephus ball. Baseball. An unorthodox pitch popularized by Pittsburgh Pirate Truett "Rip" Sewell in the 1940s. The ball floated high in the air and then fell through the strike zone. The word *eephus* was created by outfielder Maurice Van Robays lest this odd pitch remain nameless. Only one batter, Ted Williams, ever hit one of Sewell's eephus balls for a home run.

Eggies. Borrowed marbles or the act of borrowing same.

Enders. Those who turn the rope in jump rope games.

Endo. Motorcycling. When driver and machine flip end-over-end.

Eskimo roll. A complete rollover in a kayak—that is, into and under the water and up again.

Farthees. Game played with baseball cards in which the object is to see who can flip his card the farthest.

Fizgig. A loud, hissing firework.

Fletch. Archery. To put feathers on an arrow.

Girandole. Cluster of fireworks or water jets.

Glissade. Moving on snow or ice without skis.

Go-devil. A homemade vehicle made by fastening roller skate wheels at either end of a narrow piece of wood with a wooden box on the front end.

Histing. Raising one's hand from the ground when shooting in marbles.

Honda. The eye at the end of the rodeo performer's rope through which the other end of the rope is passed to form a loop.

Hoppo-bumpo. Traditional name for the game played by hopping around on one leg, trying to spill your opponent using folded arms as a bumper bar.

Hot pepper. Fast turning in jump rope. In *Jump Rope!* Peter L. Skolnik points to a number of synonyms for this term including *bullets, hot peas, hot peas with butter, pepper, vinegar,* and *whipping.* To jump as fast as you can until you miss is the *skin,* and *really* fast turning is *red hot bricks.*

Hunching. Moving one's hand forward when shooting in marbles.

J'adoubovitz. Chess. A player who annoys his opponent by making constant small adjustments to the pieces. It comes from the French *j'adoube,* for "I adjust."

Jaws. In croquet, the entrance to the uprights of a hoop.

Kimmies. One of a number of names for the target marbles in marble games. Besides *kimmies,* they are also known as *dibs, ducks, hoodles, stickers, immies, peewees, mibs, miggs, commies, crockies,* and *commons.*

Kip. Gymnastics. The move that takes one from a hanging position under the bar to a support position on the bar.

Kitchen. Shuffleboard. The minus-10 section of the scoring area.

Lagger. Hopscotch. The pebble or twig tossed in the squares. It is also known as a *peever.*

Meat hand. Baseball. The hand without a glove. Players rarely use their meat hand on a hard-hit ball.

Mication. "Shooting" or throwing fingers, such as children do when picking odd or even to see who starts a game.

Naismith's formula. Hiking. Common method of estimating the length of a hike. According to the formula you allow one hour for every three miles to be covered and add an additional hour for every two thousand feet climbed.

Nerfing bar. Car racing. A bumper that protects the wheels of one car from coming into contact with those of another.

Nock. Archery. The groove at the feather end of an arrow into which the bowstring fits.

Nurdling. Tiddledywinkese for sending an opponent's wink too close to the pot to score easily.

Pantsed. Having your pants taken off against your will. Childish prank in the same class with being *teepeed,* which is the business of covering someone's house with toilet paper (t.p., hence teepeed).

Petticoat. Archery. The white rim of a traditional archer's target. You get no points if you hit the petticoat.

Photon. Racquetball. Powerful shot.

Pips. The spots on dominos and dice. Also, the name for the tiny pimple-like projections on some Ping-Pong paddles.

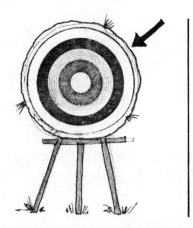

Pone. The cardplayer who cuts the cards for the dealer. The pone is usually seated to the right of the dealer.

Rainmaker. Baseball. A high, slow fly ball, also known as a *can of corn.*

Razzor. A device, usually made of rubber, that one blows into to create a low, mean noise. Pronounced razer.

Schmerltz. A ball housed in a tube sock that is thrown by twirling and releasing the end of the sock. It is caught by the tail. The Schmerltz is one of the many new games advocated by the New Games Foundation, which deemphasizes winning and losing in favor of play for the sake of play. Other New Games include: *Tweezli-Whop,* a form of pillow-fighting; *Fraha,* a cooperative paddle game in which the players try to keep the ball in the air; and *Hagoo,* a game in which a gauntlet of players works to make a person laugh.

Sclaff. Golf. Stroke in which the club hits the ground before hitting the ball.

Scoon. To skip across the water; the act of skipping a flat rock across the water.

Serpentine. Coiled colored strips of paper that are thrown and unfurled at weddings, parties, and other festive occasions.

Sights. Billiards. The diamonds on the table rail.

Sitzmark. Skiing. The mark made by a skier who has fallen over backward.

Sling. Badminton. Carrying the shuttle on the face of the racket as opposed to hitting it cleanly. Slinging constitutes a foul.

Snooger. In marbles, a close miss.

Sole. In golf, the flat bottom of the club head.

Spillikin. A small wooden peg used to keep score in games.

Squidger. Shooter in tiddledywinks.

Squoping. In tiddledywinks, freezing your opponent's winks by putting one of your winks on top of his.

Tappy. In tennis, a light stroke; a poor serve.

Taw. One of several names for the shooter in marbles. Shooters are also known as *bowlers* and *moonies.*

Tennist. One who plays tennis. An old term that is again creeping into coverage of the game.

Thimblerig. To cheat with simple sleight of hand, especially by means of three shells or thimbles and a pea or other small object that is placed under one of the shells and moved around.

Tuck. Diving. The common move in which the diver bends his knees and presses his thighs against his chest with his hands around his shins.

Void. Along with nub and lock, one of three major terms associated with jig-saw puzzles. The void is the space into which the rounded projection or *nub* is placed to form a *lock.*

Waffle face. Racquetball. To hit another player in the face with the racquet.

Waggle. The flourish of a golf club prior to the upward swing.

Whelm. Whelm, also known as *release,* or *hatch,* is the first of nine Frisbee flight periods, according to Dr. Stancil E. D. Johnson in his classic work *Frisbee.* The other eight periods in their proper order: *wedge* (insertion), *well* (climb), *wax, waft* (float), *wane, waste, warp* (turn), and *was* (touch).

Wheel sucker. Bike racing. One rider who uses the slipstream of another rider to conserve energy.

Woodpusher. Chess. Player of moderate (or worse) ability.

Yips. Golf. Pressure affecting players of that game. Not to be confused with *yip,* another golfing term that means to hit the ball poorly when putting.

HARDWARE

—A Chest of Tools and Such—

Aberuncators. A long tool for pruning tall branches. Two blades—one rigid and one movable—are attached to the end of a pole. The movable blade is worked by a rope. As common as these apparatuses are, few people call them by their proper name.

Allen wrench. A nonadjustable L-shaped tool for locking and set screws. Either of the hexagonally shaped ends of the Allen wrench can be used.

Bail. The wire handle on a bucket.

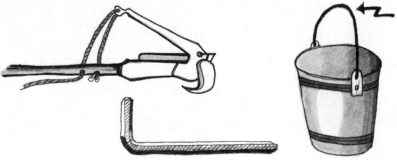

Bail rolls. The two small rubber rollers on the bar above the roller of a typewriter.

Becket. A rope grip or handle.

Bibcock. Faucet with a bent-down nozzle, also known as a *bibb* or *bib*. Outside faucets for gardening are practically always bibcocks.

Bilbo. Iron bars with sliding fetters used to shackle the feet of prisoners. From Bilbao, Spain, and its ironworks.

Bubbler. The metal portion of a drinking fountain out of which the water comes.

Cannel. Bevel on the edge of a chisel.

Chatter mark. Mark left by a tool on the surface of an object; drill or saw scars.

Chimb. The rim of a barrel. The final b is silent. Sometimes called *chime*.

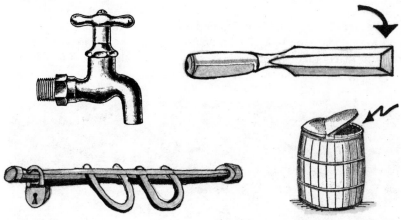

Clevis bolt. A bolt with a hole drilled through the thread end so that a cotter pin can be added for extra holding power.

Cramp. Clamp with a movable part that can be screwed in to hold things together.

Dibble. Pointed garden tool for boring holes for seeds, seedlings, and bulbs. A foot dibble is a dibble that is pushed into the earth with your foot.

Eolith. Tool shaped by natural forces and used by primitive humans.

Escutcheon. Decorative metal plate around a keyhole, drawer pull, or doorknob.

Eye. The hole in the head of an ax or hammer that receives the handle.

Fid. A sharp-pointed tool with a handle for such jobs as making holes in leather. Sometimes called a *belt awl.*

Flang. The double-pointed pick of the miner. Also known as a *beele.*

Froe. Tool used for splitting or "riving" shingles from wood. It has a heavy blade attached at a right angle to a wooden handle.

Grab. The business end of a crane.

Gusset. Triangular brace plate used to reinforce corners in a structure.

Harp. The frame on a lamp that sticks up around the bulb and holds the lampshade in place.

Helve. The handle of a hammer, ax, or similar tool.

Kerf. The channel or groove cut by a saw, ax, or knife as a marking or guide. A kerf cut in a tree indicates where it is to be cut down.

Nab. The projecting box into which a door bolt goes to hold the door.

Paper bail. Bar across the top of the typewriter that holds the paper in place.

Peavey. A lumberjack's tool named after its inventor, Joseph Peavey, a Maine blacksmith. It is a strong pole five to six feet in length fitted with a steel pike and adjustable steel hook at the end. It is used for turning and maneuvering logs.

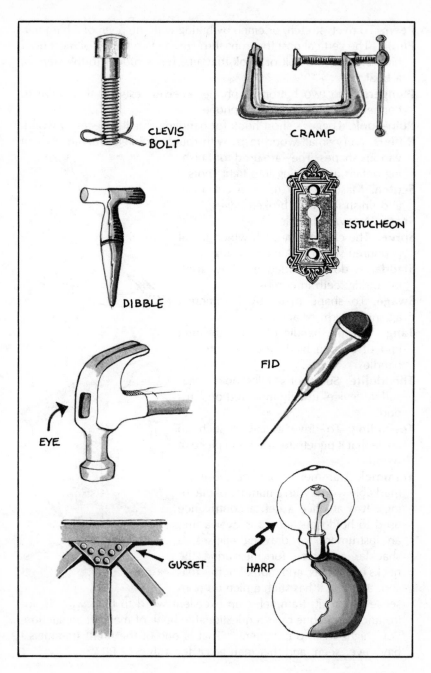

CLEVIS BOLT

CRAMP

DIBBLE

ESTUCHEON

EYE

FID

GUSSET

HARP

Paul Dickson/131

Peen. To rivet, stretch, or cinch by hitting with the peen of a hammer.

Pintle. The vertical post that runs through the two halves of most door hinges. Also, the bolt or hook that attaches a rudder to the stern of a boat.

Plungers. The two buttons a phone receiver rests on that serve to connect and disconnect the phone.

Pulp-hook. Logger's short hook for handling smaller pieces of wood.

Rifflers. Very small wood rasps with rough, pointed, curved ends of various shapes. They are used for finishing details and getting into tight spots.

Scutch. Masonry tool used to cut away and finish rough or broken edges.

Snath. A scythe handle.

Sprue. The channel through which metal is poured when making a casting.

Stadda. A double-bladed handsaw used in cutting teeth in combs.

Swage. To shape metal by hammering against a form or anvil.

Tang. The thin handle of a file; the thin end of a knife blade that fits into the handle.

Theodolite. Surveyor's telescopic measuring device, usually mounted on a tripod.

Toenailing. To drive a nail at such an angle that it penetrates a second piece of wood.

Trammel. Trammel is one of those remarkable words with a number of meanings. It is at once a net, a contrivance used to hold pots and pans over a fire, an instrument for drawing ellipses, a shackle, a device for measuring the necks of animals, and more. For this reason, and that it has such a nice no-nonsense ring to it, trammel is an excellent word to bluff with. If, for instance, someone buys a questionable hunk of metal at an auction, you might wish to comment: "That is one of the finest trammels I have ever seen, and that man got it for only $32.00."

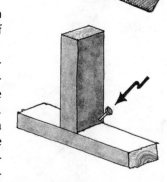

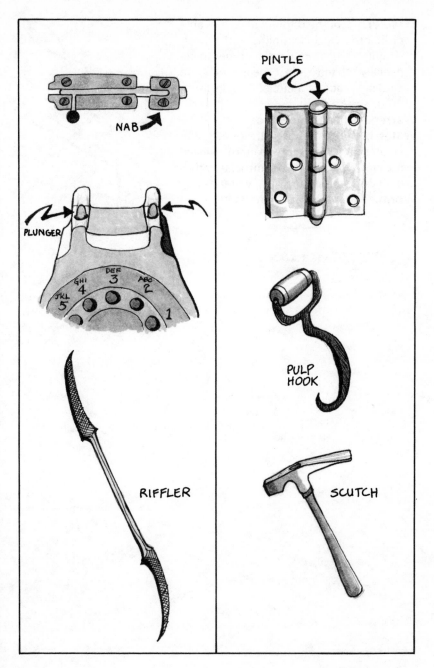

NAB

PINTLE

PLUNGER

RIFFLER

PULP HOOK

SCUTCH

Paul Dickson/133

Traveler. Hand-held tool with a movable disk, used by blacksmiths and wheelwrights to measure with. It comes in especially handy in measuring the circumference of a circle. It looks like a pizza slicer.

Warren. A heart-shaped hoe.

Water breaker. A hose attachment that creates its own spray pattern. Unlike nozzles, water breakers disperse rather than concentrate the flow water.

Worm. The thread of a screw.

HUMAN CONDITIONS

—A Congregation of Beliefs, Customs, and States—

Adamitism. Nakedness for religious reasons.

Adelphogamy. Marriage in which brothers have a common wife or group of wives.

Agathism. Belief that everything works toward ultimate good, no matter what the short-term consequences.

Allotheism. The worship of strange gods.

Androlepsy. The government of one nation seizing citizens of another to enforce some right. An obscure term that came into its own during the Iranian crisis.

Aniconism. Worshiping an object that symbolizes god. Pronounced anna-konism.

Anomie. A situation in which a society is not governed by the norms that generally regulate behavior. A period of upheaval and disorganization.

Anthropolatry. The worship of a human being as divine.

Anthropophuism. Giving god a human nature.

Autarky. State of national self-sufficiency; importing nothing.

Autolatry. Worship of oneself.

Bardolatry. Excessive worship of Shakespeare.

Bitheism. Belief in two gods.

Bourgeoisification. The acquisition of bourgeois characteristics.

Contumulation. Lying in the same tomb with another.

Couvade. A husband acting out the motions of childbirth while his wife is in labor. This custom was common in some American Indian tribes. Pronounced coo-vad.

Cryptarchy. Secret rule. This word should be in common use, given the number of Americans who believe that the Council on Foreign Relations, the Trilateral Commission, the Rockefellers, or some other force secretly runs things.

Decumbency. The act of lying down.

Ditheism. Belief in two gods.

Doulocracy. Government by slaves.

Eidolism. Belief in ghosts.

Eudemonism. The doctrine that makes well-being the ultimate goal of human action.

Eunomia. The state of being well governed.

Floromancy. The belief that flowers have feelings and will respond to kindness as well as cruelty.

Gerontocracy. Government by a council of elders; rule by old men.

Gynarchy. Government by women.

Hecatontarchy. Government by 100 people.

Heliolatry. Worship of the sun.

Henotheism. Belief in one god while not necessarily concluding that that is the only god. Pronounced henna-theism.

Hlonipa. A prohibition against saying the name of a dead person.

Hylozoism. The belief that all matter has life.

Hypergamy. The custom that allows a man—but not a woman—to marry one of lower social standing.

In-fare. A wedding reception held by the groom's family.

Inhumist. Referring to a society that buries its dead.

Jumboism. The admiration of things simply because of their largeness.

Kakistocracy. Government by the worst people.

Kleptocracy. Government by thieves.

Maffick. To celebrate with boisterous rejoicing and hilarious behavior. After the wild celebration that took place in England after the siege of Mafeking was raised by British troops on May 17, 1900.

Malism. Belief that the world and its inhabitants are essentially evil.

Mariolotry. Excessive worship of the Virgin Mary.

Mechanomorphism. The belief that god is a mechanical force and that the universe is governed by natural law.

Misosophy. Hatred of wisdom.

Monopsony. A situation in which a person or group is the only entity on the demand side of a market. For instance, a collector of used cat-food cans might qualify as a monopsonist in that field.

Moramentia. Absolute amorality.

Noyade. Mass execution by drowning, believed to be an innovation of Revolutionary France. Pronounced nwayadd.

Oligopsony. A market in which so few individuals or institutions are involved that the action of one of them can affect price.

Paedarchy. Government by children.

Pancosmism. Belief that nothing exists beyond the material universe.

Pantisocracy. Situation in which all are truly equal and all govern; a Utopian ideal.

Pelagianism. Belief in the basic goodness of nature, including human nature. Named for a heretic of the fifth century named Pelagius.

Physitheism. Giving god a physical shape.

Pseudogyny. The adoption of the woman's name by a man at the time of marriage.

Ptochocracy. Government by the poor. Pronounced tock-ock-racy.

Punaluan. Pertaining to a group marriage in which a number of sisters marry a number of brothers.

Sororate. A custom that obliges or permits a dead woman's sister to marry the widower. The male equivalent is the *levirate*.

Squassation. A form of punishment in which the victim had his arms tied, feet heavily weighted, and was jerked up and down on a rope.

Sutteeism. The practice of the widow immolating herself on her husband's funeral pyre, a custom once observed by certain Hindu women.

Teknonymy. The practice, noted among certain primitive peoples, of naming a parent after the name of his or her child.

Theanthropism. Giving human characteristics to God or the gods. Giving divine characteristics to man.

Timocracy. The ideal state in which the love of honor is the ruling principle.

Trigamy. The state of having one more spouse than a bigamist.

Tritheism. Belief in three gods; belief that the Trinity consists of three gods.

Ultimogeniture. A system of inheritance whereby the youngest son or daughter is given property or title. The commoner system whereby the eldest inherits is called *primogeniture*.

Uxorilocal. Living with your wife's family.

Vivisepulture. The practice of burying people alive.

JUNK WORDS

—A Catch of Contemporary Clichés—

"We suffer from a shortage of new catch phrases, and what you see —or hear—is what you get." These are the words of Sharon Cohen-Hager in a 1981 article in the *Tampa Tribune* on the nation's catch-phrase crisis, which has left us stuck with a stale and stuffy collection of popular words and phrases. Her point is underscored by this personal collection of buzz words that have lost their sizzle.

Absolutely.
Accession rate.
Add on.
Ambience.
Apples and oranges. A phrase used to indicate that two things cannot be fairly compared, as in "It's not fair comparing their gilhooley to ours . . . why, that's like comparing apples and oranges." Ironically, it is a poor metaphor as there are times when you do compare apples and oranges, such as when picking the best-looking fruit at the market.
At this point in time.

Back burner. "Let's push that one onto the back burner for now" is a response to an idea that is not workable at this time. Though impossible to prove, it has been estimated 99.76625 percent of all back-burner ideas will remain there forever.

Ball's in your court, the.

Ballpark figure.

Band-Aid approach.

Basically.

Best shot.

Between a rock and a hard place.

Big picture.

Biggie.

Bite the bullet.

Blah-blah-blah.

Boilerplate.

Bottom line. Presumably a bequest from the world of accounting, this term is commonly used when one chooses to avoid detailed explanations, moving directly to something on the order of "So, the bottom line is that we have to raise three-quarters of a million dollars by Monday morning at 9:00 A.M."

Broad brush.

Business as usual.

Came on board.

Can of worms. How this odd phrase for a group of problems became so popular is beyond fathoming—especially since the going price for a dozen good nightcrawlers last summer was $1.50.

Caring. A radio public-service ad proclaims that a group of "warm and caring parents" will meet to discuss summer activities for their children, and a for-profit home for the elderly boasts of its "caring staff." It is an overused and highly presumptuous word that implies that others are uncaring.

Caveat.

Charisma.

Cliché-laden.

Cluster.

Cognizant (for *aware*).

Come down on.

Communicate. When he was still part of the Carter Administration, Alfred Kahn addressed a conference on communication with this classic opening line: "I will not communicate with you, I will *talk* to you."

Community (when used for a group, such as "the vegetarian community").

Concretize.

Constraint (one of Jimmy Carter's favorites).

Cost effective.

Craft (as both noun and verb).

Crisis-oriented.

Crunch, the.

Culturally deprived.

Deaccession.

Decasualize.

Decisioned.

Déjà vu.

Depth.

Deprogram.

Détente.

Dialogue (as both noun and verb).

Disadvantaged.

Do a number on.

Dog and pony show.

Double digit.

Effectuate.

Elitist.

Enclosed herewith. One of a number of words and expressions banned in 1981 from agency correspondence by Secretary of Commerce Malcolm Baldridge. Others on the list: *maximize, finalize,* and *interface.*

End-run.

Envisage.

Exacerbate.

Eye contact.

Eyeball to eyeball.

Facilitate.

Facility.

Feasible.

Feedback. This word, along with *input,* had become so overworked that Provost John McCall of the University of Cincinnati received national attention when he ruled that any administrator who used either of these words in university communications would be fined two bits.

Finalize.

Finite.

For sure.

For your convenience. Thomas H. Middleton of the *Saturday Review* identified this as one of his favorite "twaddle terms"—modern balderdash appearing in signs and advertising. "You go into your bank," he wrote, "and there's plaster all over the floor, the ceiling has been ripped out, there are exposed wires to trip over, and you see a sign that tells you, "for your convenience, we are temporarily destroying the bank. Thank you for your cooperation."

Formulate.

Freak (as in *plantfreak*).

Free lunch.

Fully cognizant.

Game plan. The source—NFL, NBA, NHL, or organized horseshoe-pitching—notwithstanding, this sporting term is now applied to virtually every aspect of American life. It is currently used as a synonym for any kind of policy. For example, "Dear, what should our game plan be for dealing with the Nelsons if they insist on three hours of canasta before dinner?"

Gamed.

Get your act together.

Go down the tubes.

Go-fer.

Go for it.

Good news . . . bad news.

Gray area.

Ground zero.

Hang a left.

Hard ball.

Hard core.

Hard-nosed.

Have sex. The term that Eric Partridge called the "most colourless, ineffectual [and] inadequate" of all English synonyms for sexual intercourse. Partridge was reminded of a character in Nicolas Freeling's novel *What Are the Bugles Blowing For?* who says to a Frenchman, "In England we have sex. It's exceptionally depressing. In France you say 'Enjoy.' "

Heartland.

Hereby. One of the most important words in the legalistic-governmental vocabulary. James B. Minor, a lawyer and an expert on legislative drafting, has said of this word, "I think the government would have to cease operation if the word hereby were ever deleted from the language."

Herein.

Hereinabove.

Holistic.

Hot line.

Humongous. Immense; overpowering; unnaturally big. It began as college slang in the late 1960s—"He gave us this humongous assignment due Monday"—but it has spread so widely since then that it has lost its punch.

I'd like to speak to that.

If we can send a man to the moon.

Impact (as a verb).

Implement.

Implementation.

In view of.

Infrastructure.

Inoperative.

Input (along with *output* and *thruput*). In 1976 the State Department captured the annual Doublespeak Award of the National Council of Teachers of English for an announcement that said, in part, that a certain person would ". . . review existing mechanisms of consumer input, thruput and output and seek ways of improving these linkages via the consumer consumption channel."

Perhaps the final word on input was uttered in 1980 by cliché-fighter Alfred Kahn when he told a reporter from *The Washington Post,* "When I hear 'input' used as a verb I see a German golfer."

Insufficiency (when used for *shortage*).

Interdependent.

Interface. *The Wall Street Journal* found that the Air Force was so in love with this word that it managed to work it twice into one sentence of a press release. The release described engineering services as "studies, [and] analysis to further define interfaces leading to a missile design review-interface with other stages."

The man who has pushed the use of this word to new limits is Alexander Haig, who speaks of "interface areas of complexity and

difficulty" and "the great interfaces across the entire spectrum."
Into (as in "What are you into?").
Irregardless.
Irrespective.
Is of the opinion that.
Like nailing jelly to the wall.
Locked in concrete.
Low profile.
Mainstream (noun and verb).
Major breakthrough.
Major thrust.
Management team.
Manualize.
Marvelous.
Matrix.
Meaningful dialogue.
Meaningful relationship.
Megabucks.
Methodology.
Mode (especially "mode of transportation").
Modular.
Modules.
Momentum.
Multidisciplinary.
Name of the game.
No problem.
Not to worry.
Obligational limitation.
Off the wall.
Ongoing.
Opt.
Optimize.
Outreach. Alfred Kahn on outreach: "In my office we say 'outreach makes me upchuck.' "
Overview.
Painfully obvious.
Parameters.
Parcelization.
Parenting.
Past history.

Pay one's dues.
Peer group.
Phase-in.
Phase-out.
Piece of the action.
Posture (as in "credibility posture").
Practicable.
Precious few.
Prior to.
Prioritize.
Private sector.
Public sector.
Quick and dirty.
Ramifications.
Really.
Referenced.
Reinvent the wheel.
Relate (as in "Can you relate to barbecued pork?").
Resource (as a word for money).
Revise to reflect.
Role model. Along with such terms as "peer group" and "identity crisis," role model has come from the jargon of the behavioral scientist. These terms are fine things in doctoral theses but are being forced into odd places. For instance, role model is increasingly being used as a synonym for hero; for example, "When I was a kid my role model was Yogi Berra." (This refers to a time when Berra's peer group identity was as a New York Yankee.)
Root cause.
Run with the ball.
Scenario.
Sector.
Self-actualizing.
Seminal.
Sexuality (when one means sex).
Share (as used on talk shows: "Would you share with us your feelings").
Shoot oneself in the foot.
Shortfall.
Shotgun approach.
Sign off on.

Significant contribution.
Simplistic (for *simple*).
So-called (as a sign of doubt: "A so-called humanitarian").
Square one.
State of the art.
Stonewalling.
Structured.
Syndrome.
Systematize.
Take a bath.
Task force. William Safire has explained that this is nothing but a committee "given a military name to make it sound vigorous."
That's incredible.
The pits.
Third generation (as applied to technology, not people).
Throwing money at the problem.
Thrust.
Time frame.
Tip of the iceberg.
Toney.
Touch base with.
Track record.
Two-fer.
Two-way street.
Underutilization.
Up to speed.
Using a bomb for a flyswatter.
Utilize.
Value judgment.
Vector.
Verbalize.
Viability.
Viable.
Vibes.
Virgin polyester.
Visibly moved.
Whatshisface.
When deemed appropriate.
Where deemed appropriate.
Where the bodies are buried.

With the possible exception of.
Within the context of.
Within the framework of.
Would you believe?
Your dime.

KADIGANS

—Umpty-Ump Indefinite Nouns with Xteen Amorphous Adjectives Thrown In for Good Measure—

There are scrumteen scillion kadigans in English, though the soandsos who produce whatchamacallits seldom pay attention to this sortathing. Moving toward a fuller understanding of the vague precise, here is a basic majaggus.

Booznannie. Sometimes spelled boozenannie, not to be confused with a doozandassy.

Chingus. Generally a hoodus that is old, blemished, or obviously defective: a stale jiggus, for instance.

Clanth. An old tool or instrument that once had a specific use that has been forgotten. Old farm or household clanths are commonly found in the back rooms of antique shops. The word originally showed up in a quiz in the October 1973 issue of *Early American Life* magazine that sought the meanings of such early Americanisms as *holzaxt* ("a special axe with wedge-like head, designed for splitting logs") and *quern* ("simple hand mill, with revolving millstone, for grinding grain into meal"). Clanth was inserted in the quiz as a trick word whose definition was "No such word, no such thing." It seemed a shame to leave a fine construction like clanth without a meaning.

Dingbat. A gadget, but one that is suitable for throwing. According to William and Mary Morris in the third volume of the *Morris Dictionary of Word and Phrase Origins,* a dingbat is also: (1) a printer's term for a typographical ornament not easily described, (2) an Australian name for delirium tremens (the dingbats) or an acute hangover.

Dinglefuzzie. John Gould in *Maine Lingo* says that this is the Down East equivalent of Whoozit or Whatsisname: "Dinglefuzzie stopped in while you were gone, but wouldn't tell me what he wanted."

Dinglet. A small dingus.

Dingus. A thing. The word seems to derive from the South African Dutch *dinges,* for "thing."

Dofunnies. From the old West. Plural of dofunny.

Doings. No-nonsense dodibbles.

Doodad. Doodah, American style.

Doodah. British doodad.

Doowhistle. An elaborate gizwatch; a gizwatch embellished.

Eleventeen. Any amount less than a jillion, but not forty-eleven.

Eujifferous. That which is spanglorious; indefinite greatness.

Fidfad. A worthless nubbin; a fiddlestick.

Fizgig. A creation of Lewis Carroll.

Framus. An automotive thingamajig.

Gadget. Although now applied broadly, gadget was originally a Navy term for a tool or mechanical device that one could not recall the name of. One theory of its origin is that it comes from *gachette,* diminutive of the French *gache,* a "catch" or "staple."

Gidget. A gadget. Also the heroine of such films as *Gidget Goes Hawaiian.* In their *Dictionary of Word and Phrase Origins,* William and Mary Morris reveal that the name was a Hollywood writer's blending of *girl* and *midget.*

Gilguy. Clamjamtive tosh.

Gilhoolie. Once a thingamabob, now applied to a patented can opener/sealer.

Gimmick. Although the word is now widely applied, it was originally used to describe devices used to deceive, such as those that were used to rig carnival games.

Gismo. Term popularized by GIs during World War II. Also *gizmo.*

Gizwatch. A no-nonsense doowhistle.

Gowser. A recently coined indefinite noun. In an article in the April

1981 issue of the *Maine Antique Digest,* there was a report on a Plainfield, New Hampshire, auction conducted by William A. Smith during which an odd-shaped box came on the block. Smith called it a "gowser" and sold it for $45.00.

Gubbins. The singular of gubbinses.

Gubbinses. The plural of gubbins.

Hoopendaddy. An outfit; a rathob.

Hootmalalie. Seldom encountered these days, but a useful word to know should one happen to appear.

Ipses. Much the same as gimmick, save for the fact that ipses are generally edible.

Itchicumscratchy. That which irks, infatuates, inspires, irritates, etc.

Jigamaree. A new gadget.

Jiggumbob. From Samuel Johnson: "A trinket; a knick-knack; a slight contrivance in machinery."

Kajody. Doowillie for which the correct name is forgotten or unknown.

Kathob. Goofus with ethnic overtones; an imported majaggus.

Majig. Short for thingamajig; also a small thingamajig.

Oojah. Can be a majigger, majiggie, majaggus, or a majig.

Optriculum. A shebang with the look of high technology to it.

Polywhatsit. A thingamajig that obviously has more than one use.

Ringamajisser. A ringamajizzer; ringamajiggen.

Snivvie. Ringdingle with an ominous or dangerous look to it. Not to be tinkered with.

Stromm. Urbane version of a thing-jigger.

Thingummy. No such thing. See *Thingumy.*

Thingumy. An imaginary *Thingummy,* which see also.

Thinkumthankum. A cerebral thingamajig.

Thumadoodle. Generally speaking, a rinktum that can be held and manipulated in one hand. There are, of course, obvious exceptions.

Umpty-umpth. Higher than umpteenth or umptieth.

Wallage. An indefinite quality; an uncertain quality.

Whatis. An unembellished wingdoodle.

Whatsits. Currently common term in the antiques trade for mysterious old tools and objects. The Early American Industries Association, a national group of old tool buffs, has an official Whatsits Committee. Whatsits is used as both a singular and a plural noun.

Whigmaleery. Doflickety with moving parts.

Whimsey. An odd or fanciful object, for instance, an intricate carving made from one piece of wood. The word is currently popular among museum curators and antique dealers to describe objects of uncertain utility.

Whoozit. Prototype widget.

Widget. The commercial version of a whoozit. People in business are always talking about widgets when they begin talking hypothetically: "Suppose you sell 75,000 widgets, but can't get enough trucks to ship them."

Windge. Jiggus with a nautical aura about it; a whamditty of sorts.

Wingdoodle. A fanciful whatis.

LOUTISH WORDS

—More Than a Gross of Little-used but Wonderfully Apt Gibes and Taunts—

English is a fine language for insult; yet some of our finest, most precise words of derision have fallen into disuse. Here is an outlandish collection of affronts begging to be revived.

Alcatote. A simpleton; an oaf.
Ballarag. A bully.
Bawdstrot. A procuress or prostitute.
Beau-nasty. Slovenly fop. A man who is dirty but well dressed.
Belswagger. A swaggering bully.
Bezonian. A mean, low person.
Bezzler. A sot who steals for liquor money.
Blatherskite. A boaster and a loud talker.
Borborygmite. A filthy talker.
Botheration. A pest.
Bronstrops. A procuress.
Caitiff. A base, mean wretch.
Chattermucker. A blabberer, gossip.
Chuff. A fat, coarse, blunt person. Also, a fat cheek.

Clapperdudgeon. A rapscallion.

Clinchpoop. A lout or jerk.

Clodpate. A stupid fellow; a dolt; a thickskull.

Clodpoll. A stupid person.

Clumperton. A clown; a fool.

Cockabaloo. A bully; a nasty and overbearing boss.

Coistrel. A person of no account.

Cudden. A born fool.

Cullion. A mean wretch; a scoundrel.

Curship. Dogship; meanness; scoundrelship.

Cuttle. A foul-mouthed fellow; a fellow who blackens the character of others.

Dandiprat. A prattling dandy.

Dizzard. A blockhead, dimwit.

Dogberry. An ignorant and officious person who makes a lot of fuss but never takes action. From Dogberry the constable in *Much Ado About Nothing.*

Doolally. Weak in the head.

Dotterel. A sucker; one easily hornswoggled.

Drassock. A slovenly woman.

Drazel. A low, mean, worthless wretch.

Drotchel. An idle wench; a sluggard.

Drumble. A lazy person or drone.

Dunderwhelp. A detestable numbskull.

Durgen. An awkward, uncouth rustic.

Fadge. A short, obese lump of a person.

Fopdoodle. A fool; an insignificant wretch.

Franion. A man of loose behavior.

Fribble. A foppish lackwit.

Fustilarian. A low fellow; a stinkard; a scoundrel. Shakespeare's word.

Fustilugs. A filthy slob.

Fuzzdutty. A silly person; a simp.

Gangrel. Vagrant rascal; a roguish tramp.

Giddypate. Scatterbrain.

Gigg. A strumpet; a wanton woman.

Gitt. British equivalent of the American jerk.

Glump. A pouting, sulking crank.

Gnoff. A lout or boor.

Gongoozler. An idle person who is always stopping on the street to look at things.

Gormless. Stupid and unattractive.

Gossoon. A big oaf. Irish.

Grimalkin. A bossy old woman.

Grobian. A lout. St. Grobianus is the patron saint of coarse people.

Grouthead. Dunce; blockhead.

Growtnoll. A blockhead.

Grumbledory. A clod.

Gulchin. A young or little glutton.

Gundygut. An offensive, mannerless eater.

Haskard. A base and vulgar fellow.

Heanling. A base person; a wretch.

Herkel. A drip.

Hobbil. A dolt; dunce.

Hoddypeke. A cuckold; used as a term of reproach.

Honyoker. A galoot, a rube.

Humgruffin. A creep.

Jacksauce. A rude and saucy person.

Jeeter. An ill-mannered slob.

Jobbernowl. A loggerhead; blockhead.

Joskin. A bumpkin.

Kern. A rude peasant; a boor.

Knuff. Lout.

Lickpenny. A greedy, miserly person.

Lickspigot. A sponge, a revolting parasite. Also known as a *lickspittle.*

Lobcock. Sluggish lout.

Lobscouse. A lout.

Lollard. A bum; loafer.

Lollpoop. A particular type of bum who leans out of windows, watching and occasionally sticking out his tongue at those who pass by.

Looby. A hulking, lazy oaf.

Lorg. A stubborn and stupid person.

Losel. A worthless, sorry person.

Losenger. A flatterer, deceiver, or liar.

Lourd. A stupid, worthless chap (pronounced lurd).

Lungis. A ludicrous lout.

Madbrain. An especially temperamental hothead.

Micher. A loiterer who generally skulks about in corners and keeps out of sight.

Milksop. A feeble, docile person; a jellyfish.

Mobard. Boorish fool.

Mollycoddle. A weak and pampered person.

Mollygrubs. A cross and cranky person.

Mome. A blockhead; a stupid person.

Mooncalf. Imbecile, fool, daydreamer.

Moonling. A simpleton.

Muckworm. A miser.

Mudsill. A lowbred person.

Mullipuff. Twerp.

Nigmenog. A nitwit; a fool.

Ninnyhammer. A simpleton.

Nipcheese. A cheapskate.

Nithing. A base coward.

Nobbler. Swindler; sharper.

Noddypole. A simpleton; also known as a *noddypate* or *noddypeake.*

Nup. A silly person.

Nuthook. A sneak thief. From a time when thieves used hooked sticks to lift clothes and other goods from open windows.

Omadhaun. Fool or simpleton. Irish.

Pig-sconce. A pigheaded person; a boor.

Pilgarlic. A wretch who feels altogether sorry for himself and wants others to do the same.

Pinchbelly. A miserly person.

Ploot. A slut.

Princock. A pert young rogue, a conceited person.

Puckfist. A braggart.

Puler. A whiner.

Puzzlepate. One who is bewildered by the simplest ideas.

Quakebuttock. Coward.

Quetcher. A constant complainer; a bother.

Quibberdick. A nasty quibbler.

Quoob. A misfit, rhymes with boob.

Ragabash. An idler; a bum. Can be used individually or as a collective noun: "The ragabash that congregates outside the courthouse."

Rakehell. A worthless, debauched, and generally sorry fellow.

Rampallian. A general term of abuse. Used by Shakespeare to nice effect in *Henry IV,* Part II, "Away, you scullion! you rampallian! you fustilarian!"

Ripesuck. Bribable person; easy mark.

Rudesby. An uncivil, turbulent person.

Rumpot. A drunk.

Runnion. A paltry, scurvy wretch.

Scattergood. A spendthrift; a squanderer.

Scelerat. A wicked wretch.

Scomm. A buffoon.

Scroyle. A mean or shabby person. Originally, a scrofulous swelling.

Skellum. A villain, scoundrel.

Skipkennel. A lackey.

Slubber-degullion. One who slobbers his clothing, a dirty fellow.

Slummock. A cheeky slut.

Smellfeast. Person who will sniff out a major meal and show up uninvited. Sometimes this type is also called a *lickdish*.

Smellfungus. A grumbler who finds fault with everything.

Smellsmock. A lecher.

Smouger. A cheat; chiseler.

Snollygoster. A clever and unscrupulous person.

Snudge. Tightwad; miser.

Spalpeen. A rascal; knave.

Swillbelly. One who eats like a pig; a glutton.

Tatterdemalion. A ragged, dirty fellow.

Tattlebasket. A gossip.

Titivil. A rascal, especially one that tattles.

Toadeater. A sycophant.

Tomnoddy. A simpleton.

Trollybags. A repulsive and dirty person.

Troppop. A slattern.

Troublemirth. A spoilsport.

Tufthunter. A lackey; an apple-polisher.

Twittletwattle. A tattle, gabble, twit.

VUP. A Very Unimportant Person as distinguished from a VIP (Very Important Person) or PUP (Pretty Unimportant Person).

Wallydrag. An unkempt, disreputable woman.

Wheech. Scottish for twerp.

Whiffet. A whiff of air; a nobody.

Whopstraw. A boor.

Xantippe. A shrewish, tart-tongued woman. After Socrates' venomous wife.

Yazzihamper. A lunkhead.

MAGIC WORDS

—A Spell of Very Special Words (Use at Your Own Risk)—

Abracadabra. Originally a magic formula used to rid a person of illness or bad luck. According to Harry E. Wedeck in *Dictionary of Magic:*

> Usually the inscription appears on an amulet, in the form of an inverted pyramid; so that the first line reads:
>
> ABRACADABRA
>
> Each succeeding line is diminished by one letter, the last line reading:
>
> A
>
> The disease or ill fortune disappears as the magic formula itself dwindles away.

Abraxas. Word that when carved into a stone or gem is supposed to create a charm of great power. Through a numerological code, the letters add up to 365, the number of days in the year.

Agla. Magic word for the exorcism of demons. It is an acronym formed from the first letters of the four Hebrew words meaning "Thou are forever mighty, O Lord."

Alkahest. The universal solvent that the alchemists tried to find. It would have reduced all substances to their base elements. It was also called *menstruum universale.*

Amaranth. A magic flower that never fades or withers.

Ananisapta. A word that when written on parchment and worn on the body protects one from disease.

Belocolus. A stone that renders the person who holds it invisible on the battlefield.

Bilocation. The ability to be in two different places at the same time.

Enchiridion. A collection of spells and prescriptions. Used to protect against illness and bad luck.

Esbat. A weekly meeting of covens.

Exsuffiation. A form of exorcism performed by spitting and blowing on the evil spirit.

Famulus. A sorcerer's assistant.

Hocus-pocus. Next to abracadabra, the most famous magic catch-all. What is most interesting about the word are the two theories of its derivation: (1) from the name of mythical Norse demon/magician Ochus Bocus; (2) a contraction of the words *Hoc est corpus meum,* which occur in the Catholic mass when the Communion host is presented. The latter explanation is favored by those who have studied the evidence.

Hola Nola Massa. A magic formula used in the Middle Ages for banishing sickness and other emergencies. Other formulae from the period that were recorded in the works of Albertus Magnus:

> Ofano, Oblamo, Ospergo.
> Pax Sax Sarax.
> Afa Afca Nostra.
> Cerum, Heaium, Lada Frium.

Horse and hattock. The opening words of the spell used by witches when mounting their broomsticks, which was used to get them airborne. The full spell:

Horse and hattock,
Horse and go,
Horse and pelatis, Ho, ho!

Pentalpha. Design created with five interlaced *A*'s, used in magic rites.
Pyrzqxgl. In L. Frank Baum's *The Magic of Oz* the promise is made that if you can pronounce *pyrzqxgl* properly you can turn yourself or anyone else into whatever you please.
Sabbat Broth. Potion that gave the ability to see the future and fly. Traditionally made from toads, black millet, the flesh of a hanged man, the flesh of a dead child, and assorted magic powders.
VANARBI. Word used to render another incapable of having sexual intercourse. This and others—including, ironically, RIBALD—were used in the medieval period. For reasons unclear, words of impotence are capitalized.
Y Ran Qui Ran, casram casratem casratrosque. This "charme of wordes" was to be written out, put in an eggshell, and put down the throat of a dog that had been bitten by a "madde dogge," to prevent the bitten dog from becoming mad. From a 1576 *Book of Hunting*.

MARKINGS

—Everything You Ever Wanted to Know about Specks—

Aspects. Symbols used to denote positions of planets, such as * and □.

Asterism. A triangular cluster of asterisks, used to direct attention to a particular passage:

*** or ***

Caret. Mark used to show where something should be inserted (∧).

Cartouche. A scroll-inspired ornament, often used as the field for a coat of arms. ⬭

Center point. A period placed higher than the printer's base line. Used, for example, in separating syl·la·bles.

syl·la·bles

Dieresis. The two dots (¨) placed over the second of two successive vowels to indicate that they are to be pronounced separately: coöperative, for instance. Also, *diaeresis.*

Dingbat. Printer's name for any typographical ornament. Sometimes called a *flubdub*.

En. Printer's short dash used to represent the word *to,* as the years 1982–83 or pages 50–51. The next longest dash is the *em,* used to mark a faltering or turning of thought ("I—I really don't know"), and the longest, the *2-em dash,* is used for an omission: Ms.——.

End mark. Mark placed at the end of an article, chapter, or book to indicate that it is done. Common end marks: #, # # # and ㉚.

Engrailment. A ring of dots around the edge of a coin or medal.

Flabbergasterisk. A very strong exclamation point that is represented by the symbol ⸮⸮⸮. It was invented by Fred Flanagan and Stan Merritt in an article in *Printer's Ink,* who suggest it for modern advertising copywriters who have used the standard exclamation point to the point where it has become ineffectual. They also invented the *stupendapoint* and the *fluctustress* (see also).

Fleuron. Stylized flower used in printing.

Fluctustress. An underlining created for extra emphasis represented as ⌇⌇⌇⌇⌇⌇ rather than the conventional _____.

Flummux mark. Old hobo mark of danger; a house

with the mark (⊙) is to be avoided. The bone mark (◊) is, on the other hand, a good mark, and a house marked with it is likely to be the place for a free meal.

Grammalogue. A word that is shown as a sign or letter: & and @ are grammalogues. The & mark is an ampersand, but the name for the @ mark has eluded this collector.

Harlequins. Heavy decorative type elements.

Interrobang. A mark (‽) intended to express a question and an exclamation at the same time; for example, "Who needs it‽" It was invented by Martin K. Spector who created the name from *interro*gation and *bang* (printer's slang for an exclamation point). It created a lot of attention when it made its debut in the late 1960s, but has yet to really take off.

Leaders. Lines of dots used to lead the eye to the end of a line. Often used in the contents and indexes of books. Example:

Ligature. More than one letter formed as a single character.

Mackle. A printing spot or imperfection, especially one caused by slippage or wrinkles in the paper.

Macron. The horizontal mark used to show a long vowel; for example, "mā' krŏn."

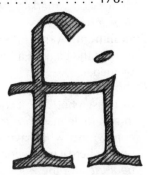

Paraph. A flourish made after a signature.

Perigraph. An inscription around something, such as the circumscriptions found on coins.

Pilcrow. The proper name for the paragraph symbol: ¶.

Postil. A note or comment made in a margin.

Quantity mark. One of two marks used to indicate whether a vowel or diphthong is to be pronounced long or short. The macron is the long sound [‾] while the breve is the short one [˘].

Schwa. The symbol (ə) in pronunciation. Used to indicate an indistinct or neutral vowel.

Semiquote. A single quotation mark, as is used in a quote within a quote; an inverted comma (').

Stupendapoint. A super flabbergasterisk represented by the symbol  . Not to be confused with the six-pointed flabbergasterisk or the overused and now enfeebled exclamation point!

Tailpiece. A small ornament or illustration at the end of a book chapter or magazine article.

Vinculum. A line over a letter or number. In math the vinculum is used to show that a group of elements are to be considered as a whole: $\overline{a+b+2}$.

Virgule. A proper name for the mark (/) that is commonly called a slash, which is used to separate fractions (1/16) to mean "per" (25 miles/hour) and to indicate "either" (has/has not). Other proper names for the same oblique stroke: *diagonal, separatrix, slant, slash,* and *solidus.*

Volle. The little circle over some Scandinavian vowels. *Volle* is Danish for little round cake (°).

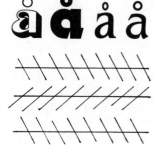

Wing. Slavic mark that commonly appears over *C* to indicate that it is to be pronounced *tch*. Čapek, for instance.

Zollner's Lines. Parallel lines crossed with other lines, which give the illusion that they are not parallel.

MEASURED WORDS

—Four Dozen Ways of
Saying How Much or How Many—

Barleycorn. One third of an inch.

Bundle. Two reams of paper; 960 sheets.

Burthen. 70 pounds, or more specifically, one firkin (56 pounds) plus one stone (14 pounds).

Coffee spoon. Cooking measure equal to a quarter of a teaspoon.

Coomb. Four bushels.

Cran. Used for fresh herring only; specifically, 45 gallons.

Dash. A scant ⅛ teaspoon.

Demy. Paper size measuring 16×29 inches.

Dessert spoon. Cooking measure equal to half a tablespoon.

Ell. A measure of length, one yard and nine inches.

Fardel. An old, not-too-accurate measure for four cloves. A clove is a fuzzy designation for 7–10 pounds of either cheese or wool.

Firkin. Both a British measure of butter—56 pounds—and another name for a ¼ of a barrel or 9 gallons.

Frail. 50 pounds of raisins.

Googol. The number one followed by 100 zeros. Coined in fun by the young nephew of mathematician Edward Kasner, the term is now accepted by mathematicians who also accept *googolplex,* which is the number 1 followed by a *googol* of zeros.

Great gross. Twelve gross; 1,728 articles.

Gross ton. 2,240 pounds.

Hairbreadth. 0.0208 inch.

Hand. A small bunch of bananas, in the banana business. A single banana is, naturally, a *finger,* while the overall bunch from which the hands come is a *stem.*

Heaped measure. A bushel in which the contents are piled high. A *struck measure,* on the other hand, is a bushel in which the contents are level with the top of the basket.

Heer. 600 yards of wool or linen yarn.

Hundredweight. A weight equal to 112 pounds in England and 100 pounds in the United States.

Kilderkin. An 18-gallon beer cask.

Kiloparsec. An immense distance equivalent to 3,259 light years. William D. Johnstone says in his definitive guide to measurement, *For Good Measure,* "The length of the kiloparsec is so great that, as an example, it would take an airplane traveling at a constant speed of 600 statute miles per hour more than 3.645 billion years to cover the distance."

Kilopascal. Metric measure of pressure. Atmospheric pressure equals approximately 100 kilopascals.

Kip. Half a ton: 1,000 pounds.

Mease. 500 herrings.

Megameter. One thousand kilometers. Since a kilometer is approximately one ten-thousandth of the earth's circumference from the equator to either pole, the circumference of the earth is forty megameters.

Mho. Reciprocal of the ohm; *ohm* spelled backward.

Oxhoft. Scandinavian measure of approximately 56–58 gallons.

Pig. A British measure of ballast equal to 301 pounds.

Pin. A beer cask of 4½ gallons.

Pottle. Four pints.

Puncheon. Enormous cask. Traditionally 120 gallons for brandy and 114 for rum.

Quad. Short for quadrillion, or 1×10. It is used when talking of energy to describe one quadrillion BTUs, or British thermal units. The term is used because it is a common unit that expresses the energy content of a fuel regardless of its source (oil, coal, uranium, or whatever).

Quartern. A measure of 5 ounces.

Quinary. In fives; pertaining to the number five.

Quintoquadagintillion. The number 1 followed by 138 zeros—larger than a googol.

Quire. Paper measure: 24 sheets, 1/20 of a ream.

Sarpler. A bale of wool that weighs a gross ton (2,240 pounds).

Seam. Eight bushels or 32 pecks.

Septipedalian. Seven feet long. Coined by British wordsman Ivor Brown for its obvious application to athletes.

Sesquipedalian. One and a half feet.

Strike. Two bushels.

Tare. The weight of a container that is sometimes deducted from total weight. For instance, the weight of the bag used to weigh a pound of peaches is the tare.

Thou. 0.001 inches.

Tun. When applied to ale or beer, a tun is a cask of 259 gallons (or 216 imperial gallons), but when it is a tun of wine, the amount is 302 gallons (or 252 imperial gallons).

Typp. Yarn measure—the number of yards of yarn in a pound, expressed in thousands. It is an acronym for Thousand Yards Per Pound and is pronounced tip.

Wrap. 3,000 yards.

MEDICAL TERMS

—A Plague of Maladies—

Accipiter. A bandage worn around the nose.
Acology. The science of remedies.
Allopathic. Relating to remedies that produce different effects from those of the disease.
Auriscope. The instrument that doctors use to look inside your ears.
Bariatrics. The branch of medicine that deals with obesity.
Bdellism. Term that covers both infestation with leeches and the practice of using leeches for bloodletting.
Beer drinker's finger. A malady described in the *Journal of the American Medical Association* as the discoloration, swelling, or maceration of one's finger as a result of pulling the rings of pop-top beer cans. This malady and hundreds of others of its type appear in a remarkable dictionary entitled *Folk Names and Trade Diseases*. It was created by Dr. E. R. Plunkett, who not only lists them alphabetically but also categorizes them by the part of the body afflicted. Plunkett, for instance, lists the following thumb maladies: *ampoule snapper's thumb, bowler's thumb, boxer's thumb, drummer's thumb, football*

keeper's thumb, gamekeeper's thumb, tennis thumb, and *vaccinator's thumb.*

Blue sweat. A blue-green discoloration sometimes observed in the sweat of copper workers.

Bull men's hand. Pain and numbness of the hand among artificial inseminators.

Circumorbital haematoma. A black eye.

Disco digit. Sore or infected finger that comes from too much finger-snapping while dancing. Disco digit first came to light in the pages of the *New England Journal of Medicine,* which is where many of our less threatening illnesses are first reported.

Edentulous. Without teeth.

Emesis basin. The small kidney-shaped basin you are given in a hospital when you feel sick.

Explorer. The pointed instrument that dentists use to check for cavities.

Flip-flop dermatitis. Form of dermatitis identified in the *British Medical Journal* as that which is caused by wearing rubber "flip-flop" shoes.

Floccillation. The deathbed habit of picking at sheets and blankets. Not to be confused with the word *carphology,* which is a neurotic picking at one's bedclothes.

45,x/46,XXq/46,XXq-dio Karyotype. The technical name for a genetic defect that appeared in the title of an article in a genetic journal. Another title: "A Family Showing Transmission of a Translocation t(3 porq−; CQ+)."

Gomphiasis. Looseness of the teeth.

Graphospasm. Writer's cramp.

Guitar nipple. Term used by the *British Medical Journal* in 1974 to describe the irritation to the breast that can occur from the pressure of the guitar against the body.

Hot pants syndrome. Term used in a 1976 issue of the *Journal of the American Medical Association* to describe a battery burn resulting from carrying a transistor battery in one's pocket.

Humper's lump. An affliction of lumber carriers that results in the swelling of the lower neck.

Iatrogenic. Diseases or symptoms that are caused by doctors. In England the acronym *DOMP* (for Diseases of Medical Practice) has come to mean the same thing.

Iatromathematics. The application of astrology to medicine.

Irroration. The custom of watering a plant with the discharge of a sick person to rid the person of the disease and give it to the plant.

Mal de raquette. Pain caused by excessive use of snowshoes. From Quebec but now used elsewhere.

Mithridatism. Immunity from poison that is realized after taking a series of small doses.

Mutagen. An agent that increases the possibility of mutation.

Optotype. Chart used to test eyesight on which random letters of diminishing size are printed.

Orchidectomy. Castration. From the Greek word for testicle, *orchid.*

Otorhinolaryngology. The proper name for the branch of medicine that deals with ear, nose, and throat.

Percussor. Doctor's hammer used in examining patients.

Phlebotomy. Opening a vein for bleeding a patient, as was common in the eighteenth century and before. The instrument used was a *fleam.*

Pruritus scroti. Proper name for jock itch.

Pyrosis. Heartburn.

Radiesthesia. Detecting and diagnosing disease by passing hands over the body.

Rectalgia. Literally, a pain in the ass.

Singultus. One hiccup in medical parlance; hiccups are singultuses.

Spansule. A capsule containing medicinal particles intended to take effect at different times. A timed-release capsule.

Sphygmomanometer. The common blood-pressure instrument.

Spit sink. The little sink next to the dentist's chair into which one can spit. Increasingly, spit sinks are being replaced by devices that suck the spit right out of your mouth and make horrible gurgling noises.

Strabotomy. Surgical removal of a squint.

Surbated. Bruised, made sore, or beaten—especially used of over-worked feet.

Trepan. A small cylindrical saw used for cutting into the human skull. Also, a powerful tool for cutting into rock, such as is needed to sink shafts. One commentator, Daniel Pettiward, writing in *Punch,* has said, "It always seems to me a most dangerous practice to have two such instruments with a single name. Imagine an inexperienced nurse on being asked by a harassed surgeon to pass the trepan handing him in her ignorance a powerful rock-boring tool. The possible consequences are too appalling even to consider."

Tympany. A swelling, such as that which comes from pride and pregnancy.

Xyster. Surgical bone-scraper.

Zipper trauma. Term used by the *Journal of the American Medical Association* for injury to the penis from catching it in a zipper. The *British Medical Journal,* on the other hand, terms it *zip injury.*

Zomotherapy. Medical treatment using raw meat or meat juices.

MONSTERS

—A Motley Mob of Demons, Beasts, Gremlins, and Other Fabulous Critters—

Save for a few superstars (Nessie, Dracula, King Kong, etc.) this is not a particularly good time for monsters. Many are all but forgotten, and those whose names we use are often used without precision. Ogre, for instance, is a term for a very particular fellow: a giant who relishes human flesh. What follows is an attempt to close the modern monster gap.

Androsphinx. Beast with a man's head and a lion's body.
Asmodeus. The demon of marital unhappiness and vanity. (One can presume that this is the patron demon of daytime television.)
Augerino. Gigantic corkscrew-shaped worm of the southwest whose main function in life is to let water out of irrigation canals.
Baldersnatch. A fierce imaginary beast, so hideous that nobody has stayed around long enough to get a description.

Belphegor. A vile, slack-jawed demon with a phallic tongue.

Billdad. With the hind legs of a kangaroo, the tail of a beaver, the feet of a duck, and the bill of a hawk, the Billdad is able to leap up to 60 yards. It lives on trout, which it leaps on and stuns with a slap of its tail.

Bingbuffer. An Ozark beast said to be able to kill other animals by throwing rocks with its hinged tail.

Bodach. A small, vile beast of the British Isles who comes down chimneys to carry off naughty children.

Boggart. Yorkshire Brownie that indulges in constant household mischief. Save for a tail, its form is human.

Bogle. A Scottish boggart.

Borogrove. An extinct shabby bird that looked somewhat like a mop and lived on veal. Borogoves appear in Lewis Carroll's *Jabberwocky* ("All mimsy were the borogoves . . .").

Bucentaur. Monster that is half-man and half-bull.

Bwbachod. A Welsh Brownie who will work free for anyone save teetotalers.

Cambions. The offspring of succubi and incubi. Incubi (male) descend on women in their sleep and have sexual intercourse with them, while succubi (female) descend on men. The cambion, incubus, and succubus are all classified as demons.

Champ. Lake Champlain's gigantic serpent.

Chessie. A monster sighted by people in the Chesapeake Bay and Potomac River. It has been named after Nessie, the familiar name for the Loch Ness monster.

Chichevache. A monster from medieval folklore who was always hungry because he lived exclusively on the flesh of virtuous women.

Criosphinx. Sphinx with the head of a ram.

Dat. A crossbred dog and cat with the worst characteristics of each.

Derodidymus. A two-headed monster.

Dipsas. A snake whose bite produces the sensation of unquenchable thirst.

Dungavenhooter. A mouthless alligator-like reptile with abnormally large nostrils. It was once common to the logging regions from Maine to Michigan. Its treacherous behavior was described in Henry H. Tyron's *Fearsome Critters:* "Concealing itself with Satanic cunning behind a whiffle bush, the Dungavenhooter awaits the passing logger. On coming within reach of the dreadful tail, the victim is knocked senseless and then pounded steadily until he becomes entirely gaseous, whereat he is greedily inhaled through the wide nostrils. . . . Rum-sodden prey is sought with especial eagerness."

Ectopagus. A double monster united laterally.

Energumen. One possessed by evil spirits.

Fifinella. Female gremlin.

Flitterbick. A flying squirrel that moves so fast it is never seen. They have known to kill an ox by hitting it between the eyes.

Galactic ghoul. Force that inhabits a point in space approximately 35 million miles from earth, 130 million miles from the sun, on the route to Mars. The term was created by space scientists after a series of mishaps with unmanned spacecraft in the area. The ghoul has been blamed for no less than three failures and three near or partial disasters.

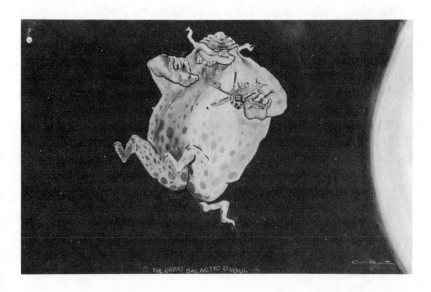

Gallinipper. A large insect capable of inflicting a sting; a big mosquito.

Gally-wampus. An amphibious monster that lived in Missouri during pioneer times. The Gally-wampus looked like a giant mink.

Galoopus. A tremendous black bird that laid square eggs and that was once common in southern Missouri. The richness of the soil in that part of the state came as a result of galoopus dung.

Giasticutus. A monstrous bird of the Ozarks capable of carrying off full-grown cattle.

Gillygaloo. Large bird that lays square eggs.

Gnomide. A female gnome.

Gollywog. A giant salamander-like monster of the Ozarks.

Gowrow. An enormous man-eating lizard said to have terrorized Arkansas in the 1880s. According to Gerald Carson, writing in *Smithsonian* magazine, a salesman named William Miller claimed to have bagged one near Marshall, Arkansas, in 1897. Nobody ever saw it because Miller claims he sent it straight to the Smithsonian (which *claims* no knowledge of it). Carson describes it as ". . . thick-skinned, 20 feet long and enormously tusked, with short legs, webbed feet, a vicious claw on each toe, a body covered by green scales and a back bristling with stubby horns."

Gremlins. Name for the little people who make things go wrong. The term dates back to the 1920s and the Royal Air Force. One theory, expounded in the *Observer* in 1942 by John Moore, is that they were called Gremlins because "they were the goblins which came out of Fremlin beer bottles." This jibes with an account that appeared in *Newsweek,* September 7, 1942, by the magazine's London bureau chief, Merrill Mueller:

> The great-grandaddy of all "bloody Gremlins" was born in 1923 in a beer bottle belonging to a Fleet Air Arm pilot whose catapult reconnaissance plane was cursed with perpetual engine trouble. This pilot was overloaded with beer the night before a practice maneuver, and he crashed into the waves when his plane's engine failed the next day. Rescued, and sobered after the cold dip, he said the engine failed because little people from a beer bottle had haunted him all night and had got into the plane's engine and controls during the flight. . . . "the bloody Gremlins did it."

Guyascutus. An American animal with two distinct characteristics: telescopic legs that enable it to graze on the steepest slopes, and a tail that can wrap around rocks for added security. In *A Dictionary of Fabulous Beasts,* by Richard Barber and Anne Riches, it is pointed out that the Guyascutus is also known as a *sidewinder, hunjus, ricaboo racker, side-hill ganger, prock gwinter,* and *cuter-cuss.*

Hieracosphinx. Sphinx with the head of a hawk.

High-behind. A bull-sized lizard with an appetite for humans. Southern United States.

Hippocampus. The great legendary seahorse that pulled the chariots of the ancient sea gods.

Hippogriff. A cross between a horse and a griffin; a winged horse.

Hodag. Given to weeping because of its extreme ugliness, the hodag has short legs, a spiny back, buck-teeth and a pointed tail. Believed to be related to the ever-weeping *Squonk,* which is covered with warts and moles and can be tracked by following its trail of tears.

Hugag. Giant animal of the north woods that is bald, covered elsewhere with pine needles, and cursed with legs without knees. Hugags must sleep standing up and routinely cause trees and buildings to lean over after napping against them.

Jackalope. Jackrabbit and antelope offspring of the Southwest. It has the body of a rabbit and the antlers of the antelope.

Je-Je Bird. Discovered by GIs stationed in Alaska during World War II. It was never seen but could be heard at night giving out its distinctive call, "Je-Je Jesus it's cold!"

Jimp. Cousin of the Gremlin. It haunts automobiles. Jimps were particularly common in England after World War II.

Jimplicute. A nocturnal dragon or dinosaur ghost that walked the roads of Arkansas in the 1870s.

Kigmy. Small animal that enjoys being kicked. Created by Al Capp.

Kingdoodle. A huge collared lizard from the American South, able to upset small buildings and uproot trees.

Kobold. Dwarf goblin or sprite that frequents mines, caves, and homes.

Lamia. A monster that assumes the form of a woman and devours or sucks the blood from human victims; a female vampire.

Luferlang. Described in Walker D. Wyman's *Mythical Creatures of the North Country* as "an animal having a distinctive feature of a tail in the middle of its back; could run in either direction; having a bite that was almost certain death." Another expert, Henry H. Tyron, has further reported: "The biting season usually occurs on July 12. An orange-colored handkerchief conspicuously displayed will invariably afford full protection. Green clothing of any shade should be studiously avoided at this season, as it serves to arouse the animal further."

Manticore. Monster with the head of a man, body of a lion, and tail of a dragon.

Merfolk. Mermaids and mermen as a tribe.

Monoceros. Not quite a unicorn, not quite a rhinoceros; it falls somewhere in between.

Nambroth. A demon that is best conjured on Tuesdays. A *Nabam,* on the other hand, is best called on Saturdays.

Oesophagus. The name of a nonexistent type of bird that appears in Mark Twain's *A Double-Barrelled Detective Story* (". . . far in the empty sky a solitary oesophagus slept upon motionless wing."). Twain later noted that very few readers caught the bluff.

Ogopogo. Canadian lake monster that has been sighted with some regularity on Okanagan Lake in British Columbia for the last 300 years.

Polyommatous. Having many eyes; a useful word to know when describing monsters.

Rath. An oyster-eating turtle with a shark's mouth, erect head, and curved forelegs (which force it to walk on its knees). Discovered by Lewis Carroll, who said it was often mistaken for a kind of green pig.

Rumtifusel. Vicious, cunning beast that is flat and covered with a luxurious, rich mink-like pelt. It drapes itself over a stump to look like an expensive fur coat to attract its human prey. If a person comes by for a close look, the Rumtifusel covers its victim and cleans him or her to the bone in seconds with its deadly ventral sucking pores.

Senocular. Having six eyes.

Side-hill hoofer. A creature that runs around Ozark mountaintops in one direction because the legs on one side of his body are shorter than the legs on the other side. Also known as a *Side-hill slicker* and a *Side-hill walloper.*

Snawfus. A white deer with great wings and flowering boughs for antlers. An Ozark species exhales blue smoke that becomes the autumn mountain haze.

Sooner-dog. An intensely ferocious American dog that would *sooner* fight than eat.

Spunkie. Goblin that preys on night travelers by tricking them with lights that lead them off cliffs.

Teratism. Love of monsters.

Thegri. The angel of wild beasts according to Gustov Davidson in his *Dictionary of Angels. Behemiel* is the angel of tame beasts and *Shakziel* is assigned to water insects.

Three-tailed Bavalorus. Now extinct half-animal, half-bird of the northwestern United States. It has a large corkscrew horn on its head, cloven hooves, and three tails, each with a different function. One was a barbed fighting tail, the second was a broad, flat tail that the Bavalorus sat on, and the last was a beautiful fantail used to ward off black flies. Its undoing was the fantail, which it would sit and admire by the hour, allowing its enemies to gain the upper hand.

Tove. Cross between a badger, lizard, and corkscrew, from Lewis Carroll's *Jabberwocky.* Toves nest under sundials and mainly subsist on cheese.

Wampus-cat. A bloodthirsty beast of the remotest Ozarks. Mean beyond belief.

Widget. A young gremlin or fifinella.

Willipus-wallipus. A big vague monster of early America.

Wowzer. A super-panther able to kill horses and cows by biting off their heads. Common to the pioneer South.

Yaksha. A Hindu gnome.

Yehudi. During World War II the American equivalent of the British gremlins were yehudis, because they were always "fiddling about."

Ziphius. A sea monster given to attacking and destroying ships in the northern latitudes. It has an owl's head and a mammoth pit of a mouth.

30

NEOLOGISMS

—A Corner for Coined Words—

Anglophobia. A dislike for England and things English. Coined by Thomas Jefferson.

Ansurge. A word that made its debut in the pages of *Word Ways* magazine, for the "irresistible urge to answer a ringing telephone, no matter how inconvenient the hour or the circumstances." It was created by Temple G. Porter, who also suggested *phonercion* and *phoneed* as alternative words for the same condition.

Anthropophaginian. A word formed by Shakespeare from anthropophagi (meat-eaters, cannibals) for the sake of a formidable sound.

Antishoopation. The feeling in the head just prior to sneezing. Word created by Bruce Pelmore of Victoria, B.C., after a radio discussion lamenting the lack of a word for this condition.

Aptronym. Franklin P. Adams's coinage for a name that sounds like its owner's occupation. William Rumhole, for instance, who was a London tavern owner. In Noah Jonathan Jacobs's *Naming-Day in Eden* we are told of a Russian ballerina named Olga Tumbelova.

Bamama. An overqualified, degree-heavy person. The term was created by columnist Ellen Goodman to describe a friend with one MA and two BAs whom she fondly called Bamama.

Barbecue mode. A term associated with the space-shuttle program. It refers to the period when the Orbiter goes into a series of slow rolls. This NASA creation stands as vivid proof that all government terms are not stuffy and overblown.

Barnacular. The quality of officialese coined by Ivor Brown, who based the term "on the Dickensian family of Tite Barnacles who clung with such tenacity to official posts."

Bladderclock. The use of your bladder as an alarm clock; drinking the right amount of water the night before to get up in time in the morning. Coinage of Bill Sherk, author of *Brave New Words,* a brilliant collection of new mintings from Canada.

Blooming verbs. In early 1981 a government official named Paul L. Bloom single-handedly disbursed $4 million in oil company overcharges to various charities. When questioned about this, he said he was "not interested in Robin Hooding." This, in turn, caused the late *Washington Star* to call such constructions Blooming verbs, after Paul Bloom.

Brillig. The time of broiling for dinner; the late afternoon. Created by Lewis Carroll for *Jabberwocky.*

Bureausis. An inability to cope with even the most reasonable, simplest rules and regulations. Attributed to a "political scientist" in *Newsweek,* September 11, 1978.

Calculatoritis. Excessive dependence on electronic calculators. The term was first introduced to the public by Marcia A. Bartusiak in a 1978 article in *Science News* on her own case, which she discovered when, as a physics student, "I was taking a test with my trusty calculator by my side and, without thinking, I actually punched up 200 divided by 2 before putting it on my paper."

Channelfido. A word that first appeared in *Personnel Administration* in 1950, which was defined as "An official, necessarily ineffective, who at all times scrupulously follows proper channels."

Copelessness. Roger Price's word for the inability to cope with life.

Cordodollars. The wood burner's woeful equivalent of the oil burner's inflated petrodollars. From Don Mitchell's article on the subject in *Boston Magazine.*

Cotton woolies. Roald Dahl's generic term for what today's children are not interested in reading about. He used it in a quote that appeared in an article about his writing in *The Hartford Courant:* "I write of nasty things and violent happenings because kids are themselves that way. . . . Kids are too tough to read about little cotton woolies."

Cremains. The end product of a cremation. The word was spotted in an ad for a Clearwater, Florida, cemetery. The ad stated, "For a free copy of an 'eye opening' article about handling of the cremains, call . . ." Presumably the term was created by someone in the funeral business.

Czardine. Assistant czar. The word appears in *Doublespeak Dictionary* by William Lambdin, who says it came from a Los Angeles police lieutenant during the days of the gas lines. In explaining how the police would make sure that service stations were remaining open the proper hours, the lieutenant said, "We have a sergeant in each area who has been appointed energy czar, and he has little czardines out helping him."

Deinstitutionalization. With 9 syllables and 22 letters, this word has been crowned by *The Wall Street Journal* as the king of all recent bureaucratic coinages, beating out such contenders as *reprioritization* and *unreprocessable.*

Democrapic. Garson Kanin's word for the expression of democratic beliefs by those who cannot tolerate democracy in action.

Dontopedalogy. Natural tendency to put one's foot in one's mouth. The creation of Britain's Prince Philip.

Ecdysiast. Stripteaser. This fine word was created in 1940 by H. L. Mencken at the request of a then famous stripper named Georgia Sothern, who felt that her profession should have a more proper name. It is based on the scientific term *ecdysis,* which refers to the act of shedding skin.

William F. Buckley, Jr., has taken the word one step further by coining *ecdysiasm* to describe what an *ecdysiast* does.

Elechiaondros. An all-purpose but entirely meaningless word created by Phyllis Richman, food editor of *The Washington Post.* It is a marvelous bluff word pronounced ella-key-andras

Eth. A member of an ethnic group, one who displays ethnicity, a subject for study by ethnographers and ethnologists. Coined by Herbert Kupferberg in his article, "Confessions of an Eth," in *Parade* magazine in reaction to the 1076-page *Harvard Encyclopedia of American Ethnic Groups.*

Extraa. Not actually a new word, but a logical and improved spelling suggested by Canadian columnist Herb Martindale. He also suggests the following spelling reforms in his book *The Caledonian Eye Opener: superfluuouss, maximuum, excesss, swarmmm,* and *glutt.*

Feaseless. The government in general and the military especially have become so infatuated with the word *feasibility* that they have created a number of awkward variations ranging from defeasible (no longer feasible) to prefeasibility (a period before something becomes feasible). Of all, however, the oddest is feaseless—presumably, something lacking feasibility.

Globaloney. Cosmic nonsense. The term was invented and introduced by Clare Boothe Luce in a speech before the House of Representatives in 1943 while commenting on the views of Vice-president Henry Wallace: "Much of what Mr. Wallace calls his global thinking is, no matter how you slice it, still 'Globaloney.'"

Glot. A person who cannot bear to waste anything. Word from poet Alastair Reid's imaginative *Ounce, Dice, Trice* (see also *gnurr, oosse, poose,* and *worg*).

Gnurr. The substance that over time collects in the bottoms of pockets and the cuffs of trousers. Gnurr is a small variety of *Oosse.* Alastair Reid.

Hippism. A philistine's resentment of a curiosity about the meaning of words. This term was coined by William F. Buckley, Jr., after reading an attack on I. Moyer Hunsberger's *Quintessential Dictionary* by a Tampa, Florida, librarian named Joseph Hipp.

Holismo. Exaggerated holism; the belief that holistic medicine is a panacea. The word was created by Fitzhugh Mullan, M.D., in response to the "outpouring of holism" offered by friends and acquaintances when he was sick. The word made its debut in Mullan's article, "The Rising of Holismo," in *Hospital Physician* magazine.

Homerism. Created by William Taaffe, who defined it in *The Washington Star:* (1) The practice of showing partiality to the home team or the side naturally favored in a broadcast area. (2) Excessive partiality, often involving distortion of fact. (3) A provincial form of announcing found in cities with few teams.

Infracaninophile. One who habitually favors the underdog. A creation of Christopher Morley.

Irage. Rage expressed during the Iranian hostage period, a term coined by an unnamed psychologist and quoted in *The Washington Post* during the crisis.

Irrevelant. Harry S Truman's way of saying irrelevant. The fact that he was wrong is not terribly revelant.

Kelemenopy. Word created by poet John Ciardi that appears in his *Browser's Dictionary.* It is a "a sequential straight line through the middle of everything leading nowhere." It is based on the *k-l-m-n-o-p* sequence of the midalphabet.

Loyalty laughter. The laughter generated by ambitious underlings when the boss tries to be funny. Fred Allen created the term, which can be applied to other situations: students and professors, sales representatives and big customers, etc.

Mecker. To visit places that have acquired some sort of shrine status. As demonstrated by its inventor, Ivor Brown, "Myriads . . . go meckering at Stratford-upon-Avon."

Metropollyanna. The belief that eventually all Americans will move in from the country and live in the cities or suburbs. The term sprang to life at the 1975 National Conference on Rural America after it had been coined by one of the delegates, Clay Cochran of the Rural Housing Authority. Metropollyanna was termed a major problem because it leads to policies that discriminate against rural and small-town America.

Monologophobe. Creation of Theodore M. Bernstein, who defined this creature in *The Careful Writer* as "a writer who would rather walk naked in front of Saks Fifth Avenue than be caught using the same word more than once in three lines." See also *synonymomania.*

Mux. A mix of many things going through one's head; a blend of mix + flux from *Time.*

Nesomaniac. A person who is mad about islands. A creation of James A. Michener, who introduced it in the January 1978 issue of *Travel & Leisure.*

Ochlotheocracy. Mob rule with religious overtones. Created in 1980 by the British magazine *The Economist* to describe the government in power in Iran.

Ocrephobia. Fear of being covered with gold paint, also known as a Gilt Complex. One of Roger Price's contributions to the language. Pronounced exactly like the word for fear of okra.

Ombibulous. H. L. Mencken's word for someone who drinks everything.

Oosse. The airy, furry matter that gathers under beds. Also known as *dust bunnies, trilbies, kittens.* Alastair Reid.

Plentieth. Franklin P. Adams's adjective of indefinite older age, as in "he is about to celebrate his plentieth birthday."

Plimp. To participate à la George Plimpton in a professional sport for the sake of participatory journalism. The creation of *Time* magazine.

Plobby. A word created by P. G. Wodehouse to describe a pig eating. He actually used it in conjunction with another word of his own invention to marvelous net effect: it was a "plobby, wofflesome sound."

Poose. A drop that hangs on the end of the nose and glistens. A poose is likely to appear when one has a cold or comes out of the water after swimming. Alastair Reid's word.

Proxmites. Those who oppose new technology, especially that which comes from the Pentagon or the Space Agency. The term first appeared in an editorial in the newsletter *Space Daily* in 1971, where it was presented as the modern counterpart to the Luddites, who opposed labor-saving machinery in nineteenth-century England. Although he was not named in the editorial, the term recognizes Senator William Proxmire as the leader of the Proxmites.

Quatressential. Not quite quintessential. One of a number of new words that Lewis Burke Frumkes has offered the English language via his article, "A Volley of Words," in *Harper's* magazine. Two other examples of his fine work:

> **Copulescence.** The healthy afterglow that attends successful sexual intercourse.
>
> **Ossis.** The contents of a black hole.

Queuetopia. Winston Churchill's blending of queue + Utopia. He created it circa 1950 to describe the Utopia of the Socialist nations where people waited in line for everything.

Quiz. The product of a wager. The manager of a Dublin theater named Jim Daly bet that he could take a word with no meaning and make it the talk of the town in twenty-four hours. He won the bet with q-u-i-z chalked on walls all over the city. At first the word was synonymous with practical joke, but later came to have the meaning it has today.

Not all the experts accept the story as authentic, but usually retell the story anyhow because it is the only explanation that has ever been given for this word, which is listed in most dictionaries as "origin unknown." In the *Morris Dictionary of Word and Phrase Origins,*

William and Mary Morris say that the story "smacks a bit more of 100-proof Irish whiskey than of 100 percent accuracy."

Ratomorphic. Arthur Koestler's term for a view of human behavior modeled on the behavior of laboratory rats and other experimental animals.

Reaganaut. Government official loyal to Ronald Reagan and his policies. Term created by Richard Allen, once Reagan's national security advisor, to distinguish the loyalists from the rest.

Rendezwoo. Columnist Earl Wilson's word for a rendezvous that is clearly romantic.

Renovation. A fresh start beginning with a Reno divorce. Walter Winchell.

Roomscanitis. An affliction of some partygoers that makes their eyes flit about looking for someone more interesting or less dull than you to talk to. Created by John H. Corcoran, Jr., who introduced it in an article in *The Washingtonian* magazine.

Semantiphony. One who is continually raising alleged semantic questions in an effort to conceal his lack of knowledge and wisdom. Like *channelfido,* this word made its debut in the magazine *Personnel Administration* in 1950. An example was given: "If someone says something no more esoteric than 'How about going to lunch?', the semantiphony is likely to rejoin: 'We have to define terms first. Just what does "going to lunch" mean?' "

Semordnilap. A word that spells another word in reverse. It is the creation of Martin Gardner, who made it by spelling "palindromes" backward. A palindrome is, of course, a word, phrase, or passage that spells the same thing forward as well as backward. Some choice semordnilaps: *straw, reknits, doom,* and *repaid. Serutan* is an intentional semordnilap trade name, whereas *Tums* probably is not.

One can make the case that if we have gone far enough to accept semordnilap, we can go one step further to embrace *quasisemordnilap* for words that come close to spelling something else backward. A good example is *air raid.*

Serendipity. A word created by Horace Walpole, which made its debut in his *Three Princes of Serendip.* It refers to the ability to make favorable discoveries by accident.

Significa. Term created by Irving Wallace, his daughter Amy, and his son, David Wallechinsky, for "unusual or little-known facts which have too much significance to qualify as mere trivia."

Snoblem. The concern of a small group who see prestige value in the issue; a blend of snob + problem. The word made its debut in *The New York Times* in December 1964.

Spart. "Spart is pretty much the same as fight or pep or gumption. Like the *Spart of St. Louis,* that plane Lindbergh flowed to Europe in." Dizzy Dean.

Synonymomania. A word created by Theodore M. Bernstein to describe the "compulsion to call a spade successively a *garden implement* and an *earth-turning tool.*" Both this term and the complementary *monologophobia* appear in Bernstein's *The Careful Writer.*

Tangibilate. Word created by Father Divine when he became disgusted with the theoretical and highly theological musings of others in his field. "The trouble with the world today," he said, "is that there are too many metaphysicians who don't know how to tangibilate."

Urbanality. James Thurber's term for self-conscious and plodding urbanity. He used it to describe, among other things, the early issues of *The New Yorker.*

Verbicide. C. S. Lewis's word for the killing of a word.

Videot. The late Red Smith's word for those who watch anything that flickers across the tube. He created it in the days when Liberace and Gorgeous George were major TV figures, but the term is just as useful today. It rhymes with idiot.

Watchpot. Creation of Alexander Haig spotted by William Safire, who wrote, "A watchpot is, presumably, a pot that bears watching to make certain that it does not boil over."

Worg. A plant that never grows. Created by Alastair Reid.

OCCUPATIONS

—A Corps of Job Descriptions—

It would seem as if there is no such thing as a job without a name. With the help of various editions of the Labor Department's *Dictionary of Occupational Titles* (hereafter referred to as DOT) and a number of other sources, here are some unusual examples.

Almanagist. Compiler of almanacs.

Astrologaster. A lying or deceitful astrologer.

Ballast scorer. One who inspects and scores the ballast on a railroad line. Ballast is the material—usually crushed stone—in which the railroad ties are imbedded.

Bee hunter. One who follows bees back to their hives for the purpose of taking their honey.

Bersatrix. An old word for baby-sitter, not in general use since the eighteenth century.

Blue-collar worker supervisor. The new official term for foreman at the Department of Labor. It may work on paper, but it is hard to imagine a factory worker calling out, "Where's the blue-collar worker supervisor, we've got a problem over here."

Paul Dickson/187

Bung puller. A slaughtering/meat-packing job described in the 1949 DOT: "Removes bung from intestines, for use as sausage casing: Grasps bung with one hand and, holding guts down with other, tears bung loose from other guts. Washes bung under water spray and hangs it on rack. Replaces remaining guts on conveyor." The kind of job that could lead one to drink, or at least to work as a:

Bung remover. One who removes the plugs, or bungs, from full whiskey barrels in preparation for blending. DOT.

Button layer. Lays reflective, ceramic traffic tiles on roads and parking lots.

Camoufleur. Person skilled in use or application of camouflage.

Campanologist. One skilled at bell ringing.

Clicker. An old term for the person who stands at the door of an establishment to invite customers.

Cliometrician. One who uses modern economic techniques to study the past.

Cod tonguer. One of a group of workers likely to be found on a fish-dressing gang, according to the 1949 DOT. A cod tonguer removes the cod's tongue with a sharp knife. Other members of the gang: *blooder, gibber, giller, gutter, header, idler, ripper, scraper, spawner, spitter,* and *throater.*

Dreamer. Officially defined in the DOT: "Sells lucky numbers, which she claims to select by occult means, to policy game bettors. May sell horse-race tips which are derived from similar sources."

Drifter. Runs machines that remove scale from the inside of pipes. DOT.

Faller. In logging, the faller is the logger who

puts the initial cut in a standing tree that indicates where it will fall.

Feather renovator. Cleans feathers for reuse in pillows. DOT.

Fellmonger. A dealer in furs and pelts.

Fogger. One who is paid to feed farm animals; sometimes called *fodderer.*

Funambulist. A rope walker.

Haruspex. One who practices divination from examining the entrails of animals.

Heresimach. One who combats heresy.

Hypertrichologist. The professional name for a person who treats excessive or unsightly facial hair.

Leacher. Tends leach tanks that recover soda ash from black ash. DOT.

Leguillon debeader. One who removes bead wire from scrap automobile tires using a Leguillon wire puller. DOT.

Longshore worker. Neutered form of *longshoreman* adopted by the U.S. Department of Labor. There are many others, including *bat handler* for *bat boy.*

Lump inspector. Inspects lumps of tobacco for defects in wrapper leaf. DOT.

Maturity checker. Tends machine that mashes peas and registers force required to crush them to ascertain hardness. DOT.

Meringue spreader. Fills pies; a pie topper. DOT.

Mesquite grubber. Laborer who clears land of mesquite so that it can be used for cattle. *Cactus grubber* does the same with cactus. DOT.

Moirologist. Mourner for hire.

Mother repairer. One who repairs the mental phonograph matrix, also known as a *mother.* DOT.

Myropologist. One who sells unguents or perfumes.

Necker. Stitches around the neckline of neckties. DOT.

Peruker. A wig maker.

Right-fly raiser. A sewing-machine operator who turns under the edge of the right-fly lining and sews it to the fly along the seam that joins fly to trousers. The DOT, second edition, lists this but not the *left-fly raiser.*

Santa Claus. The DOT *claims* that this is someone who "impersonates Santa Claus during the Christmas season."

Sequins stringer. Tends machine that automatically interlaces thread around strings of sequins in such a manner as to separate, space, and hold fast sequins. DOT.

Shoyhoy. A boy hired to scare birds.

Siffleur. A professional whistler. A woman professional whistler is a *siffleuse.*

Slab smoother. The person who smooths off large ice cream slabs with a large spatula. DOT.

Slubber doffer. In a textile mill, removes full bobbins from slubber frames and replaces them with empty ones. A slubber is a machine that processes raw cotton and is operated by a *slubber tender.* DOT.

Smasher. Person who operates a power press to crease the folds of the signatures of books before they are bound. Presumably a smasher has helped bring this book to you. Smashers are also known as book compressors. DOT.

Squeal, rattle, and leak repairer. Drives automobiles of service customers to determine origin of noises and leaks, and repairs or adjusts components to eliminate cause of complaint. DOT.

Tea-bag tagger. One of three DOT names for the person who ties tags to individual tea bags. The other two: *tea-bag stringer* and *tag threader.*

Visagiste. An expert in cosmetics; a makeup person.

Whizzer. Tends a machine that spins felt hat bodies to remove excess water. DOT.

32

ODDITIES

—A Sideshow of Very Special Words—

Some words are important for reasons that may not be immediately obvious.

Adder. One of a select group of words in English that was created by the misplacement of a letter. Originally an adder was *a nadder,* but somewhere along the way the *n* migrated to the *a.* The same thing happened to *a napron* (but not to *a napkin,* which is closely related).

Asphodel. One of a list of words identified some years ago by Dr. Wilfred Funk as the most beautiful in English. The others: *fawn, dawn, chalice, anemone, tranquil, hush, golden, halcyon, camellia, bobolink, thrush, chimes, murmuring, lullaby, luminous, damask, cerulean, melody, marigold, jonquil, oriole, tendril, myrrh, mignonette, gossamer, alysseum, mist, oleander, amaryllis,* and *rosemary.* The asphodel, incidentally, is a flower.

Balloonnoonnookkeeppoobah. The creation of Joel D. Gaines, an English teacher in Honolulu, who fashioned it to set a record for consecutive pairs of like letters (it has nine). The word that was submitted to and appeared in *Word Ways* magazine describes "an agent who sits on balloons at noon in a corner in order to earn his keep."

Bologna. One of those words that the experts cannot agree how to spell. Various dictionaries yield *balogna, baloney, bolony, bologny,* and *boloney.* Phonetically, *baloney* looks best.

Cleave. A word with opposite meanings: to stick together and to part.

Cuspidor. The word that James Joyce singled out as the most beautiful in the English language.

Designated hitter. The rarest of terms, one that was accepted by the editors at the G. & C. Merriam Company on first hearing and without the need for further evidence that it belonged in the dictionary. The term, of course, refers to the 1973 American League ruling that allows for a tenth player, or designated hitter, to be put in the lineup to bat for the pitcher. It was correctly reasoned that the name for a tenth player would come into immediate use.

Dord. This word, which first appeared in the *Merriam-Webster International* edition of 1934 as a synonym for density, was, in fact, an error. It slipped into the dictionary from an abbreviation file that had an entry "D or d"—meaning a capital or small *d*—as an abbreviation for the word *density.* Although it was taken out of the next edition of the *Merriam-Webster,* it has shown up in other dictionaries. *Dord* was brought to public attention by Professor Allen Walker Read of Columbia University at the 1976 meeting of the Modern Language Association in a paper on "ghost words."

Facetiously. One of a handful of words in which the vowels appear in proper order. Other examples include: *bacteriously, abstemiously,* and *arteriously.* They appear in reverse order in even fewer words. One example is *duoliteral.*

Flatulent. One of ten words that were voted the least euphonious in the language by the National Association of Teachers of Speech. The other nine: *phlegmatic, crunch, cacophony, treachery, sap, jazz, plutocrat, gripe,* and *plump.*

Floccinaucinihilipilification. The longest word in the *Oxford English Dictionary* (OED). It means "to estimate as worthless." The word is actually used. In January 1979, Senator Daniel P. Moynihan of New York used it in a press conference in response to a question about New York City's fiscal problems when he said, "The floccinaucinihilipilification problem is not behind us." There are many longer words in science and technology, especially science. In his book *Beyond Language,* Dmitri A. Borgman points to a chemical term with 1,185 letters in it. Incredibly, a year after Borgman's initial discovery he came up with a 1,913-letter chemical monster, which was announced in the first issue of *Word Ways.*

Fog. The word that Professor Raven McDavid, editor of the forthcoming *Linguistic Atlas of the United States,* said distinguished the different linguistic backgrounds of the candidates in the 1980 presidential campaign. Carter, Reagan, and Kennedy respectively pronounced it "fawg," "fohg," and "fahg."

Glottochronology. In the *Morris Dictionary of Word and Phrase Origins* (Volume II), William and Mary Morris cite this word and *lexicostatistics* as the ugliest words from the decade (the 1960s) in which they were coined. What fascinates the Morrises is that both words were coined by *linguists.* Both words are technical names for techniques used to date the age of a word.

Walter de la Mare held that ". . . of all names, perhaps those which grammarians have given to the various species of words themselves are the most unalluring: *adjective, adverb, preposition, conjunction,* for example."

Hungry. Aside from *angry,* the only other common English word that ends in *-gry.* For reasons unclear, the commonest query that is addressed to the editors at the G. & C. Merriam Company goes like this: "There are three English words that end in *-gry.* Hungry and angry

are two of them, what is the third?" Among the 450,000 entries in *Webster's Third New International Dictionary,* there is only one other, which is *anhungry,* an obsolete word for hungry that is allowed to stay in the dictionary because it shows up in Shakespeare. Editors at Merriam have found a few others buried deep within the OED, usually as variant spellings. One is *puggry,* one of several spellings of *pugaree* (also *pugree, puggree, puggaree*), which is a scarf wound around a sun helmet.

I. The most commonly spoken word spoken in America. *You, the,* and *a* come in second, third, and fourth.

Kinnikinnik. An Indian smoking mixture made of bark and leaves but no tobacco. According to John Ciardi it is the longest palindromic word in *Webster's Third New International Dictionary.*

Kudos. One of those few words that is the same in the singular and the plural. Another is *shambles. Kudos* is an old university colloquialism that was brought back to life by *Time,* which began to use it as the title of an annual listing of honorary degrees in 1926.

Monosyllable. A monosyllable. Ralph Woods, who listed *monosyllable* as a monosyllable in his book *How to Torture Your Mind,* also lists *oxyopia,* which is a seven-letter word with five syllables.

Muzz. British slang for "to study," also "to confuse." The author's research leads him to believe that this would be the last word in the dictionary if all the words in *The Random House Dictionary* were spelled backward. It would also be the first word if the dictionary were completely reversed.

NOON. Noon, when capitalized, comes out the same backward, forward, and upside down.

Oslo. An important city in Czechoslovakia, right in the middle of Czecho*slo*vakia, as a matter of fact. This was once a clue in a crossword puzzle in the London *Observer.*

Ouija. The name of a once-popular board for divination. It is rarest of words in that it has roots in two languages and is in fact a combination of the word *yes* in French and German.

Pikes Peak. One of the few legislated punctuation bans in history. In 1978 the Colorado legislature outlawed the apostrophe in Pike's Peak.

Pneumonoultramicroscopicsilicovolcanoconiosis. The longest word in *Webster's Third New International Dictionary.* It is a lung disease caused by inhaling fine particles of silicon dust. It can also be spelled with a *k* in place of the last *c* in the word.

Rhythm. One of the longest—if not the longest—words possible without using *a,e,i,o,* or *u.* Other fairly long oddities of this nature: *tryst, Gypsy,* and *lymph.*

Set. According to *The Guinness Book of World Records,* this is the most overworked word in the English language, with 58 noun uses, 126 uses as a verb, and 10 as a participial adjective. For a long time there were those who claimed that *jack* was the most overworked word, but it has only a mere 52 uses. Other words with a multitude of uses: *through, strike, serve, run, draw, cut, cast,* and *point.*

Strengths. The Reverend Solomon Ream claims in his *Curiosities of the English Language* that this is probably the longest word in English with only one vowel.

Typewriter. One of a small number of longer words that can be typed by using only the top row of letters on a standard typewriter. *Proprietory* is another, and *flagfalls* is one of the few that comes from the middle row only. The vowelless bottom line yields no words.

According to an item in the February 1968 issue of *Word Ways,* the champion "top row" words are two 12-letter medical words: *pituitotrope* (person with a constitution strongly influenced by his pituitary gland) and *uropyoureter* (an infected urourerer).

Unquestionably. Good answer to the question "Are there many English words containing all five vowels?" See also *facetiously.*

Usher. A word containing four personal pronouns: *us, she, he, her.*

Victuals. "The ugliest word in the language," according to the late Harry Golden, who explained, "You can't say it or write it. The best thing is to forget it." Those who do use it usually pronounce it *vittles.*

Yy. It has been claimed that no English word contains a double *y,* although one can find the word *snarleyyow* in Webster's Second.

Zyxomma. An Indian dragon fly. It also stands as the best possible seven-letter word that can be used in a Scrabble game (30 points). Zyxomma emerged as the best Scrabble word after a book was published in 1974, *The Best* by Peter Pasell and Leonard Ross, which claimed that "the best" Scrabble word was *jonquil* at 23 points and, if one could use a blank tile, that *quiz-er* at 24 points was even better. Immediately, Scrabble buffs began coming up with better offerings such as *squeeze* (25) and *popquiz* (29) until zyxomma appeared to best them all.

Zyzzyva. The last of the last words in the major dictionaries. The zyzzyva is a South American weevil and is the last word in *The American Heritage Dictionary,* beating such other last words as *zyzzogeton* (a type of South American leaf hopper from *Webster's Third*), and *zyrian* (a Uralic language, from the *Random House Dictionary*).

According to William and Mary Morris—who have used the word *zyzzyva* to end their *American Heritage Dictionary*—the *Grolier Universal Encyclopedia,* and the *Dictionary of Word and Phrase Origins,* the word is pronounced ziz-ih-vuh.

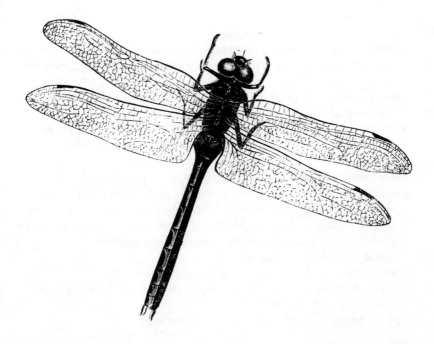

OUTDOORS WORDS

—Calls of the Wild—

Aiguille. A steep, pointed mountain as opposed to one with rounded, soft outlines. The term is used by mountain climbers and rhymes with wheel.

Alpenglow. The reddish glow that appears on mountaintops just before sunrise or just after sunset.

Astrobleme. Scar on the face of the earth made by a meteorite.

Balk. The piece of ground in a field that remains unploughed.

Benthos. The flora and fauna of the sea bottom.

Berm. An earth wall; the shoulder of a road, river, canal, etc.

Cabatoe. A plant that grows potatoes underground and cabbage above. It is one of a number of such creations offered in the catalog of Lakeland Nurseries of Hanover, Pennsylvania. Another is the *topeperatoe,* which grows potatoes for roots and bears peppers and tomatoes above ground.

Chiminage. A toll paid for going through a forest.

Copse. A thicket of small trees. This word is used a lot in nineteenth-century English novels.

Culm. An individual shoot or cane of bamboo.

Dendrochronological. Tree-dating.

Detritus. Debris, such as the mixture of leaves, twigs, and pebbles found on the forest floor.

Disgorger. Instrument used to remove the hook from the mouth of a fish.

Ejecta. Matter thrown out, such as volcanic ejecta.

Espalier. The lattice or trellis on which a fruit tree is trained to give it an unusual shape. Also the name of a tree so shaped.

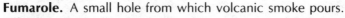

Eyot. A small island in a river or lake. Sometimes called an *ait.* Eyot is pronounced ite and ait sounds like ate.

Foehn. A warm, dry wind that comes off a mountain. Foehns commonly blow in from the north side of the Alps. Rhymes with main.

Fumarole. A small hole from which volcanic smoke pours.

Gilpoke. Originally a lumberman's term for a stuck log protruding into a stream that hampered log drives. The term has been adopted by canoeists, who also see gilpokes as hazards.

Gnarr. A knot in wood; an abnormally dense or hard place.

Gnat-ball. A dense swarm of gnats or other small insects. Ozarkian.

Gore. A small, irregular piece of land that can't be fitted into a township. The term is common to Maine, where the map is dotted with such places as Misery Gore and Coburn Gore.

Gowt. A sluice in an embankment for letting water out.

Grike. A narrow opening in a wooden or stone fence that allows people but not farm animals to get through.

Hill-nutty. The outdoor equivalent of cabin fever. According to a column in the *Arizona Republic,* it is "a neurosis brought on by too many months of solitude in the hills."

Hornito. A low, smoke-emitting volcanic mound.

Interamnian. Between two rivers.

Intercolline. Between hills.

Logan. New Englandism for a bog or swamp.

Mephitis. A foul odor from the earth; a great stink.

Misly. Raining in minute drops.

Moraine. Piles of debris carried by a glacier.

Onding. Scottish term for a pelting rain. Ivor Brown, among others who have expressed concern over our lack of good terms to describe weather, wrote in his *No Idle Words,* "My degrees and terminologies of rainfall are onding for a pelting storm, snifter for a moderate shower and a smurr for a longish drizzle or incidence of mist."

Orogeny. The process by which mountains are formed.

Pergola. An arbor, or a passageway over which plants have been trained to grow.

Piddock. A mollusk that burrows into wood, soft rock, etc.

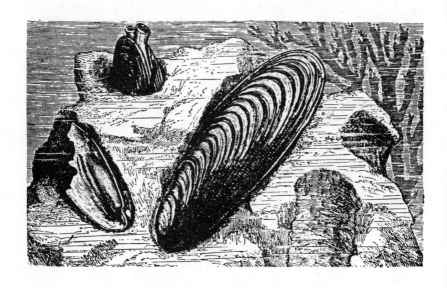

Pudding stick. Canoeist's term for a stiff paddle with little or no give in its shaft.

Pung. A low box sled. Also, the place in a sled where one sits.

Rime. Frozen fog deposited on objects as a light, feathery coating of ice.

Riparian. Having to do with the bank of a river or stream.

Rockmill. A hole in a streambed created by rotating stones.

Rorulent. Dew-covered.

Scarp. A cliff on the moon.

Schizocarp. A seed pod that breaks into two or more pieces at maturity. Those winged seeds that fall from maple trees and that kids put on their noses are schizocarps.

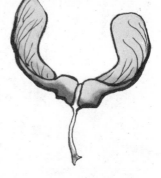

Slatch. An area of quiet water between areas of disturbed water; the space between breakers.

Slip. An area of uniform width between two townships. Butterfield Slip, for instance.

Snye. A natural channel that leaves the main body of a river or stream and bypasses rapids or a waterfall. Canoeists love snyes.

Spile. Device for tapping sap from maple trees. It is a hollow spike that drips into a sap pail that is often hung from it.

Paul Dickson/201

Subtopia. Area between outer suburbs and open country.

Surplus. A surveyor's mistake, such as Andover North Surplus, which appears on detailed maps of the State of Maine.

Swale. A depression in a stretch of otherwise flat land, which is usually moister than its surroundings.

Swallet. Place where a stream disappears underground. Term commonly used by cave explorers.

Tramontane. Located beyond the mountains. *Transmontane* is an alternative form of the same word.

Virga. Rain that falls but evaporates before it hits the ground.

Wattle. To bind or intertwine with twigs.

Xenolith. A piece of rock embedded in another rock.

Zuckle. Old slang word for a withered tree stump.

PEOPLE

—Terms to Fit a Flock of Folks—

Acersecomic. One whose hair has never been cut.

Ademonist. Person who denies the existence of the devil or demons.

Agelast. One who never laughs.

Ailurophile. Cat lover.

Ambidexter. A double-dealer.

Ambivert. One who is neither an introvert nor extrovert.

Angelolater. One who worships angels.

Antiscians. People who live in the same longitude but on opposite sides of the equator; northern New Zealanders and New Yorkers, for instance.

Benedick. A newly married man. An eponym from young Benedick in *Much Ado About Nothing*.

Boeotian. A person who opposes words of literature or art because he does not understand them. The term comes from the ancient Greek farming district of Boeotia, which the Athenians thought to be loaded with bumpkins. Pronounced bee-ocean.

Burdalone. A solitary person.

Cacographer. One who spells or writes badly.

Centimillionaire. Millionaire with more than $100 million.

Chasmophile. A lover of nooks and crannies.

Cockalorum. A very confident little man.

Deipnosophist. One who is good at dinner-table conversation.

Dilling. A child born to parents who are past the age when parents commonly have children.

Dudette. A female dude. According to Ramon F. Adams in *Western Words,* "[a dudette is] described by the cowboy as a young lady who comes west to marry a cowboy." *Dudine* means the same thing.

Dudolo. A Westerner who lives by sponging off dudes and dudettes.

Earthlubber. One who has not been in space.

Ecodoomster. One who forecasts ecological calamity.

Fancymonger. One who deals in tricks of the imagination.

Gnof. A curmudgeon.

Gongoozler. One who spends an inordinate amount of time staring at things that are out of the ordinary.

Gradgrind. A person who measures everything, allowing nothing for human nature. From the character Thomas Gradgrind in Dickens's *Hard Times.*

Grammaticaster. A mean verbal pedant; one who views the misuse of the word *hopefully* as a major threat to Western civilization.

Ignicolist. A fire worshiper.

Leptorrhinian. A person with a long, thin nose.

Lychnobite. One who works at night and sleeps in the day.

Marplot. One who frustrates a plan by his officious interference.

Minimifidian. One who puts the least possible faith in something—an afterlife, astrology, UFOs, or whatever.

Misocapnist. A hater of smoking. An old and all but forgotten word with obvious modern possibilities.

Mumpsimus. A person who refuses to correct an error, habit, or practice even though it has been shown to be wrong. It comes from a pigheaded sixteenth-century priest who always said *mumpsimus* when reciting the mass even though he had been shown many times that *sumpsimus* was correct.

Myrmidon. Someone who carries out commands without hesitation or pity. To speak of a policeman or sheriff as a myrmidon of justice is not a compliment.

Mythoclast. Destroyer of myths.

Nemophilist. One who loves the woods.

Omphalopsychite. One of a sect who practice gazing at the navel as a means of producing hypnotic reverie. *Omphaloskepsis* is the state of contemplation while gazing at the navel.

Oncer. One who does something once and never again; one who has had a number of "once was enough" experiences. A oncer may have had one airplane ride, smoked a single cigarette in 1967, and can still recall that singular occasion when he walked when the signal said, "Don't Walk."

Opsimath. One who has learned late in life.

Paedophage. A child-eater.

Perpilocutionist. One who talks through his hat.

Philodox. One who loves his own opinions.

Pickmote. One who habitually points out and dwells on petty faults.

Plebiocologist. One who flatters the common people.

Pyrrhonist. An absolute skeptic.

Quadragenarian. A person in their forties.

Quidnunc. One who seeks all the latest news and gossip. From the Latin *quid nunc,* for "What now?" This rather uncommon word was brought into the limelight in a 1977 ad from Citicorp, which suggested that our own era "is on the way to becoming the Quidnuncs' Golden Age."

Quintroon. A person who is 1/16th black: the offspring of an octoroon and a white.

Salariat. A person with a salary and the security that goes with it. It is in contrast to the word *proletariat.* It is an uncommon word, but Ivor Brown has argued that it is a useful word of distinction at a time when words like *middle class* have become so imprecise.

Spermologer. One who gathers seeds. By extension, a trivia-monger, a gatherer of gossip.

Stegophist. Person whose pastime is climbing the outside of buildings.

Tetrarch. The governor of one part of a country that has been divided into four parts.

Thaumaturgist. One who works wonders.

Utopographer. One who depicts Utopias.

PERFORMING WORDS

—A Cast of Show Business Terms—

Academy leader. Standardized film beginning showing a backward countdown from 10 to 3. So called because it was specified by the Academy of Motion Picture Arts and Sciences.

Annie Oakley. Free pass to the theater.

Barney. Sound-deadening housing for a camera, used to prevent camera noises from being picked up by microphones.

Belcher. A person who comes on the air with a frog-like voice or a "frog" in his throat.

Bird feed. Transmission (feed) from an earth-orbiting satellite (bird).

Bloom. A sudden flash on the TV screen caused by a reflection from an object being televised, such as the sun hitting the windshield of a car.

Business, the. The television field, not to be confused with "the Industry," which is the motion picture field.

Camerature. A distorted photograph; a photographic caricature.

Capo. A movable bar fitted over the fingerboard of a guitar or banjo to change the pitch of the instrument.

Captation. An attempt to obtain applause or recognition.

Chromakey. Videotape technique in which a person can be inserted over another background.

Clapper. Combination blackboard and noisemaker used to note the scene number and coordinate the sound at the beginning of a "take." The person who holds the board and makes it clap is known as the "clapper boy" or "clapper girl."

Claque. Hired applauders. Those who show approval for a fee or self-interest.

Closet drama. A play that is written to be read rather than performed —Shelley's *The Cenci,* for instance.

Contour curtain. Curtain that can be opened by loops or scallops.

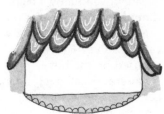

Cucalorus. Cutout or shade placed over a spotlight to produce a shape on the backdrop of a stage. Also called a *cookie, cuke,* and *cuckoolorus.*

Dakota. Lines spoken immediately before a song. "Then, in 1927 I wrote," is a Dakota.

Digitorium. A silent piano; for practicing.

Drive time. Radio term for the two periods during a weekday when commuting is at its peak, usually 6 to 9 A.M. and 4 to 7 P.M.

Drooling. Unrehearsed talking to fill in allotted radio or TV program time. Sometimes referred to as *yatata-yatata.*

Early fringe. TV time before prime time.

Eejay. Short for "electronic journalism," the term created some years ago by Eric Sevareid to distinguish television from print journalism.

Flies. The area over the stage, generally out of the audience's sight.

Foreshortening. The compressed distortion caused by telephoto lenses.

George Spelvin. A fictitious name sometimes used in theater programs to indicate that an actor is playing two or more parts. The actor's real name is used for the main role and Spelvin's for the minor role or roles.

Guard band. Buffer of unused frequency space on either side of a television channel to insure clear transmission.

Halation. The tendency of light to spread in film.

Halflap. TV or movie shot in which two different scenes appear at the same time side-by-side.

Hammocking. Putting a new television show between two established hits.

Hiccup. Opening a movie with a dramatic scene and then bringing on the title and credits.

Iris-in/Iris-out. The classic beginning and ending of a cartoon is to start with the iris-in and end with the iris-out. The iris-in begins with a small dot in the center of the screen, which spreads to reveal the whole scene. The iris-out occurs when the full scene recedes to a dot.

Kilroy. Television camera shot in which the performer's chin is missing. Term comes from the "Kilroy was Here" cartoon in which you cannot see Kilroy's chin.

Kinephantom. The illusion of reverse movement in a fast-moving object, as the spokes of a wheel in a movie.

Lap dissolve. Fading from one scene to another as one is superimposed on the other.

Lavaliere. Small microphone hung around the neck.

Legs. Hollywood talk for a movie with a long box-office life. " 'Star Wars' has great legs," said *Newsweek* a few years back. " 'Jaws' was said to have 'fins.' "

Limbo. Situation in which a television performer is left standing without a background or with the wrong one.

Lip flap. When a person on television can be seen talking but not heard.

Mike stew. Unwanted background noise picked up by a microphone.

Monomorphic station. Radio station with one thrust—all news, Country and Western, or whatever.

Mooz. A fast zoom-out shot.

MOR. Broadcasting term for a station that plays Middle of the Road music.

Motor cue. The circular mark that appears in the upper right-hand corner of a film just before the reel is to end (there is actually 12 feet of film left). The motor cue alerts the projectionist that he should be ready to switch to the second projector and the new reel. A second cue, the *changeover cue,* appears when there is only a foot of film remaining and the time has come to switch to the second projector.

Noodling. Music that is played as titles or credits roll.

Nostril shot. Derogatory term for an extreme close-up.

Omnies. In broadcasting, background sound of crowd noises.

Peripeteia. A dramatic turnaround in the action of a play—for instance, learning that the hero and heroine are one and the same. Pronounced pear-a-pa-tee-a.

Pixillation. Stop-motion photography that gives live actors the appearance of cartoon characters.

Plosives. Explosive sounds that are sometimes produced in broadcasting when a *p* or *b* is overstressed.

Proscenium. The front part of the stage, through which the audience views the play. It is set off at the top by the *proscenium arch.*

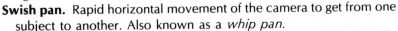

Scrim. A curtain that can be opaque or transparent, depending on how it is lit.

Scumble. Making a set look old.

Sustainer. The piano pedal on the right.

Swish pan. Rapid horizontal movement of the camera to get from one subject to another. Also known as a *whip pan.*

Tally light. Red light on a television camera indicating which camera is on.

Thribble. To be vague about your lines while acting.

Upanga. Nose flute.

Verismo. Using everyday material as opposed to the epic or legendary, especially when applied to operatic themes.

Voice wrap. The use of a broadcaster's voice to begin and end a piece of tape or film.

Wipe effect. In film or TV, when one scene appears to be wiped off the screen by a line that reveals a new scene.

"PHILOPHILY"

—A Collocation of Collections and Collectors—

What could be a more natural thing to accumulate than other collectors? The urge is hereby dubbed "philophily."

Aerophilately. Air mail-stamp collecting.

Arctophilist. A collector of teddy bears. Believed to be the coinage of Peter Bull, English actor and bear collector.

Argyrothecology. Collecting money boxes.

Atrocibilia. Term used in the *American Collector* to describe "horrible heirlooms," relics associated with mass murder, execution, etc. It was used in connection with a surge of collector interest in things having to do with Son of Sam.

Baptisaphily. Christian names.

Bibliopegist. A collector of fine book bindings. Also, a bookbinder.

Brandophily. Cigar bands. Also, *cigrinophily.*

Cagophily. Keys.

Cartophily. Cigarette cards. Collectors in this field are likely to belong to the British-based Cartophilic Society.

Comiconomenclatury. Funny names. This word appears in a recent book published in Australia, Peter Bowler's *Superior Person's Little Book of Words.* Bowler writes, "The serious collector of funny names accepts only those of real people, and abides by certain rules of the game. . . . Chinese names are not fair game, and no self-respecting comiconomenclaturist would include in his collection a Ho Hum, a T. Hee, or a Jim Shoo."

Conchology. Shells.

Copoclephily. Publicity key rings.

Cumyxaphily. Matchbox collecting, not to be confused with *phillumeny,* which is the collecting of matchbooks.

Deltiology. Picture postcards.

Discophily. Phonograph records.

Errinophily. Stamps other than those used for postage (Christmas seals, tax stamps, etc.).

Exonoumiast. A collector of trade, subway, and other tokens.

Hostelaphily. Inn signs.

Hughesiana. Artifacts that relate to the late Howard Hughes.

Labeorphily. Beer bottle labels.

Laclabphily. Cheese labels.

Lepidopterology. Butterfly collecting.

Moxiana. Memorabilia relating to the soft drink Moxie.

Notaphily. Bank notes.

Onomastics. Name collecting. George Hubbard, a leading onomasticist from New York, has a collection that includes such gems as Aphrodite Chackess, Three Persons Appleyard, and Sistine Madonna McClung.

Oologist. A collector of bird's eggs.

Peristerophily. Love of pigeons; pigeon collecting.

Phillumeny. Matchbook collecting. What this hobby may lack in numbers, it makes up for in terminology. Collectors talk of *jewelites* (sparkling covers), *royal flashes* (covers with 40 matches), *odd strikes* (covers with a striking surface in an odd place), and *matchoramas* (covers with full-color photos). Matches are commonly referred to as *strikes.*

Philographer. Term coined by famous autograph dealer Charles Hamilton for serious autograph collectors. Hamilton was quoted in the *American Collector* as saying that such a word "is needed to describe autograph collectors which will instantly establish them as specialists in assembling letters and documents of historic interest, rather than seekers of celebrities' signatures."

Philometry. Envelopes with postmarks.

Plangonologist. Doll collector.

Receptary. A recipe collection.

Scripophily. The collecting of antique stock and bond certificates. The term was coined in 1979 as the result of a contest held by a London newspaper to find a name for the stock-collecting craze that was then sweeping England.

Tegestology. Beer coasters and mats.

Timbromania. Along with *timbrophily,* one of the early names proposed for stamp collecting. Philately won out.

Tyrosemiophily. Camembert cheese labels. One would be hard-pressed to come up with a more specific collector-term than this one, which was culled from Philippe Julian's book *Collectors.*

PIDGIN

—Many Half Talks—

By all accounts, it came into being some 300 years ago along the China coast as an intensely loose, linguistic shorthand with a severely limited vocabulary. The words were English and the syntax Chinese, which provided enough common ground for Western sailors and Chinese merchants to talk with one another. It was called a business language, but it was hard for the Chinese to pronounce *business,* which came out as something that sounded like *bijin.* It eventually became known as *pidgin.*

Over time other pidgin languages evolved: African pidgins, a Hawaiian version, an Anglo-Indian pidgin (known as Hobson-Jobson), pidgins based in French and Portuguese, and the rich pidgins of the South Seas. The latter are largely compatible languages spoken in Melanesia and Australia. In his *Many Hues of English,* Mario Pei was tempted "to describe as pidgin the Pennsylvania 'Dutch' of York and Lancaster counties, which is not at all Dutch, but a blend of English and High German."

Although there are some who hold pidgin in disregard (it was dismissed in one edition of the *Encyclopaedia Britannica* as a jargon

composed of "nursery imbecilities, vulgarisms and corruptions"), it is immensely practical—something that its severest critics will admit. It is especially useful when people from two cultures are trying to communicate. It is also used: pidgin in one form or another is spoken by an estimated 30 to 50 million people worldwide.

Besides being useful, pidgin can also be charming, expressive, and amusing—a magnet for word collectors. Here are some fine examples from the Pacific islands and Australia.

Airmail. Paper-yabber along big fella hawk.
Artery. Rope he-got blut.
Ashes. Shit belong fire. (The phrase for gray is "all-same shit belong fire.")
Automobile. Eat 'im wind cart.
Beard. Grass belong face.
Bishop. Top-side-piecee-Heaven-pidgin-man.
Bottom of . . . Arse belong . . .
Butcher. Man-belong-bullanacow.

Contradict. Sack-im talk.

Copulate with. Pushim. (Also make-im, push-push-im, savvy 'long, etc.)

Cough. Kuss. A sneeze is "kuss 'long nose," which is not to be confused with the phrase for snot, which is "kuss belong nose."

Elbow. Screw belong arm.

Fifteen. Two-fella hand one-fella foot.

Foreigner. Man belong far-way place.

Frenchman. Man-a-wee-wee. (The man who says *oui-oui*.)

God. Big Name; Big Boss. In *Pidgin English* by Edgar Sheappard Sayer, the author translates the Twenty-third Psalm in Australian pidgin. The first few lines:

> Big Name watchem sheepysheep:
> watchum black fella.
> No more belly cry fella hab.
> Big Name makum camp alonga grass,
> taken black fella walk-about longa,
> no fightem no more hurry watta
> Big Boss longa sky makum inside glad;
> takem walk-about longa too much good fella.

Helicopter. Mixmaster belong Jesus Christ.

Hospital. House sick.

Intellectual. Think fella too much.

Is the water drinkable? Good fella water?

Lantern. Lamp walkabout.

Onion. Apple belong stink.

Only child. One-fish.

Piano. Hit 'im in teeth, out come squeal allasame pig. (Southeast Asian pidgin for piano is "Bokkis [box] you fight him, him call out.")

Pocket. Basket belong trouser.

Poor. Rubbish long money.

Pour the coffee. Capsize him coffee along cup.

Put out the fire. Make-im die fire.

Ruin. Bugger-im-up-im.

Secret. Talk he-hide.

Set the table. Put clothes belong table.

Sun. Lamp belong Jesus. Robert Graves once wrote of an Englishman who told a pidgin speaker to tell others of an impending eclipse of the sun. It came out as: "Him kerosene belong Jesus Christ bimeby all done, bugger up, finish."

Swear (to take an oath). Talk true 'long ontop.

Tent. House sail.

Thunder. Fire-up belong cloud.

Toe. Finger belong leg.

Train. Big fella firesnake.

Twenty. One-fella man. (This refers to the total number of fingers and toes. Ten is "two-fella hand.")

Unripe. He-no mow yet.

Violin. Scratch 'im in belly, out come squeak allasame pussycat.

Whisper. Talk-talk easy.

Word. Half talk.

Worm. Liklik (little) snake.

You need a bath. Skin belong you 'im stink.

PROPHETIC WORDS

—A Gathering of Omens—

Several summers ago I found a copy of the 1859 edition of *Webster's Unabridged,* was browsing through it, and came upon the word *tyromancy.* It means to foretell the future by the examination of cheese. I still have no idea how one performs tyromancy, nor have I found a way to work it into polite conversation (save for contrived comments about words that are almost impossible to work into conversation). However, the very idea that the jargon of divination had become so specific as to include cheese set off a search for other ancient words of prophecy.

Aeromancy. From the state of the air or weather, or by the state of ripples on the surface of water.

Aichomancy. By sharp points.

Alectryomancy. By means of a cock picking up kernels of corn. Commonly the cock would be encircled by grains placed on the letters of the alphabet, and words would be put together from the order in which they were eaten. There is a vivid description of this custom in Thornton Wilder's *Ides of March.*

Aleuromancy. By means of flour. The Chinese, among others, have practiced the custom of baking fortunes in dough. The fortune cookie is a modern example.

Alomancy. By means of salt.

Alphitomancy. By barley and barley cakes. This was once used as a means of determining guilt. If the person could not swallow or was made sick by the barley cake, he was deemed guilty. This was also known as *critomancy*.

Amathomancy. By the arrangement of dust.

Ambulomancy. Through taking a walk.

Amniomancy. By observing the caul on a child's head at birth.

Anthomancy. From flowers—presumably the process at work in "She loves me, she loves me not!"

Anthracomancy. By means of burning coals.

Anthropomancy. By examining human entrails. This horrid form of divination was practiced by the Roman emperor Heliogabalus.

Anthroposcopy. The deduction of a person's character, ability, and/or future from his or her face.

Apantomancy. By objects that appear haphazardly.

Arithmancy. By numbers.

Aruspicy. By the entrails of animals.

Aspidomancy. By sitting on a shield within a magic circle and going into a trance.

Astragalomancy. By dice or knucklebones.

Astromancy. By the stars. Astrology.

Augury. By observing birds and serpents.

Auspicy. By the appearance of things being sacrificed.

Austromancy. By observing winds.

Axinomancy. By means of an ax and a stone placed on a bed of hot embers.

Belomancy. By drawing arrows at random from a container.

Bibliomancy. By randomly opening a Bible and using the first passage one sets eyes on to predict the future. The practice had become so common in the fifth century A.D. that several church councils were formed to study and forbid it.

Botanomancy. By means of plants.

Brizomancy. By the inspiration of Brizo, goddess of sleep.

Brontomancy. By thunder.

Capnomancy. By means of smoke wreaths.

Captromancy. By the fumes rising from a poppy thrown on hot coals.

Cartomancy. By the dealing of playing cards.

Cartopedy. By the lines on the soles of the feet.

Catoptromancy. By means of a mirror or lens.

Causimomancy. By fire, specifically flammability. It was often seen as a good omen if something did not burn or took a long time to ignite.

Cephalomancy. By burning the head of an ass on hot coals.

Ceraunoscopy. By the combined phenomena of the air (rain, thunder, etc.).

Ceromancy. From figures produced by dropping melted wax into water. Sometimes spelled *ceramancy.*

Chalcomancy. By brass vessels.

Chaomancy. Through the appearance of clouds; through airborne apparitions.

Chartomancy. By writing.

Cheiromancy. Palmistry.

Chirognomy. A branch of palmistry that deduces a person's intelligence from the shape of his or her hand.

Cledonomancy. By listening to utterances of mantric significance.

Cleidomancy. By a key hanging from a young girl's third-finger nail.

Cleromancy. By throwing dice, bones, or black and white beans. Casting lots. It can also be accomplished by studying the shapes formed as pebbles are thrown into still water.

Clidomancy. By means of a Bible and a hanging, moving key.

Conchomancy. By seashells.

Coscinomancy. By means of a sieve (it is usually suspended and the divination comes from observing its motion).

Crithomancy. By grain or particles of flour strewn during sacrificial rites—sometimes over the bodies of sacrificial victims.

Cromniomancy. By means of onions placed on the altar at Christmas.

Cromnyomancy. By means of onions.

Cryptomancy. By mysterious means.

Crystallomancy. By gazing into a crystal ball, precious stone, or bright metal surface.

Cubomancy. With dice.

Dactyliomancy. By means of a finger ring.

Demonomancy. With the aid of demons.

Dophnomancy. By laurel or, more specifically, interpreting the crackle of a laurel branch on a fire. Also spelled *daphnomancy.*

Dririmancy. By dripping blood.

Elaeomancy. By observing a liquid surface.

Empyromancy. By observing objects on a sacrificial fire.

Eromancy. By exposing objects to the air.

Extispice. From entrails plucked from a fowl.

Gastromancy. From (1) the sounds coming from the belly (2) marks on the stomach. (3) ventriloquism.

Geloscopy. By laughter.

Geomancy. By throwing a handful of dirt on a flat surface to see what figure is suggested. Also, by jotting dots at random on a piece of paper.

Graphomancy. By handwriting.

Gyromancy. By someone walking around in a circle until he falls from dizziness.

Halomancy. By the shape of salt thrown on a flat surface.

Hepatoscopy. By studying the livers of animals.

Hieromancy. By observing things offered as sacrifices.

Hippomancy. By observing a horse's pace.

Horoscopy. By horoscopes; determining one's future by the position of heavenly bodies at the time of one's birth.

Hydromancy. By water (commonly a young boy was used as a medium to report on images he saw in water).

Hyomancy. By the tongue bone.

Ichthyomancy. By the heads or entrails of fishes.

Iconomancy. Through images.

Idolomancy. By idols.

Keraunoscopy. By thunder and lightning.

Knissomancy. With incense.

Labiomancy. By lip reading.

Lampadomancy. By observing substances burned in a lamp or by a candle.

Lecanomancy. By inspecting water in a basin.

Libanomancy. By incense smoke.

Lithomancy. By stones, by meteorites.

Logomancy. By magic words or formulae.

Lycanthropy. The power of turning a human into a wolf.

Machairomancy. With swords or knives. Sometimes, *macharomancy.*

Macromancy. By the largest thing at hand.

Maculomancy. By spots.

Magastromancy. By magic or astrology.

Manticism. The practice of divination. From *mantic,* for one who has been blessed with prophetic powers.

Margaritomancy. By means of a pearl.

Mazomancy. With the help of a suckling baby.

Meconomancy. By drug-induced sleep.

Meteoromancy. By thunder, lightning, and meteors.

Metoposcopy. From the lines of the forehead.

Micromancy. By the smallest thing at hand.

Mineramancy. By found minerals.

Molybdomancy. By noting images in molten lead.

Moromancy. Through nonsense; foolish divination.

Myomancy. By the movements of mice.

Necromancy. Through communication with the dead. Black magic.

Nectromancy. The perception of the inner nature of things.

Necyomancy. From the inspected nerves of the dead.

Nephelomancy. By the clouds.

Nephromancy. By the kidneys.

Nomancy. Determining the fate of a person by the letters that form their name. Also called *onomancy.*

Odontomancy. By examining teeth.

Oenomancy. By the color, sediment, or other wine variations.

Ololygmancy. By the howling of dogs.

Omphalomancy. By the navel.

Oneiromancy. Through dreams.

Onomancy. By interpreting the person's name.

Onychomancy. By the fingernails. Alternatively spelled *onycomancy, onimancy,* and *onymancy.*

Oomancy. By means of eggs (usually broken). Also, *ooscopy.*

Ophiomancy. By watching snakes.

Orthinomancy. By observing the flight of birds. Also, *orniscopy, ornithoscopy,* and *ornomancy.*

Osteomancy. From bones.

Pedomancy. By observing the soles of the feet.

Pegomancy. Observing the way that air bubbles rise in fountains or springs.

Pessomancy. From tossed pebbles.

Petchimancy. By brushing clothes.

Phrenology. By examining the skull.

Phyllomancy. By leaves.

Phyllorhodomancy. By rose leaves.

Pneumancy. By blowing. Joseph T. Shipley points out in his incomparable *Dictionary of Early English,* ". . . a vestigium of this is the blowing out of candles on a festival cake."

Psephomancy. By heaped pebbles.

Pseudomancy. False divination.

Psychomancy. By conjuring the dead.

Psychometry. Determining something about a person from an object, such as a piece of clothing, connected with that person. Also known as *psychometrics.*

Pyromancy. By interpreting flames.

Retromancy. By looking over one's shoulder.

Rhabdomancy. Divining. Finding water by means of a rod.

Rhapsodomancy. Through verses. Sometimes this is performed as a needle is stuck through a closed book.

Scapulimancy. Observation of the shoulder blade of an animal. Also known as *omoplatoscopy* and *scapulomancy.*

Scatomancy. Through examination of excrement.

Scrying. Crystal-gazing.

Selenomancy. From the moon.

Seyomancy. By means of a cup.

Sideromancy. By burning straws on a red hot iron.

Sortlige. By casting lots.

Spasmatomancy. By observing spasmodic movements.

Spatalamancy. Through skin, bones, or excrement.

Sphondulomancy. By means of spindles.

Spodomancy. By ashes, specifically those of a sacrifice.

Stercomancy. By studying seeds in dung.

Stichomancy. By lines and passages in books.

Stigonomancy. By writing on the bark of a tree.

Stolcheomancy. By opening a poet's book at random and reading from the first verse that presents itself.

Stolisomancy. From the manner of dressing.

Sycomancy. By fig or sycamore leaves.

Tephromancy. By writing in ashes.

Teratoscopy. By monstrosities.

Theiromancy. By observing wild animals.

Theomancy. By the response of oracles.

Topomancy. By the shape of the terrain.

Transataumancy. On the basis of omens seen unexpectedly.

Trochomancy. By wheel tracks.

Turifumy. By incense smoke.

Tyromancy. By examining cheese. Sometimes spelled *tiromancy.*

Uromancy. By urine.

Xenomancy. By the first stranger that appears.

Xylomancy. By interpreting the positions and shapes of twigs and other pieces of wood found on the ground.

Zygomancy. Through weights.

"PSYCHONEOLOGISTICS"

—A Drove of Manias and Phobias—

There is nothing amusing about mental illness; but there is something downright amusing about the way psychological professionals feel compelled to construct a new word each time they come on a poor soul with a very rare—perhaps unique—fear or fantasy.

Aboulia. Loss of willpower.
Acarophobia. Fear of small insects such as mites and ticks.
Acoria. Unnatural or morbid appetite for food.
Amathophobia. Fear of dust.
Anhedonia. The inability to be happy.
Anthophobia. An abnormal fear of flowers.
Anuptaphobia. Fear of remaining single.
Arachibutyrophobia. Fear of peanut butter sticking to the roof of your mouth, according to *The People's Almanac*.
Astraphobia. Fear of being struck by lightning.
Batrachophobia. Fear of frogs and toads.
Blennophobia. Morbid fear of slime.
Boanthropy. The madness in which a man imagines himself to be an ox.

Botanophobia. Fear of plants and flowers.

Bulimy. Insatiable hunger.

Castrophrenia. Belief that your thoughts are being stolen by an enemy.

Cathisophobia. Fear of sitting.

Chrematophobia. Fear of money.

Clinophobia. Fear of going to bed.

Counterphobic. Seeking out what is feared; preferring that which one is afraid of.

Cremnophobia. Abnormal fear of cliffs and precipices.

Cynanthropy. A form of insanity in which the person imagines himself to be a dog.

Doramania. The compulsion to own furs.

Dromomania. A compulsive longing for travel.

Ecophobia. Fear of home.

Eidetic image. A memory that is as intense and fresh as actual experience.

Eleutheromania. A compelling desire for freedom. Pronounced i-luth-era-mania.

Emacity. An itch to be buying.

Eosophobia. Fear of dawn.

Epicaricacy. Taking pleasure in the misfortunes of others.

Ergasiophobia. Fear of work.

Euphobia. Fear of good news.

Formication. A feeling that ants are crawling over one's skin.

Friendorphobia. Fear of forgetting a password—one of several new phobias suggested by readers of J. Baxter Newgate's *National Challenge*. Another: *charminphobia,* fear of being squeezed.

Galeanthropy. Belief that one has become a cat.

Gamomania. A form of insanity characterized by odd or extravagant proposals of marriage.

Geniophobia. Fear of chins.

Gephyrophobia. Morbid bridge fear.

Gymnophobia. Fear of nudity.

Hagiophobia. Fear of holy objects, people, and concepts.

Hamartia. A single defect of character in an otherwise decent person. The classic tragic flaw.

Helminthophobia. Morbid fear of becoming infested with worms. Not to be confused with *scoleciphobia,* which is a simple fear of worms.

Homichlophobia. Fear of fog.

Homilophobia. Fear of sermons.

Hydrophobophobia. According to the *Psychiatric Dictionary,* this is the fear of hydrophobia. Hydrophobia, incidentally, not only means fear of water but is also a medical word for rabies.

Hygrophobia. Fear of liquids.

Hypercatexis. Intense desire or mania for some object.

Iatrophobia. Fear of going to the doctor.

Inficious. Given to denying, not accepting, blame.

Jocasta complex. The desire of the mother for her son.

Kathisophobia. Fear of sitting down.

Levophobia. Fear of things on the left; the opposite of *dextrophobia.* These would seem to have obvious political application.

Linonophobia. Fear of string.

Lycanthropy. The affliction that turns an ordinary human being into a raging beast—usually a wolf. A mainstay of horror movies.

Macrophobia. Fear of prolonged waiting.

Misocainea. Abnormal dislike of all things new.

Myophobia. Fear of mice.

Mysophobia. Fear of dirt.

Nebulaphobia. Fear of fog, clouds.

Neurasthenia. Neurosis characterized by boredom, laziness, and fatigue.

Nostopathy. Morbid fear of returning to a familiar place or places.

Nucleomitaphobia. Irrational fear of death by nuclear weapons. Oddly, this is a rare phobia.

Ombrophobia. Fear of rain.

Onomatophobia. Fear of hearing a given word or words.

Optophobia. Fear of opening one's eyes.

Orestes complex. The desire of a son to kill his mother.

Paedophobia. Fear of dolls.

Parthenophobia. Fear of virgins.

Pathophobia. Abnormal fear or dread of disease or germs.

Pediophobia. Dread of dummies, dolls, and mannequins.

Phaneromania. The habit of picking at scabs, biting one's nails, or poking at pimples.

Phobophobia. Dread of fear itself.

Pica. A craving for unnatural food; dust, for instance.

Placophobia. Fear of tombstones.

Pogonophobia. Morbid fear of beards.

Porphyrophobia. Dread of purple.

Sciaphobia. Fear of shadows. (This word tends to get a lot of play around Groundhog Day, when editorialists muse on groundhog psychology.)

Selenophobia. Moon fear.

Stenophobia. Morbid fear of narrow spaces.

Storge. Parental instinct.

Taphephobia. Fear of being buried alive.

Tarantism. The irresistible urge to dance.

Theomania. Belief that one is god.

Topophobia. Intense stage fright; fear of performing.

Trichotillmania. The compulsion to pull out one's hair.

Triskaidekaphobia. Dread of the number 13. Pronounced trisk-a-deck-a-phobia.

Tropophobia. Fear of making changes or moving.

Uranomania. The delusion that one is of celestial origin.

Uranophobia. Fear of heaven.

Zeigarnik effect. The tendency to recall an uncompleted task more vividly than one that has been completed.

PUNKS

—Also, Punkers, Punkesses, Punkaroos, Punkettos, Punkhornes, and Punkabillies—

Punk is an unattractive little word. It sounds mean and decadent and for that very reason fits nicely with a new fad of music, dress, and behavior that emerged in the mid-1970s. This new use of the word *punk* fascinated me and led to the question, How many other uses and variant forms has the word had?

The question led to a punk hunt that in turn led me to a variety of places including the collection of slang dictionaries at the Library of Congress and the citation files at the G. & C. Merriam Company in Springfield, Massachusetts. Humility aside, I believe this to be the definitive work on punk.

Punk. (Army.) Pre-World War I slang for bread. It was often used specifically for light bread. According to Eric Partridge in his *Dictionary of the Underworld,* it also has had the same meaning among prisoners and tramps. Some have said that this use of the word came from the French word *pain;* Partridge contended that it was a new application of punk in the sense of dry, decayed wood—the kind of bread a tramp, prisoner, or soldier might get.

Punk. (Australian.) Sea wood; driftwood.

Punk. Bad or inferior liquor; also, *punkeroo.*

Punk. (Black jargon.) A homosexual.

Punk. (Boxing.) A poor or worn-out fighter.

Punk. Bunk; insincerity.

Punk. (Carnival.) A toy cat used in a game.

Punk. Chinese insect-repellent.

Punk. Cigarette; cigar. (I have also found an unattributed reference to punk meaning "smoking paper." I am not sure whether this means paper used in smoking—e.g., cigarette paper—or paper that is smoldering.)

Punk. (Circus.) A young animal, such as a baby lion. Any circus youngster, whether it be an elephant or a human.

Punk. (College.) Below par; off.

Punk. (College.) A box of good things from home, limited use dating from a report on college slang in the 1880s.

Punk. (Construction.) A general term for any beginner on a construction job. Usually designated as carpenter punk; ironworker punk; or even a coffee punk—novice who goes for coffee.

Punk. (Criminal.) Low-level thief; an apprentice hoodlum. An earlier criminal meaning dating back to the turn of the century is that of a boy thief; a very young criminal.

Punk. Decayed and rotten wood.

Punk. (Fire fighting.) Charred and partly decayed material, such as old wood in which fire smolders unless carefully overhauled and extinguished.

Punk. A foolish argument.

Punk. A form of incense.

Punk. A fungus (polyporus fomentarius, etc.) sometimes dried and used as tinder.

Punk. A harlot or prostitute. This use of the word was common from the sixteenth through the eighteenth centuries and used with this meaning by a number of writers including Shakespeare in *The Merry Wives of Windsor* ("This punk is one of Cupid's carriers . . .") and *Measure for Measure* ("She may be a punk, for many of them are neither maid, widow nor wife").

Punk. Having a dry and flavorless flesh; used of fruits and vegetables.

Punk. (Hobo.) A homosexual boy who travels with an older man.

Punk. (Horse racing.) An inefficient rider.

Punk. An insignificant person; a nobody.

Punk. Knot cut from crabapple tree, a regional use of the word found in Joseph Wright's *English Dialect Dictionary*.

Punk. A little whore.

Punk. (Logging.) The meanings are listed in Dean Walter F. McCulloch's *Woods Words:* "a. The man or boy who passes signals from the choker setters to the donkey puncher. b. A green kid, or any youngster in the woods. c. Rotten wood." Still another meaning appears in *Logger's Words of Yesteryear* by L. G. Sorden and Isabel J. Ebert: "A bad spot in the wood caused by an injury to the tree when it was young."

Punk. A new nihilism, which began in the mid-1970s; what *Life* termed "hip nihilism."

Punk. A person who has adopted the punk style in music, clothing, and behavior. Some have gone as far as to capitalize the word, as if it were the name of a nationality. "The Punks are also rebelling against a very repressive atmosphere," reads a breathless article on the phenomenon in the *New York Post* for June 9, 1977.

Punk. (Photography.) A photographer's assistant.

Punk. (Prison.) According to the 1976 *Dictionary of Desperation,* it has the following meanings in prison parlance: "An informer; or an inmate who can't do his own time well; the kept lover of a homosexual." Partridge says in his *Dictionary of the Underworld* that it also means any young prisoner.

Punk. A punctured bicycle tire. (Late-nineteenth-century slang.)

Punk. Short for *punk rock* or *punk rocker.*

Punk. Small-time character; chiseler.

Punk. A stick covered with a certain paste that burns very slowly when ignited, commonly used to light fireworks.

Punk. A style of dress and a manner associated with punk rock. From a 1977 *Time* article "The Punks are Coming!" ". . . punk fans have cultivated an aggressively dumb look: strategically torn T-shirts; safety pins stuck through clothes, cheeks and ear lobes; fishnet hose; cropped and dyed hair." Other elements of the style: skintight pants, stiletto-heeled pumps, black eye-makeup, ugly sneakers.

Punk. (Theater.) Child actor; a "juve."

Punk. To be very poor.

Punk. A verb, to procure.

Punk. A verb, to puncture a tire.

Punk. Worthlessness; a thing of no value.

Punk. A young elephant.

Punk. A young man; a novice.

Punka. Secondary spelling of *punkah* listed in the *Oxford English Dictionary.*

Punkabilly. Defined in the Arts section of a 1979 issue of *Saturday Review* as a style characterized by "adolescent country pickers with a flair for masochism and audience abuse."

Punkah. A large screenlike fan hung from the ceiling, which is kept in motion by machinery or a servant. The term is from India. It can also describe a portable fan.

Punkah. World War II code name.

Punkah wallah. Servant who operates a punkah. *The Random House Dictionary* lists "punkah coolie" as synonymous.

Punkapog. An Indian village that existed outside Stoughton, Massachusetts.

Punkaroo. (Sports.) Second-rate player.

Punkateero. A pimp or panderer. It comes from punk in the sense of a harlot.

Punkatunk. Popular name for the American bittern, a tawny brown heron.

Punkaw. Variant spelling of punkah found in the *Oxford English Dictionary.*

Punkdom. The state of punk. Spotted in an article by Blair Sabol in *Vogue,* "Female punks?" which opens with the line, "Some insist punkdom is just a chip off the old rock."

Punker. According to an article entitled "A Glossary of Jam Joint Terminology," which appeared in *The Philadelphia Inquirer* in 1972, a punker is "A kid chosen from the audience to help in the tip man's illusion act; child of the richest looking parents."

Punker. (Baseball.) Ball hit between the infield and outfield; a Texas Leaguer.

Punker. Man of loose morals in the old days.

Punker. Neophyte to crime; young criminal.

Punker. Punk rocker.

Punker. A wencher; a user of harlots. "He is a very honest Younker, A bonny Lad and a great Punker" is a line from Charles Cotton's *Scoffer Scofft* of 1670.

Punkeroo. Bad liquor.

Punkery. Another variation found in Blair Sabol's article in *Vogue,* "Female punks?" "But punkery was already established by the likes of Brando, Dean, and Mineo," it says at one point in the article.

Punkess. Feminine form of punk, a term that may only live in the October 1976 issue of *Vogue* where it was found. "I see punkesses as a whole new (yet old) type of female character," says writer Blair Sabol, who goes on to define them in terms of "feistiness and endurance." Tuesday Weld and Jane Fonda are termed "classic celluloid punkesses."

Punkette. Diminutive punk, a word appearing in *The New York Times, Vogue,* and *Women's Wear Daily.*

Punketto. A rare and obsolete term for a minute point of behavior.

Punkhead. Still another variation from *Vogue.* It seems to be just another name for a punk rather than, as one might suspect, a punk who is involved in drugs. In context, "Barbra Streisand was one of the few born punkheads, but she lost it in her Hollywood heist."

Punkhorne. A horn for holding punk (i.e., rotten wood) when used as tinder. This word comes from B. W. Green's *Word Book of Virginia Folk Speech,* published in 1912.

Punkie. Tiny biting fly; "no-see-'em."

Punkin. Pumpkin in some American dialects.

Punkin. Yorkshire term for footsteps of horses or cattle in soft ground.

Punking it up. Affecting punk rock mannerisms. An article in *Mother Jones* for December 1980 asks of Chinese youth, "Are they punking it up at the Peace Cafe?"

Punkish. Feeling ill; also, *punky.*

Punkish. Meretricious.

Punkish. In the punk rock style. *People* magazine for July 27, 1981, described John McEnroe's haircut as "punkish."

Punkishness. Term for punk quality appearing in *The New York Times* on October 5, 1975.

Punkism. The state or quality of punk. *Rolling Stone* for April 8, 1976, speaks of Bruce Springsteen's "street punkism."

Punkitudes. Title of a 1978 French book on punk rock.

Punkling. A young harlot.

Punko. Word appearing in Norman Mailer's article "Miami Beach and Chicago" in the November 1968 *Harper's.* Mailer uses it in the sense of punk meaning "of poor quality." Mailer writes, "The acoustics ranged from punko to atrocious."

Punkwood. Rotten wood.

Punky. Dirty; a dirty person, especially a chimney sweeper. This is a Yorkshire term from Joseph Wright's *English Dialect Dictionary.*

Punky. Rotten and soft; like a dead tree.

Punky. Variant spelling of punkie (a minute fly, midge).

Punk-box. A tinder box.

Punk-boy. (Logging.) A small hook at the end of a loading line or chain.

Punk-eye. Affliction reported in a letter to the *New England Journal of Medicine* by Dr. Thomas F. Caspari, a Boston area physician. He described it as "bilateral subconjunctival hemorrhages: or broken blood vessels under the surface of the eyes." It is caused by too much pogoing.

Punk-funk. Musical style that marries white punk with black funk.

Punk-grafter. A tramp who has a boy to do his chores.

Punk-hole. A hole or pit in moss; a "peat-pot." British.

Punk-jazz. Music that is part punk rock and part jazz. The term appeared in the *Record Round Up* (a record catalog) for January–March 1980.

Punk-knot. A protuberance in wood that indicates inner decay.

Punk-star. Term used by *New York* magazine for a new wave rock star.

Punk and gut. (Hobo.) Bread and sausage.

Punk and plaster. (Hobo.) Bread and butter.

Punk and white wine. Prison slang for bread and water; prison food in general. Also *piss and punk.*

Punk culture. Library of Congress subject heading for books on modern punk along with punk rock.

Punk day. Children's day at a circus or carnival.

Punk dunk. (Basketball.) "Any sort of dunk that humiliates the defender," according to *The In-Your-Face Basketball Book* by Chuck Wielgus, Jr., and Alexander Wolff.

Punk for. (Theater.) To act as a foil or straight man to a comedian.

Punk hit. (Baseball.) Short hit.

Punk kid. A catamite, according to Eric Partridge's *Dictionary of the Underworld.*

Punk oak. A tall water oak of the southeastern United States, sometimes called the possum oak.

Punk out. Slang from the early 1950s for quitting.

Punk out. (Street gang slang.) To get scared; to refuse to fight.

Punk out. To inform; to rat.

Punk pills. Tranquilizing pills; "red devils."

Punk pusher. (Circus and Carnival.) A boss who supervises work done by locals, like the boys hired to set up tents.

Punk rack. (Carnival.) Row of funny, fuzzy animals used in games. Normally these are cats that baseballs are thrown at.

Punk ride. (Carnival.) Rides that cater to children.

Punk rock. A style of rock music defined by its lack of style. It has been variously described as "minimal art," "two and three chord pedantry," "wind-up monkey musicianship," and "raw, nerve flaying, an aggregate of amplified guitars in a tin garage." The sound was pioneered by such groups as the Buzzcocks, Ramones, Dead Boys, and Sex Pistols. Sometimes it is simply referred to as "punk."

Punk show. (Carnival.) Insiders' name for the shows that display abnormal fetuses in glass jars. See also *Pickle punk.*

Punk stuff. Something useless or contemptible.

Punk tree. Another name for the cajuput, an Australian tree having a pungent smell.

Dental punk. Obsolete term from the time when dentists used dry fungus to dry cavities before they were filled.

Funk-punk. Variation of punk-funk, presumably applied when the influence of funk is stronger than punk. Found in a 1981 article in *The Washington Post* by Mike Joyce on Rick James: "James, the self-annointed high priest of funk-punk, presided over a sold-out celebration of outrageous party music."

In the punk. In bad condition; the opposite of "in the pink."

Mess punk. (Nautical.) Waiter or steward.

Pickle punk. (Carnival.) Name for the abnormal fetuses that are preserved in glass and exhibited. See also *Punk show.*

Pretty punk. From *English as It Is Spoken in New Zealand* (1970): "Pretty punk does some of the work performed in America by *lousy.*"

Whistle punk. (Logging.) A signalman; one employed to signal the operations of machinery.

PUNC. Acronym for Practical, Unpretentious Nomograph Computer.

Punke. Old form of punk in the sense of a harlot. "Soe fellowes," runs an old ballad quoted in J. S. Farmer and W. E. Henley's *Slang and Its Analogues,* "if you be drunke, of ffrailtye itt is a sinne, as itt is to keepe a puncke."

Punquetto. A very old variation punk in the sense of a harlot. From Ben Jonson's *Cynthia's Revels:* "Marry, to his cockatrice, or punquetto, half a dozen taffeta gowns . . ."

SEXY WORDS

—A Lusty Lexicon—

Aischrolgia. The frank expression of obscenities.

Algolagnia. A term for both masochism and sadism.

Alpha androstenol. The name of a recently isolated substance found in the sweat of human males, which is believed to create sexual excitement in women.

Ambisextrous. Attractive to both sexes; involving both sexes.

Amober. "Maiden fee" paid by a groom to prevent his new bride from having to spend her wedding night with the lord of the manor. The term and the practice come from Wales.

Ampallang. According to Charles Winick's *Dictionary of Anthropology,* "A metal rod with balls or brushes fixed to the ends. This device is worn transversely through a perforation in the end of the penis by Dyak men and is said to heighten sexual pleasure of their wives."

Anaphroditous. Without sexual desire.

Andromania. Excessive sexual desire in the female.

Antaphrodisiac. Something that reduces sexual desire. The legendary quality of saltpeter.

Antipudic. That which covers the private parts of the body.

Apistia. Faithlessness in marriage.

Arrhenotoky. The bearing of male offspring only.

Bathykolpian. Deep-bosomed.

Blisson. Lusty; with strong sexual desire; in rut.

Brocage. A pimp's wages. An old word that appears as far back as Chaucer.

Callipygian. Having beautifully proportioned buttocks.

Cataglottism. A lascivious kiss; a tongue-kiss.

Catamite. A boy kept by a pederast.

Cornuto. A cuckold; a man horned.

Copesmate. Someone with whom you cope; a lover.

Croodle. A portmanteau word combining crouch and cuddle that sometimes shows up in Victorian novels as a lover's indulgence.

Cullion. A testicle.

Dasyproctic. With hairy buttocks. It is commonly applied to apes.

Dyscalligynia. Dislike of beautiful women.

Ecdemolagnia. The tendency to be more lustful when away from home.

Embonpoint. A plumpness of figure, especially at the bust.

Endogamy. The compulsory custom of marrying within one's own group. Inbreeding.

Eonism. A synonym for transvestism. From Chevalier d'Éon, who for years at a time lived alternately as a man and woman.

Ertomania. Abnormally powerful sex drive.

Fanny. An archaic British slang word for vagina, which became popular after John Cleland's *Memoirs of a Woman of Pleasure,* better known as *Fanny Hill.*

Ferk. To jig up and down. In his *Scholar's Glossary of Sex,* Ray Goliad writes, "The word *ferk* is largely forgotten today, but it is the probable source of our most frequently unprinted four-letter word."

Frottage. The practice of rubbing one's genitals against another person, usually of the opposite sex and usually in public. This word is also used to describe the technique of rubbing a raised design with a crayon and a piece of paper to produce an image.

Gere. A sudden fit of passion.

Iatronudia. The desire of a woman to expose herself to a doctor while feigning illness.

Iconolagny. Sexual stimulation by means of pictures.

Idiogamist. A man who is only capable of coitus with his wife.

Infibulate. To fit with a chastity belt.

Lectual. Proper for bed.

Lupanarian. Pertaining to a brothel or brothels.

Meable. Easily penetrated.

Melcryptovestimentaphilia. Fondness of women's black underwear. This marvelous word appears in Willard Espy's *Words at Play* and very few other places. It also contains *cryptoscopophilia,* the desire to look into the windows of homes that one passes, and *genuglyphics,* the practice of decorating the female knee to make it more erotic.

Meretricium. A tax on prostitution.

Merkin. A woman's pubic wig.

Mixoscopy. The secret observation of the sexual act.

Moschate. Musk-like smell, the goal of many perfumes.

Nympholepsy. Trance induced by erotic daydreaming.

Ophelimity. The ability to give sexual pleasure.

Opsigamy. Marriage late in life.

Osphresiology. The study of aromas and olfactory reactions, especially in regard to sexual relationships.

Paizogony. One of a cluster of synonyms for necking and petting. Other high-sounding terms for the same activity: *contrectation, sarmassation,* and *paraphilemia.*

Pansexualism. Total sexual obsession; seeing sex in all activities; belief that sexual instinct is at the basis of all human activity.

Parnel. The mistress of a priest.

Passion purpura. The proper medical name for a hickey, or as it is defined in *A Dictionary of Dermatological Words, Terms and Phrases,* ". . . the erythematous and later ecchymotic mark of a playful bite or pinch, usually on the cheeks (of the face or buttocks), the neck or breasts, inflicted or incurred in hanky-panky."

Penotherapy. Regulating prostitutes as a means of VD control.

Pernocation. The act of spending the night; an overnighter.

Philematology. The art of kissing.

Poke. To brusquely fornicate with. A British term.

Polyandry. A woman who has more than one husband: the opposite of polygamy.

Pornerastic. Addicted to harlotry.

Pornocracy. Government by whores. The term is sometimes used to describe Rome during the first half of the tenth century.

Pornogenarian. A dirty old man. Word created by Norma S. Vance of Florissant, Missouri, for the "National Challenge," a syndicated newspaper game.

Priapus. A penis of enormous size. From Priapus of classic times, who was born with a phallus so large that his horror-stricken mother disowned him.

Pronovalence. Only being able to have sexual intercourse in the prone position.

Pyrolagnia. Sexual arousal from watching fires.

Renifleur. One who gets sexual pleasure from body odors.

Roger. To screw. British slang.

Sam. An Egyptian amulet in the shape of a phallus. It was used to foster erotic relationships.

Sarcology. The study of the fleshy parts of the body.

Satyriasis. A condition of intense male lustfulness.

Secundipara. A woman who has borne two children. A *primipara,* on the other hand, has an only child, and a *nullipara* is a woman with no children.

Shunammitism. Contact—visual, tactile, or carnal—with younger girls by old males to encourage or restore their sexual vigor. A practice that was common in biblical times.

Starkers. British equivalent of bare-ass. *Starko* is the same thing.

Stasivalence. The inability to have sexual intercourse in any but the standing position.

Syndyasmian. Pertaining to temporary sexual union. A syndyasmian relationship would be a one-night stand.

Tentiginous. Lust provoking.

The 3Ps. Current medical slang for "the pill, permissiveness, and promiscuity." It is used when explaining the spread of certain forms of VD.

Thelyphthoric. That which corrupts women.

Theogamy. Marriage of gods.

Urtication. Flagellation with fresh nettles. In ancient Rome urtication was a common means employed to arouse sexual appetites.

Uxoravalent. Pertaining to a man who is only able to have sexual intercourse outside of marriage. *Uxorovalent* men, on the other hand, can only perform with their wives.

Uxorious. Excessively or foolishly fond of one's wife.

Uxorium. A tax imposed on male citizens in ancient Rome for not marrying.

Viripotent. Fit for a husband; marriageable.

Wittol. A man who encourages infidelity in his wife, the *wittee.*

Xeronisus. The inability to reach orgasm.

SMALL TALK

—A Toddick of Tiny Terms—

Perhaps it is because of the excess of Madison Avenue, the NFL, the Pentagon, and other modern institutions; but we have become overburdened by the big, the stupendous, and, recently, the humongous. The result is that we are losing our ability to think and speak small. A modest, antidotal offering:

Animalcule. An animal that is either invisible or nearly so.
Bavin. A piece of waste wood.
Bindle. A small or trifling amount.
Bort. Ground fragments of diamond; diamond dust used in polishing.
Doit. A trifle. The word occasionally shows up in crossword puzzles.
Dole. A scanty share; a lesser allowance.
Flinders. Small things the size of splinters; splinters.
Fribble. Something of little or paltry value.
Funicle. A small cord or fiber.
Glim. A bit; small amount.
Gry. An old, little-used word for anything of little value; for instance, nail parings.

Jerp. A small quantity usually used in reference to sweets. The term comes from the Ozarks.

Jot. A tiny particle.

Minikin. Of small and delicate form.

Monad. Something ultimately small and indivisible.

Noil. Piece or knot of short hair or fiber.

Opuscule. A small or minor work.

Piff. Something insignificant; a trifle.

Pigwidgeon. Anything especially small.

Pismire. The hoarding of small things.

Pledget. A small mass of lint, such as that which accumulates at the human navel.

Quiddit. A trifling nicety.

Scantling. A little piece.

Scrid. Tiny portion, as in accepting a "scrid of pie" as a second helping. Scrid is a term from New England.

Scuddick. Anything small or paltry.

Sermuncle. A short sermon.

Skimption. Southern talk for a small amount; not enough to bother with.

Snick. A small cut or mark.

Snip. A small person.

Snippety. Ridiculously small.

Sop. A thing of little or no value.

Sup. A small bite or mouthful.

Tittle. A particle; an iota.

Toddick. A very small quantity.

Trig. A stone, brick, or anything placed under a wheel or barrel to keep it from rolling.

Vug. A small cavity in a rock. Also, *vugg* and *vugh*.
Waf. Worthless.
Wem. Blemish or spot.
Whit. The smallest imaginable particle.

43

SOUNDS

—A Cacophony of Words
That Make Noise—

Armisonant. Resounding with the noise of clashing weapons.
Blatter. To make a rattling or senseless noise.
Borborygm. Bowel noise; the noise of a fart.
Bourdon. A bass drone, as can be made by a bagpipe.
Brontide. Seismic noise; the earth making a sound like distant thunder.
Cachinnation. Excessive laughter.
Canorous. Sweet-sounding.
Chirr. Insect sound made by rubbing rough surfaces together. Grasshoppers chirr.
Churr. The sound made by a partridge.

Conflation. Blowing together, as many wind instruments in a concert.

Crepitation. A small crackling; a slight, rapidly repeated sound. Rice Krispies, for instance, are crepitant.

Feep. Computerese for the soft bell associated with a display terminal. A melodious bleep or beep.

Frantling. The mating call of a peacock.

Fritiniency. The noise of insects.

Gothele. The noise that water makes when a hot iron is dropped in it.

Hirrient. Heavily trilled—as in Hirrrrrrrient.

Horrisonant. Making a horrible noise.

Kinclunk. The sound of a car going over a manhole cover. Word created by poet Alastair Reid (see *ploo,* which is also his creation).

Kyoodle. To make loud, meaningless noise.

Lallation. Pronouncing *r* as *l*.

Lumbrage. A term from the Ozarks for a loud rumbling or crashing noise.

Mugient. A lowing or bellowing. This word, which has been out of use for centuries, was recently reintroduced by the Unicorn Hunters, the organization that annually attacks overused words, which felt that it had modern application, especially in election years. Anyone enjoying mugient should also like *remugient,* to bellow or low again.

Parasigmatism. The inability to pronounce the sound of the letter *s*.

Plangent. Making a sound like the breaking of waves on the shore.

Ploo. The sound of a breaking shoelace.

Poppling. A bubbling sound such as is made when rain falls on water.

Psithurism. Whispering sound of wind through leaves.

Pule. To cry like a chicken.

Raucity. A loud, rough noise.

Reboation. The echo of a bellow.

Rhinophonia. Strong nasality in one's voice.

Rote. Noise made by the surf.

Skirl. The distinctive sound of a bag-pipe.

Skirr. Whirr of birds in flight.

Soughing. A soft rustling or murmuring sound. It is pronounced suhf-ing and is both a noun and an adjective. In their book *A Play on Words* a group of word lovers called VERBIA say of this word, "A soughing sound is soft or gentle or muted: It is soft like the deep sigh of a sleeping baby; it is gentle like the rustle of a taffeta gown; it is muted like the shuffle of an old man's carpet slippers."

Stomatolalia. Speech produced when one's nostrils are clogged.

Thrum. To play an instrument coarsely or artlessly.

Tinnitus. A ringing sound in the head.

Tintinnabulation. The sound of bells; bell ringing.

Tonant. Making loud, deep noise.

Tucket. A trumpet flourish.

Ululate. To howl or hoot.

Vagitus. The cry of the newly born.

Wamble. To rumble from the stomach.

Whurr. To pronounce the letter *r* too forcefully.

SOUSED SYNONYMS

—Exactly 2,231 Words and Phrases for Drunk—

As far as can be determined the first person ever to publish a list of slang terms for drunkenness in the English language was Benjamin Franklin, who came out with his *Drinker's Dictionary* in 1733. It contained 228 terms for intoxicated including these remarkably quaint expressions:

Has stole a Manchet out of the brewer's basket
Has drank more than he has bled
He's kissed black Betty
He's had a thump over the head with Samson's jawbone
He's heat his copper
He cuts his capers
Sir Richard has taken off his considering cap
It is a dark day with him
He's a dead man
He's Prince Eugene
He's eat[en] a load and a half for breakfast
He owes no man a farthing
His flag is out

He's a king
The king is his cousin
He makes indentures with his legs
He's well to live
He's eat[en] the cocoa nut
He's eat[en] opium
He smelt of an onion
He drank till he gave up his halfpenny
He's as good conditioned as a puppy
He's contending with Pharaoh
He's wasted his paunch
He's eat[en] a pudding bag
His shoe pinches him
It is starlight with him
He carried too much sail
He's right before the wind with all his studding sails out

"HE DIDN'T KNOW IT WAS LOADED."

He makes Virginia fence
The malt is above the water

Others followed Franklin's lead in this admirable pursuit.

Edmund Wilson came out with a long list of them in 1927, H. L. Mencken added some in *The American Language* and its supplements, and nearly 1,000 appeared in Lester V. Berrey and Melvin Van Den Bark's monumental *American Thesaurus of Slang*. Over the years *American Speech* has carried several extensive lists contributed by various authors, and a number of books have recorded other terms. Some of the most important have been Eric Partridge's *A Dictionary of Slang and Unconventional English*, Harold Wentworth and Stuart Berg Flexner's *Dictionary of American Slang*, and Richard A. Spears's recent *Slang and Euphemism*.

All this inspired this word collector to begin work on a master drunk list, a list that not only incorporates all the previous lists but draws from a wide variety of additional sources ranging from "research" conducted by friends and scribbled on the back of cocktail napkins to material from the editorial offices of the forthcoming *Dictionary of American Regional English* (DARE).

The list that follows contains 2,231 entries (including the thirty-one already listed from Franklin's collection) without resorting to slight variations in syntax or spelling and resisting the temptation to include one-liners that start with "He's so drunk that——" (such as the nineteenth-century expression, "He's so drunk that he opens his collar to piss," or "He's so drunk the dogs wouldn't piss on him"). The author soberly contends that this is a world's record that will stand until the first person comes along and adds a couple of new ones to it.

Two final points before starting: (1) All the words and phrases are in "as found" condition, which means that mostly all of the terms that have a place for a personal pronoun refer to men (e.g. Dipped his bill,

Paul Dickson/249

Has his pots on, etc.). No slight to besotted women is intended. (2) A number of fine people have helped add terms to the list. For their help in this regard I would like to thank:

Jim Agenbrod
Reinhold Aman
Ryan Anthony
Alan Austin
Terence Blacker
F. G. Cassidy
Terry Catchpole
Mary H. Claycomb
Martha Cornog
Don Crinklaw
Alan Currey
Frederick C. Dyer
A. Ross Eckler
Darryl Francis
Dan Gardner
Joseph C. Goulden
Dave Hackett
Nancy Hackett
Ray Lovett
John McGuire
Peter T. Maiken
Meghan Mead
Russell Mott
Fitzhugh Mullan
Dennis Panke
Denys Parsons
Dan Rapoport
Richard E. Ray
Barbara Rifkind
Somers Ritchie
William Safire
Robert Skole
Marshall L. Smith
Robert C. Snider
Robert Specht
Jim Steigman

William C. Stokoe
Bill Tammeus
John Thornton
Elaine Viets

Stephen Wells
Robert T. West
Hal John Wimberley

250/WORDS

A bit lit
A date with John Barleycorn
A guest in the attic
A real bender
About blowed his top
About drunk
About full
About gone
About had it
About half drunk
About right
About shot
About to cave in
About to go under
About to pass out
Absolutely done
Abuzz (A-buzz)
Aced
Acting silly
Activated
Acts like a fool
Adam's apple up
Addled
Adrip
Afflicted
Afloat
Aglow

Alcoholic
Alcoholized
Alecie (pronounced ale-see)
Alight
Alkied
Alkied up
Alky soaked
All at sea
All fucked up
All geezed up
All gone
All he can hold
All in
All liquored up
All lit up
All mops and brooms
All organized
All out
All pink elephants
All schnozzled up
All shucked up
All there
All wet
Almost froze
Almost intoxicated
Altogetherly
Amuck
Anchored in sot's bay
Antifreezed
Antiseptic
Aped
Apple palsy
Arf an' arf
Arfarfanark
Arseholed
A-showin' it
Ass backwards
Ass on backwards
A-tappin' the bottle
At one's ease

At rest
At rights
Ate the dog
Awash
Awry-eyed

Bacchi plenus
Bacchus-bulged
Bacchus-butted
Back-assward
Back home
Back teeth afloat
Bagged
Ball-dozed
Balmy
Bamboozled
Banjaxed
Baptized
Barleysick
Barmy
Barreled-up
Barrelhouse
Barrelhouse drunk
Bashed
Basted
Bats
Batted
Battered
Batty
Beargered
Bearing the ensign

Beastly drunk
Been among the Philippines
Been among the Philistines
Been at an Indian feast
Been at Geneva
Been before George
Been elephants
Been in the bibbing plot
Been in the sauce
Been in the sun
Been to a funeral
Been to France
Been to Barbados
Been to Jericho
Been to Mexico
Been to Olympus
Been to the saltwater
Been too free with Sir John Straw-
    berry
Been too free with Sir Richard
Been too free with the creature
Been with Sir John Goa
Beerified
Beer-soaked
Beery
Beginning to fly
Beginning to get a glow on
Beginning to stagger
Behind the cork

Belly up
Below the mahogany
Belted
Bemused
Bending over
Bent
Bent and broken
Bent his elbow
Bent out of shape
Benused
Besoppen
Besot
Besotted
Better if he's gone twice after the
    same load
Bewildered
Bewitched
Bewottled
Beyond salvage
Beyond the fringe
Bezzled
Bibacious
Bibulous
Biffy
Biggy
Binged
Bingoed
Bit by a fox
Bit teed up
Bit tiddley
Bit tipsy
Bit wobbly
Biting the brute
Biting them off
Bitten by a barn-mouse
Black jacked
Blacked out
Blanked
Blasé
Blasted

Bleary-eyed
Blewed
Blighted
Blimped
Blind
Blind drunk
Blind, staggering drunk
Blind staggers
Blinded
Blinders
Blindo
Blinking drunk
Blinky
Blissed out
Blistered
Blithered
Blitzed
Bloated
Block and block
Bloody drunk
Blotto
Blowed

Blowed-away
Blown
Blown away
Blown out
Blown over
Blown up
Blowzy
Blue
Blue around the gills
Blued

Blue-eyed
Boggled
Boggy
Boiled
Boiled as an owl
Boiled to the gills
Boiling drunk
Bollixed
Bombed
Boned

Bongo
Bongoed
Bonkers
Boosy
Booze blind
Boozed
Boozed as the gage
Boozed up
Boozie
Boozified
Boozy
Boozy-woozy
Borracho
Bosco absoluto
Boshy
Bosky
Both sheets in the wind
Bottle-ached
Bottled

Bought the black sun
'Bout had it
Bowzed
Bowzered
Boxed
Boxed out
Boxed up
Brained
Brandy-faced
Breath strong enough to carry coal
  with
Breezy
Bridgey
Bright-eyed
Bright in the eye
Bruised
Bubbled
Bubby
Buckled

Budgey
Buffy
Bug-eyed
Bull-dozed
Bulletproofed
Bummed out
Bumpsy
Bung
Bunged
Bung-eyed
Bungey
Bungfu
Bungy
Bunned
Bunnied
Buoyant
Buoyed
Burdock'd
Buried
Burned to the ground
Burns with a low blue flame
Burnt
Burst
Busky
Busted
Buzz

Buzzed
Buzzey
Buzzy

Cached
Caged
Cagrin'd
Candy
Canned
Canned up
Canon
Can't hit the ground with his hat
Can't see through a ladder
Capable
Capernoited
Cap-sick
Cargoed
Carrying a heavy load
Carrying a load
Carrying the dark dog on his back
Carrying two red lights
Cast
Casting up his accounts
Cat
Catch'd
Catsood
Caught
Caught off his hobbyhorse
Certified drunk
Chagrin'd
Chap-fallen

Charged
Cherry-merry
Cherubimical
Chickery
Chipper
Chock-a-block
Chucked
Clear
Clear out
Clipped the King's English
Clobbered
Clinched
Coagulated
Coarse
Cocked
Cocked as a log
Cocked to the gills
Cockeyed
Cockeyed drunk
Cogey
Cognacked
Coguy
Cold
Comboozelated
Comfortable
Comin'
Comin' on
Commencin'
Commencin' to feel it
Completely out of it
Completely squashed
Concerned
Conflummoxed
Conked out

Cooked
Copey
Copped a crane
Corked
Corked-up
Cork high and bottle deep
Corkscrewed
Corky
Corned
Cornered
Cracked
Cramped
Crapulous
Crashed
Crashed and burned
Crazed
Crazy drunk
Creamed
Crocked
Crocko
Crocus
Cronk
Cropsick
Cross-eyed
Crump
Crump footed
Crumped
Crumped out

Crying drunk
Crying jag
Cuckooed
Cup-shot
Cupped
Cupshotten
Curved
Cushed
Cut

Daffy
Dagged
Damaged
Damp
Daquifried
D and D
Dead drunk
Dead to the world
Decayed
Decks awash
Deep drunk
Defaced
Deleerit
Derailed
Detained on business
Dew drunk
Dewed
Did the job up right
Ding-swizzled
Dinged-out
Dingy

Dinky
Dipped
Dipped his bill
Dipped too deep
Dipsy
Dirtfaced
Dirty drunk
Discombobulated
Discomboobulated
Discouraged
Discumfuddled
Disguised
Disgusting
Disorderly
Distinguished
Dithered
Dizzy
Dizzy as a coot
Dizzy as a goose
Dog drunk
Done a Falstaff
Done a vanishing act
Done an Archie
Done got out
Done over
Done up

Doped
Doped over
Dotted
Dotty
Double-headed
Double-tongued
Doubled up
Down and out
Down for the count
Down with the fish
Dramling
Draped
Draw a blank
Drenched
Drinkative
Dripping tight
Drowned
Drowning brain cells
Drunk
Drunk and disorderly
Drunk and down
Drunk as a badger
Drunk as a bastard
Drunk as a bat
Drunk as a beggar
Drunk as a besom
Drunk as a big owl

Drunk as a boiled owl
Drunk as a brewer's fart
Drunk as a cook
Drunk as a coon
Drunk as a coot
Drunk as a cooter
Drunk as a cootie
Drunk as a dog
Drunk as a fiddler
Drunk as a fiddler's bitch
Drunk as a fish
Drunk as a fly
Drunk as a fowl
Drunk as a Gosport fiddler
Drunk as a hog
Drunk as a king
Drunk as a little red wagon
Drunk as a log
Drunk as a loon
Drunk as a lord
Drunk as a monkey
Drunk as a Perraner
Drunk as a pig
Drunk as a piper
Drunk as a poet
Drunk as a rolling fart
Drunk as a sailor

Paul Dickson/259

Drunk as a skunk in a trunk
Drunk as a soot
Drunk as a sow
Drunk as a swine
Drunk as a tapster
Drunk as a tick
Drunk as a top
Drunk as a wheelbarrow
Drunk as an owl
Drunk as Bacchus
Drunk as blazes
Drunk as buggery
Drunk as Chloe
Drunk as Cooter Brown
Drunk as David's sow
Drunk as hell
Drunk as hoot
Drunk as mice
Drunk as muck
Drunk as the devil
Drunk as Zeus
Drunk for sure
Drunk up
Drunken
Drunker than a boiled owl
Drunker than a cannon
Drunker than a hoot owl
Drunker than a monkey
Drunker than hell
Drunker than Scootum Brown

Drunker than whiskey
Drunkulent
Drunkok
Drunky
D.T.'s (Delirium Tremens)
Due for drydock
Dull-eyed
Dull in the eye
Dumped
DWIed (Driving While Intoxicated)

Ears are ringing
Ears ringing
Eating his oats
Ebrios
Ebriose
Ebrious
Edged
Electrified
Elephant's trunk
Elevated
Eliminated
Embalmed
Enter'd
Exalted
Exhilarated
Extinguished

Faced
Faint
Fairly ripped
Fallen off the wagon

Falling down drunk
Fap
Far ahead (Farahead)
Far gone
Fearless
Fears no man
Featured
Feeling
Feeling aces
Feeling dizzy
Feeling drunk
Feeling excellent
Feeling frisky
Feeling funny
Feeling glorious
Feeling good
Feeling groovy
Feeling happy
Feeling high
Feeling his alcohol
Feeling his booze
Feeling his cheerios
Feeling his drink
Feeling his liquor
Feeling his oats
Feeling his onions
Feeling it
Feeling it a little
Feeling juiced up
Feeling no pain
Feeling pretty good
Feeling real well
Feeling right royal
Feeling the effect
Fell off the wagon
Fettered
Feverish
Fiddled
Fighting drunk
Fighting tight

Paul Dickson/261

Fired up
Fish-eyed
Fishy
Fishy about the gills
Fixed up
Fizzed up
Fizzled
Flabbergasted
Flag is out
Flakers
Flako
Flared
Flat-ass drunk
Flatch kennurd
Flat-out drunk
Flawed
Floating
Floating high
Flooded
Floored
Flooey
Floppy
Florid
Flown with the wild turkey
Fluffy

Flummoxed
Flummuxed
Flush
Flushed
Flusterated
Flustered
Flusticated
Flyblown
Fly-by-night
Flying blind
Flying high
Flying light
Flying one wing low
Flying the Ensign
Fogged
Foggy
Fogmatic
Folded
Fool if you don't quit
Foolish
Footless
Foozlified
45 degrees listed
Fossilized
Fou

Four sheets to the wind
Foxed (Foxt)
Foxy
Fozzed
Fractured
Frazzled
Freaked
Freefall
Fresh
Freshish
Fried
Fried on both sides
Fried to the gills
Fried to the hat
Fried up
Frozen
Froze his mouth
FUBARed (Fouled Up Beyond All
    Recognition)
Fucked out
Fucked over
Fucked up
Fuddled
Full
Full as a boot
Full as a bull
Full as a fiddler
Full as a goat
Full as a goog egg
Full as a goose
Full as a lord
Full as a tick
Full as an egg
Full cocked
Full flavored
Full of courage
Full to the bung
Full to the gills
Full up
Full up to the brain

Fully soused
Fully tanked
Funny
Fur brained
Fur on his tongue
Furry
Fuzzled
Fuzzy
Fuzzy headed

Gaffed
Gaga
Gaged
Galvanized
Gambrinous
Gargled
Gaseous
Gassed
Gassed up
Gassy
Gay
Gayed
Geared up
Geed up
Geezed
Geezed up
Generous
Get Chinese
Getting a glow
Getting a jag on
Getting a little boozy

Getting a little high
Getting a little inebriated
Getting a little whizzy
Getting a load on
Getting a snootful
Getting a thrill
Getting about all he needs
Getting an answer
Getting barreled up
Getting bleary-eyed
Getting boozed up
Getting boozy
Getting charged up
Getting crocked
Getting dopy
Getting full
Getting goofy
Getting him
Getting his ears back
Getting in
Getting inebriated
Getting intoxicated
Getting kind of high
Getting kind of woozy

Getting light-headed
Getting likkered up
Getting lit
Getting lit up
Getting loaded
Getting looped
Getting loose
Getting on one
Getting on the band wagon
Getting polluted
Getting pretty full
Getting pretty high
Getting pretty well lit
Getting ready
Getting right
Getting shaky
Getting shot
Getting soft
Getting soused
Getting started
Getting tanked up
Getting teed up
Getting the habit
Getting there

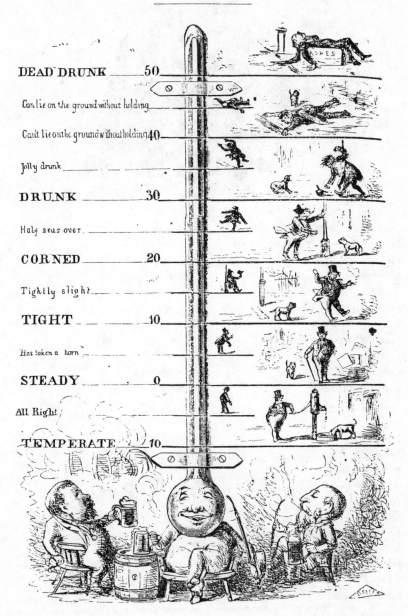

The Inebriometer.

DEAD DRUNK — 50

Can lie on the ground without holding

Can't lie on the ground without holding — 40

Jolly drunk

DRUNK — 30

Half seas over

CORNED — 20

Tightly slight

TIGHT — 10

Has taken a horn

STEADY — 0

All Right

TEMPERATE — 10

Getting to be a drunkard
Getting to feel his liquor
Getting too full
Getting topsy
Getting under the influence
Getting under way
Getting up high
Getting warmed
Getting warmed up
Getting wasted
Getting woozy
Giddy
Giffed
Giggled
Gilded
Gin crazed
Gin soaked
Gingered up
Ginned
Ginned up
Ginny
Glad
Glassy
Glassy-eyed

Glazed
Globular
Glorious
Glowed
Glowing
Glued
Goat drunk
God-awful drunk
Goes out
Goggle-eyed
Going
Going overboard
Going to Jerusalem
Going under
Gold-headed
Gone
Gone Borneo
Gone down in flames
Gone maximum Southern Comfort
Gone out
Gone over the hill
Gone to Mexico
Gone to Olympus
Gone to the devil

Good and drunk
Good-humored
Goofy
Googly-eyed
Gory-eyed
Got a blow on
Got a brass eye
Got a bun on
Got a buzz on
Got a dish
Got a jag on
Got a little polly on
Got a load on
Got a rum nose
Got a snootful
Got about enough
Got by the head
Got corns in his head
Got his shoes full
Got his snowsuit on and heading
   north
Got kibbled heels
Got on his little hat
Got one going
Got some in him
Got the blind staggers
Got the glanders
Got the good feeling
Got the gout
Got the gravel rash
Got the horns on
Got the Indian vapors
Got the nightmare
Got the pole evil
Got the treatment
Got too much
Gowed
Gowed to the gills
Grade-A certified drunk
Grapeshot

Graveled
Greased
Groatable
Grogged
Grogged up
Groggy
Guarding the gates of hell
Gutter drunk
Guttered
Guyed out
Guzzled

Had a bun on
Had a couple of drinks
Had a couple of shooters
Had a dram
Had a few drinks
Had a few too many
Had a kick in the guts
Had a little too much
Had a number of beers
Had a shot or two
Had a skinful and a half
Had a snort
Had enough
Had enough to make him noisy
Had it
Had one or two
Had one too many
Hair on his tongue
Half-a-brewer

Half and half
Half-assed
Half bent out of shape
Half-blind
Half-bulled
Half-canned

Half-cocked
Half-cockeyed
Half-corned
Half-crocked
Half-cut
Half-doped

Half-drunk
Half geared-up
Half-gone
Half-high
Half in the bag
Half in the boot
Half in the tank
Half-lit
Half-looped
Half nelson
Half-on
Half-out
Half-pickled
Half-pissed
Half rats
Half-rinsed
Half-screwed
Half-seas over
Half-seas under
Half-shaved
Half-shot
Half-slammed
Half-slewed
Half-slopped
Half-snapped
Half-sober
Half-soused
Half-sprung
Half-stewed
Half-stiff
Half-stoused
Half-tanked
Half the bay over
Half the bay under
Half-tipsy
Half-under
Halfway over
Halfway to Concord
Hammered
Hammerish

Hanced
Hang one on
Happy
Happy drunk
Hard up
Hardy
Harry flakers
Has a bag on
Has a big head
Has a brass eye
Has a brick in his hat
Has a bun on
Has a can on
Has a cup too much
Has a drop in his eye
Has a drop too much taken
Has a full cargo
Has a full jag on
Has a full load on
Has a glow on
Has a jag on
Has a load on
Has a load under the skin
Has a package on
Has a pretty good glow on
Has a shine on
Has a skate on
Has a skinful
Has a slant on
Has a snootful
Has a turkey on one's back
Has an edge on
Has been kicked in the guts
Has bet his kettle (also Has het . . .)
Has burnt his shoulder
Has froze his mouth
Has his flag out
Has his gage up
Has his head full of bees

Paul Dickson/269

Has his head on backwards
Has his pots on
Has hung one on
Has lost a shoe
Has made an example
Has made too free with John Bar-
    leycorn
Has scalt his head pad
Has sold his senses
Has spoke with his friend
Has taken a chiruping glass
Has taken Hippocrates' Grand
    Elixir
Has the Indian vapors
Has the Mexican vapors
Has the screaming meemies

Has the shakes
Has the whoops and jingles
Has the yorks
Has the zings
Hasn't got no pain
Haunted with evil spirits
Hazy
He couldn't find his ass with two
    hands
Heading into the wind
Heady
Hear the owl hoot
Hearty
Hee-hawing around
Heeled
Heeled over

Helpless
Hepped
Hepped up
Het-up
Hiccius-doccius
Hickey
Hicksius-doxius
Hiddey
High
High as a cat's back
High as a fiddler's fist
High as a Georgia pine
High as a kite
High as Lindbergh
High as the sky
High in the saddle
High lonesome
Higher than a kite
Hipped
His elevator's stalled
His hair hurts
His head is smoking
His lee scuppers are under
His nose is getting red
His teeth are floating

Hitting 'em up
Hitting it a little
Hitting the jug
Hitting the sauce
Hoary-eyed
Hockey
Hocus
Hocus-pocus
Hog drunk
Holding up the wall
Honked
Hooched
Hooched-up
Hoodman
Hooted
Hopped
Hopped up
Horizontal
Horseback
Hosed
Hot
Hot as a red wagon
Hotsy-totsy
Hotter than a skunk
How-come-ye-so?

Paul Dickson/271

Illuminated
Imbibed giggle water
Imbibed too freely
Impaired
Impixocated
In a bad way
In a drunken stupor
In a fix
In a fog
In a fuddle
In a glow
In a head
In a muddle
In a rosy glow
In a stew
In a trance
In a vise
In armor
In color
In good fettle
In his airs
In his altitudes
In his cups
In his elements
In his glory
In his habits
In his pots
In his prosperity
In it now
In liquor
In Mexico

In orbit
In soak
In the bag
In the cellar
In the clouds
In the gun
In the gutter
In the ozone
In the pen
In the pink
In the pulpit
In the rats
In the sack
In the satchel
In the suds

In the sun
In the tank
In the wind
In tipium grove
In uncharted waters
Incog
Incognitibus
Incognito
Indisposed
Inebriated
Infirm
Influenced
Injun drunk
Inked
Inkypoo
Insobriety

Inspired
Inter pocula
Into the suds
Intoxed
Intoxicate
Intoxicated
Inundated
Iron-plated
Irrigated
Ishkimmisk
It's beginning to kick
It's getting to him
It's got ahold of him and he can't
  let go
It's showing on him
It's working on him

Paul Dickson/273

Jag on
Jagged
Jagged up
Jambled
Jammed
Jarred
Jazzed
Jazzed up

Jiggered
Jingled
Jocular
Jolly
Jolly fu'
Joplined
Jug-bitten
Jug-steamed
Jugged
Jugged up
Juiced
Juiced up
Juicy
Jungled
Just about drunk
Just about half-drunk
Just plain drunk
Just showing signs

Kentucky-fried
Keyed
Keyed up
Keyed to the roof
Killed
Killed his dog
Kind of high
Kind of woozy
Kisky
Kited
Knapt
Knee-crawling, commode-hugging, gutter-wallowing drunk
Knee-walking drunk
Knocked for a loop
Knocked off his pins
Knocked out

Knocked over
Knocked-up
Knockered
Knows not the way home
Ky-eyed

Laced
Laid
Laid out
Laid right out
Laid to the bone
Lame
Lapped the gutter
Lappy
Larruping drunk
Lathered
Laying out dead drunk
Leaning
Leaping
Leary
Leathered
Leery
Legless
Leveled
Lifted
Light
Light-headed
Lighting up
Lights out
Like a rat in trouble
Likker-soaked

Paul Dickson/275

Likkered

Likkered up

Likkerous

Limber

Limp

Lined

Lion drunk

Liquefied

Liquor plug

Liquor struck

Liquored

Liquored up

Liquorish

Liquor's talking

Listing to starboard

Lit

Lit a bit

Lit to the gills

Lit to the guards

Lit to the gunnels

Lit up

Lit up a little bit

Lit up like a cathedral

Lit up like a Christmas tree

Lit up like a church

Lit up like a kite

Lit up like a skyscraper

Lit up like a store window

Lit up like Main Street

Lit up like the Commonwealth

Lit up like the sky

Lit up to show he's human

Little bit on the go

Little off the beam

Little round the corner

Little tight

Little woozy

Living up a bit

Loaded

Loaded for bear

Loaded his cart

Loaded to the barrel

Loaded to the earlobes

Loaded to the gills

Loaded to the guards

Loaded to the gunnels

Loaded to the gunwales

Loaded to the hat

Loaded to the muzzle

Loaded to the Plimsoll mark

Loaded to the tailgate

Loading up

Lock-legged

Logged

Longlong (pidgin English)

Longwhiskey (pidgin English)

Look lively

Looks boozy

Loony

Looped

Looped-legged

Loop-legged

Loopy

Loopy-legged

Loose in the hilt(s)

Loosening up

Loppy

Lordly

Lost his rudder

Loud and proud

Lousy drunk

Low in the saddle

Lubricated

Lumped

Lumpy

Lush

Lushed

Lushed up

Lushington

Lushy

Maggoty
Main-brace well spliced
Making a trip to Baltimore
Malted
Marinated
Martin drunk
Mashed
Mastok
Maudlin
Mauled
Mawbrish
Maxed out
Mean
Mellow
Mellowing
Melted
Merry
Merry as a Greek
Mesmerized
Messed
Methodistconated
Mexican-fried
Mickey-finished
Middlin'
Middling
Miffy
Milled
Miraculous
Mitered
Mixed-up

Mizzled
Moist around the edges
Mokus
Moon-eyed
Moonlit
Moony
Moored in sot's bay
Mopped
Moppy
Mops and brooms
Mortal
Mortallious
Mortally drunk
Motherless
Mountous
Mouthy
Muckibus
Muddled
Muddled up
Muddy
Muffed

Paul Dickson/277

Mug blotto
Mugg blots
Mugged
Mugged up
Muggy
Mulled
Mulled up
Muzzy

Native (as in "He went native")
Nazy
Nearly off his rocker
Needing a reef taken in
Newted
Nice
Nimptopsical
Nipped
Noddy-headed
Noggy
Nolo
Non compos
Non compos poopoo
Not able to see through a ladder
Not all there
Not feeling any pain
Not in any pain
Not suffering any
Numb
Nuts
Nutty
N.Y.D.

Nappy
Nase
Nasty drunk

Obfuscated
Obfusticated
Oenophlygia
   (pronounced ee-no-fly-gia)
Off
Off at the nail
Off his bean
Off his feet
Off his nut
Off nicely
Off the deep end
Off the nail
Off the wagon
Off to Mexico
Off to the races
Oiled
Oiled up
Oinophluxed
On
On a bat
On a bender
On a binge
On a brannigan
On a bus
On a bust
On a drunk
On a jag
On a merry-go-round
On a skate
On a spree

On a tear
On a tipple
On a toot
Ona
On his ass
On his ear
On his fourth
On his last legs
On his oats
On his way down
On his way out
On his way to a good drunk
On instruments
On sentry
On the booze
On the floor
On the fritz
On the go
On the grog
On the juice
On the lee lurch
On the ooze
On the randan
On the razzle dazzle
On the sauce
On the shikker
On the skyte
One over the eight
One too many
Oozy
Organized
Orie-eyed
Oscillated
Ossified
Out
Out cold
Out for the count
Out in left field with a catcher's
   mitt on
Out like a lamp

Paul Dickson/279

Out like a light
Out like Lottie's eye
Out of altitudes
Out of commission
Out of funds
Out of his mind
Out of his mind drunk
Out of key
Out of one's element
Out of register
Out of the picture
Out of the way
Out on the roof
Out to it
Out to lunch
Over the bay
Over the mark
Overboard
Overcome
Overloaded
Overseas
Overseen
Overserved
Overset
Overshot
Oversparred
Overtaken
Over-wined
Owled
Owl-eyed
Owly-eyed
Oxycrocium (pronounced oxy-
    crock-eum)

Packaged
Padded
Pafisticated
Paid
Painted
Paintin' his nose
Palatio
Palled
Paralytic
Paralyzed
Parboiled
Pass out cold
Passed

Past going
Pasted
Peckish
Pee-eyed
Pegged too low
Peonied
Pepped
Pepped up
Peppy
Pepst
Perked
Perpetual drunk
Pertish
Petrificated
Petrified
Phfft
Pickled
Pickled the mustard
Pie-eyed
Pied

Piffed
Pifficated
Piffle
Piffled
Pifflicated
Pigeon-eyed
Pilfered
Pinked
Pinko
Pious
Piped
Pipped
Pipped up
Pissed
Pissed as a newt
Pissed in the brook
Pissed up
Pissed up to the eyebrows
Pissing drunk
Pissy-arsed

Pissy-drunk
Pixillated
Pixy-laden
Pixy-led
Pizzacato
Plain drunk
Plain old drunk
Plastered
Plated
Played out
Pleasantly intoxicated
Pleasantly plastered
Plenty drunk
Plonked
Plootered
Plotzed
Ploughed
Ploughed under
Plowed
Plumb drunk

Paul Dickson/281

Pocito
Poddy
Podgy
Poffered
Poggled
Pogy
Polished
Polished up
Polite
Polled-off
Polluted
Poopied
Popeyed
Potched
Pot-eyed
Pots on
Potsed
Pot-shot
Pot-sick
Potted
Potted off
Potty
Potulent
Potvaliant
Powdered
Powdered up
Practically down
Preaching drunk
Preserved
Prestoned
Pretty drunk
Pretty far gone
Pretty happy
Pretty high
Pretty silly
Pretty well intoxicated
Pretty well organized
Pretty well over
Pretty well plowed
Pretty well primed

Pretty well slacked
Pretty well started
Priddy
Primed
Primed to the barrel
Primed to the muzzle
Primed to the trigger
Primed up
Pruned
Psatzed
Puggled
Puggy drunk
Pulled a Daniel Boone
Pungey
Pushed
Put to bed with a shovel

Putrid
Putting one on
Pye-eyed

Quarrelsome
Quartzed
Queer
Queered
Quisby
Quilted

Racked
Racked-up
Raddled
Ragged
Raised
Raised his monuments
Rammaged
Ramping mad
Rather high
Rattled
Ratty

Ratty as a jaybird
Raunchy
Razzle-dazzled
Reached a hundred proof
Ready
Ready to pass out
Real drunk
Real tipsy
Really
Really feeling his drinks
Really gassed
Really got a load
Really had a load
Really high
Really lit
Really lit up
Really saturated
Really soused
Really tied one on
Reeking
Reeling
Reeling and kneeling
Reeling ripe
Reely
Relaxing
Religious
Re-raw
Rich
Right down and out
Right royal
Rigid
Rileyed
Ripe
Ripped
Ripped and wrecked
Ripped to the tits
Rip-roaring drunk
Roaring
Roaring drunk
Roasted

Rocky
Rolled off the sofa
Rolling
Rolling drunk
Roostered
Rorty
Rosined
Rosy
Rosy about the gills
Rotten
Round as a glass
Royal
Royally plastered
Rum-dum
Rum-dumb
Rummed
Rummed up
Rummy
Running drunk
Rye-soaked

Salt junk
Salted
Salted down
Salubrious
Sank like a brick
Sank like a rock
Sank like a stone
Sap-happy
Sapped
Saturated

Sauced
Saw Montezuma
Sawed
Scammered
Schicker
Schizzed-out
Schlitzed
Schlockkered
Schnockered
Schnockkered
Schnoggered
Scooped
Scorched
Scotch mist
Scrambled
Scratched
Scraunched
Screaming drunk
Screeching
Screeching drunk
Screwed
Screwy
Scronched

Scrooched
Scrooched up
Scrooped
Seafaring
Seasick
Seeing a flock of moons
Seeing bats
Seeing by twos
Seeing double
Seeing pink elephants
Seeing the bears
Seeing the devil
Seeing the elephants
Seeing the French king
Seeing the snakes
Seeing the yellow star
Seeing two moons
Seguéd
Semibousy
Sent
Served-up
Set-up

Several slugs behind the midriff
Sewed
Sewed up
S.F. (Shit-faced)
Shagged
Shaggy
Shaky
Shaved
Sheet and a half to the wind
Sheet in the wind
Shellacked
Shellacked the goldfish bowl
Sherbetty

Shicer

Shicker

Shickered

Shifassed

Shikker

Shikkered

Shined

Shined up

Shiny

Shiny drunk

Shipwrecked

Shit-faced

Shitty

Shot

Shot away

Shot down

Shot full of holes

Shot in the arm

Shot in the mouth

Shot in the neck

Shot in the wrist

Shot-up

Showing his booze

Showing his tipsiness

Showing it

Silly

Silly drunk

Sinking like a rock

Six sails to the wind
Six sheets to the wind
Sizzled
Skunk drunk
Skunked
Skunky
Slap drunk
Slathered
Slewed
Slewy
Slick
Slightly buzzed
Slightly clobbered
Slightly draped
Slightly drunk
Slightly high
Slightly looped
Slightly tightly
Slightly under

Slightly woozy
Slippery
Slipping
Slobbered
Slopped
Slopped over
Slopped to the ears
Slopped to the gills
Slopped up
Sloppy
Sloppy drunk
Sloshed
Sloshed to the ears
Sloughed
Slued
Slugged
Slurks
Slushed
Slushed-up

Smashed

Smashed out of his mind

Smashed to the gills

Smeared

Smeekit

Smelling of the cork

Smitten by the grape

Smoked

Snackered

Snapped

Snerred

Sniffed the barmaid's apron

Snockkered

Snockkered up

Snoot full

Snooted

Snoozamorooed

Snotted

Snozzled

Snubbed

Snuffy

Snug

So

Soaked

Soaked to the gills

Soaked-up

Soaken

Soako

Soapy-eyed

Sobbed

Socked

Sodden

Soft

Soggy

Somebody stole his rudder

Sopped

Sopping

Sopping wet

Soppy

Sore footed

Soshed

So-so

Sot drunk

Sotted

Sottish

Sotto

Soul in soak

Soupy

Soused

Soused to the ears

Soused to the gills

Southern-fried

Sow-drunk

Sozzled

Sozzly

Spak (pidgin English)

Speared

Speechless

Spiffed

Spifficated

Spiffilo

Spiffled

Spiflicated

Spliced

Sploshed

Sponge-eyed

Sponge-headed

Spoony drunk

Spotty

Spreed

Spreed up

Sprung

Squamed

Squared

Squashed

Squiffed

Squiffy

Squirrelly

Squished

Staggering around

Staggerish
Staggers
Staggery
Stale
Stale drunk
Standing too long in the sun
Starched
Starchy
Stark drunk
Starting to feel pretty good
Starting to feel rosy
Starting to get lit up
Starting to glow
Starting to show his drink
State of elevation
Staying late at the office
Steady
Steamed
Steamed-up
Steeped
Stewed
Stewed as a fresh boiled owl
Stewed to the ears
Stewed to the gills
Stewed-up
Sticked
Stiff
Stiff as a carp
Stiff as a goat
Stiff as a plank
Stiff as a ramrod
Stiff as a ringbolt
Stiffed
Stiffo
Still on his feet
Stimulated
Stinkarooed
Stinking
Stinking drunk
Stinko

Stitched
Stocked-up
Stoked
Stolled
Stone blind
Stone cold drunk
Stoned
Stoned out of his mind
Stoned to the gills
Stoney blind
Stonkered
Stove in
Stozzled
Striped
Strong
Stubbed
Stuccoed
Stumble-drunk
Stung
Stunko
Stunned
Stupefied
Stupid
Sucked
Sucky

Paul Dickson/289

Suffering no pain
Sun in the eyes
Sunk like a brick
Super-charged
Sure feeling good
Sure 'nuff drunk
Sure petrified
Sure tied one on
Suttle
Swacked
Swacko
Swallowed a hare
Swallowed a tavern token
Swamped
Swatched
Swatted
Swattled
Swazzled
Sweet
Swigged
Swiggled
Swilled
Swilled up
Swillo
Swine-drunk
Swiney
Swinnied
Swiped

Swipey
Switchy
Swivelly
Swizzled
Swozzled

Tacky
Taken a segue
Taken a shard
Taking a trip
Taking it easy
Talking loud
Tangled
Tanglefooted
Tanglelegged
Tanked
Tanked out
Tanked up
Tanned
Tapped
Tapped out
Tapped the admiral
Tap-shackled
Tattooed
Taverned
Tead up
Teed
Teed up
Teeth under
Temulent
Temulentious

"YOU'LL NEVER MISS THE WATER"

Temulentive
That way
Thawed
There
There with both feet
There with the goods
There with what it takes
Thick-lipped
Thick-tongued
Thoroughly drunk
Thoroughly intoxicated
Three bricks short of a load
Three sheets in the shade
Three sheets in the wind and the
  other one flapping
Three sheets to the wind
Three sheets to the wind's eye
Tiddled
Tiddley
Tied one on

Tiffled
Tight
Tight as a brassiere
Tight as a drum
Tight as a fart
Tight as a goat
Tight as a mink
Tight as a tick
Tight as the bark on a tree
Tilted
Tin hats
Tinned
Tip merry
Tipium grove
Tipped
Tipping
Tippling
Tipply
Tippsified
Tippy

Paul Dickson/291

Tipsy
Tip-top
Tired
Tired and emotional
Tishy
Toasted
Tol-lol
Tongue-tied
Too many clothes on the wind
Too numerous to mention
Toped
Toper
Top-heavy
Top-loaded
Topped
Topped off his antifreeze
Topper
Toppy
Topsy-boozy
Topsy-turvy
Tore-up
Torrid
Tossed
Tosticated
Tostified
Totaled
Totally drunk

Touched
Touched as a boiled owl
Touched off
Toxed
Toxicated
Toxy
Trammeled
Translated
Trashed
Trifle maudlin'
Tripping
Tubed
Tumbling
Tumbling drunk
Tuned
Tuned up
Tuned up a little
Turned on
Twisted
Two sheets to the wind
Two-thirds kicked in the ass

Ugly
Ugly drunk
Umbriago
Uncorked
Under
Under full sail
Under full steam
Under the affluence of incohol
Under the influence

Under the table   Unsober
Under the wagon   Unsteady
Under the weather   Up a tree
Underway   Up in one's hat
Unkdray   Up on blocks

Up on Olympus
Up the pole
Up to the ears
Up to the gills
Upholstered
Uppish
Uppity
Upsey

Valiant
Varnished
Very
Very drunk
Very high
Very relaxed
Very weary
Vulcanized

Walking on his cap badge
Wall-eyed
Wallpapered
Wam-bazzled

Wamble crop'd
Wapsed down
Warming up
Wassailed out
Wassailed up
Wasted
Watered
Waterlogged
Water-soaked (also
    water-soaken)
Waxed
Weak jointed
Wearing a barley cap
Weary
Weaving
Well away
Well bottled
Well fixed
Well heeled
Well in for it
Well jointed
Well lathered
Well lit
Well loaded
Well lubricated
Well oiled
Well on his way
Well primed
Well soaked
Well sprung
Well under
Wet
Wet both eyes
Wet-handed
Wettish
Whacked out
Whacky
What-nosed
Whazood
Whiffled

Whipped
Whipsey
Whiskeyfied
Whiskey-frisky
Whiskey-raddled
Whiskey-shot
Whiskied
Whistle drunk
Whittin stewed
Whittled
Wholly-wassailed
Whooshed
Whoozy
Whopped up
Wide-eyed and legless
Wild

Wilted
Wine-potted
Winey
Wing-heavy
Winterized
Wiped
Wiped out
Wiped over
Wired
Wired up
Wise
With a binge on
With a bun on
With a jag on
With a load on
With a skate on

Paul Dickson/295

With a slant on
With an edge on
With the sun in one's eyes
With the topgallant sails out
With too many cloths in the wind
With too much sail
Wobbly
Woggled
Woggly
Womble-ty-cropt
Wooshed
Woozy
Wrapped up in warm flannel
Wrecked

Yappy
Ydrunken

Zagged
Zapped
Zigzag
Zigzagged
Zipped
Zippered
Zissified
Zoned
Zonked
Zorked
Zozzled

STUDIOUS WORDS

—An Academic Assortment—

ABD. Abbreviation for "all but dissertation"; applied to doctoral candidates who have completed all the required courses but who have yet to write their dissertations. Used facetiously in some circles, as M.A. and Ph.D. are.

Algriology. Study of savage customs.

Autology. The scientific study of oneself.

Axiology. In philosophy, the science of values in general. A relatively recent coinage.

Balneology. The study of the therapeutic effects of bathing in mineral waters.

Biometeorology. The effect of weather on people.

Cart. Campus-course slang for cartography. There are many of these —*trig, calc, Brit lit, poli sci,* etc.—but they reach their highest form as rhyming pairs such as *rocks for jocks* for introductory geology. A fine collection of these appears in an article, "Course Names" by Paul A. Eschholz and Alfred F. Rosa, in the Spring 1970 issue of *American Speech.* Among them:

Slums and bums: Urban local government.
Nuts and sluts: Abnormal psychology.
Stones and Bones: World prehistory.
Chokes and Croak: First aid and safety education.

Donnism. Academic self-importance.

Enigmatology. The study of enigmas and puzzles. According to an Associated Press story of March 1981, there is only one academically confirmed specialist of this sort in the United States. He is Will Shortz, who designed his own course of study in enigmatology at Indiana University.

Ichnology. The study of footprints commonly applied to those who study fossilized prints.

Kalology. The study of beauty.

Ktenology. The science of putting people to death.

Lirripoop. A learned person who lacks common sense; an academic dolt. Also applied to the hood and long tail of an academic gown.

Melittology. The study of bees.

Momilogy. The study of mummies.

Nassology. The science of taxidermy.

Nidology. The study of birds' nests.

Oikology. The science of housekeeping.

Orology. The study of mountains.

Osmics. The scientific study of smells.

Osmology. The study of odors.

Parietal. Of or relating to life within a college or university.

Phobiology. The study of phobias.

Photics. The scientific study of light.

Polemology. The study of war.

Polymath. One who has mastered many fields of knowledge.

Pomology. The science of fruit growing.

Pteridology. The study of ferns. The *p* is silent, as it is on the next word.

Pterylology. The study of the distribution of feathers on a bird's body.

Pyrgology. The study of towers.

Sphragistics. Study of engraved seals.

Teacherage. Housing provided for a teacher; the academic equivalent of a parsonage or vicarage.

Telmatology. The study of swamps.

Theogony. The study of the genealogy of the gods.

Toponomy. The study of place names.

Trichology. Study of the hair, especially as it relates to baldness.
Vexillology. The study of flags.

Wonk. Current slang for one who studies excessively. A student who
wrote to William Safire on the occasion of a column on student slang
suggests that *wonk* is *know* spelled backward.

TEMPORAL TERMS

—Words of Diverse Duration—

Baton. The stroke that is sometimes used on a clock or watch instead of a number.

Bezel. The rim, usually metal, that holds the glass of a watch or clock in position.

Biduous. Lasting two days.

Bimester. Two months.

Bissextile. The correct term for leap year. The day itself, February 29, is called the *bissextus*.

Chiliad. A period of 1,000 years; a millennium.

Chronon. One billionth of a trillionth of a second.

Decennium. A period of ten years.

Enneaeteric. Occurring every nine years. Pronounced any-ate-eric.

Gnomon. The pin or plate of a sundial that throws its shadow on the dial.

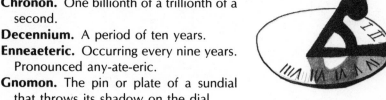

Grandfather Paradox. Science-fiction dilemma that classically occurs when a time-traveler goes back and murders his grandfather before his father is born. The paradox: If this happened, the murderer not only would have never been born, but also would be incapable of going back in time to perform the deed.

Hebdomadal. Happening every seven days. Pronounced heb-do-maddle.

Hesternal. Pertaining to yesterday.

Kalpa. About 4,320 million years in the Hindu calendar.

Light-foot. One billionth of a second.

Lug. The shaped portion of a watch to which the wristband (or, in the case of a pocket watch, the strap) is attached.

Lustrum. A period of five years.

Matutine. Relating to the early morning.

Noctivagant. Wandering by night.

Nudiustertian. Relating to the day before yesterday.

Nycthemeron. The space of 24 hours; day plus night.

Octongentenary. The 800th anniversary. In his book *British Self-Taught: With Comments in American,* Norman W. Schur points out that this is essentially a British word, because Americans are still piddling around with things like bicentennials.

Penteteric. Recurring every five years.

Picosecond. One trillionth of a second. Pronounced peak-o-second.

Piscean Epoch. The 2,000-year era that preceded the present Aquarian Age. The Piscean Epoch ended in March 1948.

Pissing-while. An instant; a short period of time. Used, according to J. E. Barlough in his book *The Archaicon,* from the sixteenth through the nineteenth centuries. He adds, "The allusion is blatantly obvious."

Premundane. Before the creation of the world. *Postmundane* refers to the period after the end of the world.

Quadragenarian. Between 40 and 50 years of age; a person of that age.

Quadrennium. A period of four years.

Quinquennial. An event that occurs every five years.

Quotidian. Recurring each day, especially what is ordinary.

Raith. A Scottish word for three months; a quarter of a year.

Sennight. The space of seven days and nights; half a fortnight.

Shake. One hundred millionth of a second.

Sublapsary. Occurring after the fall of man.

Tertian. Occurring or recurring every third day.

Trinoctial. Lasting three nights.

Vicennial. Every 20 years.

Widdershins. Counterclockwise; to go against the natural direction.

Yestreen. Yesterday evening.

TONGUES

—A Babble of English Languages—

Some of the many ways we speak and write.

Agglomerese. A shortening of language common to people in the military and the civilian bureaucracy. It is typified by the use of initials, acronyms, and portmanteau words. If someone in the U.S. Navy says "CINCLANT is dismayed that BUPERS has not gotten JCS the information it needs to get to SHAPE for the upcoming NATO meeting," you are listening to pure Agglomerese. The term was coined by writer Robert C. Doty in a 1959 article in *The New York Times Magazine* entitled "Parlez-Vous NATO?"

Bafflegab. Alternative term for gobbledygook. Can be used to greater effect with the words *sheer* and *utter.* Term coined by former counsel for the U.S. Chamber of Commerce, Milton Smith, who is quoted in William Lambdin's *Doublespeak Dictionary:* "I decided we needed a new . . . word to describe the utter incomprehensibility, ambiguity, verbosity and complexity of government regulations."

Baltimore-ese. Howard K. Smith once had this to say of Baltimore: "They can't speak English there. They call their city this: Balamer,

Murlin. They call garbage gobbidge. Legal is pronounced liggle. Paramour is their word for power mower. And if you ever ask directions there, remember that Droodle Avenue means Druid Hill Avenue." Some other examples:

Umpahr: Person who calls balls and strikes at Awrioles games.
Pahret: Name of the Pittsburgh baseball team.
Council: Cancel.
Idn't: Is not.

A recent master's thesis written by Ann Marie Hisley of the University of Maryland claims that the key influence in all of this came from the settlers from northern England who colonized Maryland.

Basic English. The invention of Professor C. K. Ogden of England's Orthological Institute, it stands for "British, American, Scientific, International, Commercial" English. It was introduced in 1933 as a quick and easy way of teaching someone to write and speak English. The Basic vocabulary is limited to 850 words that its inventor felt were able to express all fundamental thoughts in English. It features only 400 nouns ranging from *account* to *year.* One gets a flavor of Basic from an article in *The Baltimore Sun* that used Basic to tell how the words were selected:

The selection of the 850 words came about after deep thought about this complex business and the words given were taken because they were the most simple and most necessary. They go around the dangers of connection with tricky groups of letters in words and strange ways of sounding them.

The language was used during World War II to teach Chinese and other Orientals enough English to function with American and English units. "It takes only 400 words of Basic to run a battleship," one advocate told *Time* in 1945; "With 850 words you can run the planet."

Basic has had many staunch supporters—Winston Churchill and Franklin D. Roosevelt to name two—and only a few critics. One critic was Alden H. Smith, who waggishly suggested it would not work as it left out such basics as *ouch* and *plop.*

Cablese. A particular form of expression based on the compression of as much meaning into as few words as possible. It is predicated on the fact that telegram charges have been based on so much per word no matter how long or short the word. Many years ago this took the first prize in an English contest for the longest 12-word cable.

> ADMINISTRATOR-GENERAL'S COUNTER-REVOLUTIONARY INTER-COMMUNICATIONS UNCIRCUMSTANTIATED STOP QUARTERMASTER-GENERAL'S DISPROPORTIONABLENESS CHARACTERISTICALLY CONTRA-DISTINGUISHED UNCONSTITUTIONALIST'S INCOMPREHENSIBILITIES STOP

Cincinnada Dutch. Term used by author and novelist Dorothy Weil in an article in the *Cincinnati Enquirer* magazine to describe the manner of speaking in that city. Some of Weil's prime examples:

> **Wer's ziz office:** Where's his office.
> **Denist:** Dentist.
> **Quarder:** Quarter (not to be confused with *quata,* which is New Yorkese).
> **Er:** Or.
> **Wat's zat fer:** What's that for.

Crosswordese. A vocabulary that is little used outside the confines of crossword puzzle box. They are usually short, vowely, and obscure. In a statement that clears the air of any pretense about crosswords, Eugene T. Maleska, crossword puzzle editor of *The New York Times,* says in his *A Pleasure in Words,* "Who cares that an *anoa* is a Celebes ox, a *moa* is an extinct bird or an *Abo* is a member of an Australian tribe?" Not to be too harsh, some of these words have a certain presence about them, although their use in daily conversation is severely limited. *Oese,* for instance, is the name for the small looped wire used by bacteriologists in making cultures and is pronounced U-say.

Constabulese. The talk of police when they are on duty that dictates that they say "in the vicinity of" instead of *near,* "ascertain as to whether" when they want to *find out,* and "as to why" when *why* would do. This manner of speaking is not limited to the United States. British writer Spike Hughes points out in *The Art of Coarse Language* that in his country the same high-sounding language is used—that is, "utilized and employed." Hughes has collected a number of favorite examples including that from a mobile unit running about "taking informationary numbers."

This is different from the information station house slang that police use among themselves: *hole* for subway, *poke* for pickpocket, *KG* for known gambler, and so forth.

DCD. DCD, or the D.C. Dialect, is an argot that was revealed to the nation during the Watergate era. In their book *The D.C. Dialect* authors Paul Morgan and Sue Scott explore the new language in terms of ten easy lessons (be impersonal, be obscure, be pompous, be evasive, be repetitious, be awkward, be incorrect, be faddish, be serious, be unintelligible) and end with a glossary of DCD words and phrases. A few examples are in order:

English	*DCD*
begin	implement
break-in	entry operation
cover-up	contain the situation
criminal conspiracy	game plan
fired	selected out
kidnap	segregate out
won't work	counterproductive
workable	viable

Educanto: High educational jargon. For instance, proper *Educanto* for textbook is an "empirically validated learning package" and a library is a "media access center." A teacher who is able to operate a movie projector is an "Audio-visually qualified person," and if older kids are allowed to help younger ones, it is known as "cross-age tutoring." A few years ago a group of Texas parents were sent a note from a school principal that baffled the parents but showed the principal's mastery of the jargon. It read in part:

> Our school's cross-graded, multi-ethnic individualized learning program is designed to enhance the concept of an open-ended learning program with emphasis on a continuum of multi-ethnic, academically enriched learning.

In some circles it is known as *Pedageese*.

Gobbledygook. Term for bureaucratic language coined by Representative Maury Maverick when he was the wartime chairman for

FDR's Smaller War Plans Corporation. Maverick was so infuriated with the bloated language in the memos that were landing on his desk that he wrote a scathing memo of his own on the subject, containing such direct lines as, "Anyone using the words 'activation' or 'implementation' will be shot." In 1977 his son, Maury Maverick, Jr., wrote to *The Christian Science Monitor* to reveal how his father came up with the name: "He stated at the time that most bureaucratic language reminded him of his days as a boy back in Texas when he could hear a foolish old turkey gobble endlessly, saying 'gobble, gobble, gobble' and then ending it with a 'gook.'"

Everybody has their pet examples; here are mine:

Anticipatory retaliation: Attacking your enemy on the assumption that he would do the same if given the chance.

Health alteration committee: The name the CIA once gave to one of its own assassination teams.

Individualized learning station: A desk renamed by the U.S. Office of Education.

Information processing center: A typing pool.

Intermodal interface: A term that was translated by former Transportation Secretary William Coleman as, "When you get off the train, a bus is waiting."

Personalized, recreational eco-unit: A garden.

Mellowspeak. Term popularized by Doonesbury cartoonist Garry Trudeau for the "laid back" hip and slangy new language of ego and emotion—a whole new "language trip" that includes such "upfront" expressions as "to go with the flow," "I hear you," "I know where he/she is coming from," "to die for," "to make some space," "to get one's head together," "can/can't relate to it," "high energy," "swing with," "mellow out," and more.

It is called *psychobabble* in a book of the same title by R. D. Rosen, who writes of it as "a set of repetitive verbal formalities that kills off the very spontaneity, candor and understanding it pretends to promote."

Meta-Talk. It has been given various names—"Meta-talk" in a book of the same title by Gerard I. Nierenberg and Henry Calero, "meta-communication" in Julius and Barbara Fast's *Talking Between Lines,* and "super language" by others—but it amounts to the silent messages that are generated when we talk. Examples abound. One that

Paul Dickson/307

is used by the Fasts is the line that bosses use on employees: "Are you sure you're feeling all right this week?" In reality the boss is not asking about the person's health but saying that the person's work is unsatisfactory. The authors of *Meta-Talk* cut through such classic lines as "Oh, don't worry about me" and "I'll do my best" to reveal that the first is often an appeal for help and the second is an admission of failure before the fact.

Noo Yawkese. Sometimes called Brooklynese (though not limited to that borough), this is one of the few distinct manners of speaking that people actively try to shed. One linguist, William Labov, told *The New York Times* in 1971, "A great many New Yorkers feel that it's a compliment to be told 'You don't talk like a New Yorker,' " adding, "The average working-class Philadelphian doesn't see anything wrong with Philadelphia speech but in New York City the average working-class person feels there is something wrong with the way he talks." Some classic examples:

> **Toidy toid and toid:** 33rd and Third.
> **Waddaya dune?** What are you doing?
> **Alodda dem.** A lot of them.
> **Jalettum?** Did you let him?

Padress. Awkward manner of speaking that afflicts those who begin speaking into public address systems, especially at airports. Some of the commonest words in Padress include *de-plane, pre-board,* and *equipment* for airplane. For example, "Due to the late arrival of equipment in the area, the pre-boarding period has been extended." The rules of Padress require that all announcements of great inconvenience ("All planes have been delayed 48 hours"), end with the line "Thank you for your cooperation."

Pittsburghese. One of the more pronounced and easy-to-recognize urban dialects, which, according to University of Pittsburgh linguist Dr. Robert Parslow, has unique speech patterns heard no place else in the world. Some of the words with which to recognize a Pittsburgher:

> **Still:** Steel.
> **Dauntaun:** Downtown, where the streets get "slippy" when it snows.

Yuns: You ones, used the way "You all" is further south.
Gumband: Rubber band.
Worsh: As in Worshington, D.C.
Igle: The national bird, which it is "illigle" to shoot.

Plannish. Plannish is the term that Lloyd A. Kaplan, an analyst for the New York City Planning Commission, created in the late 1960s to cover the "epidemic technicalese used by urban planners to confuse the public." Kaplan told a reporter for *The New York Times* that the single most useful word in plannish is *facility,* meaning "things." "For example, there are waterfront facilities, health facilities, recreation facilities, and," Kaplan added, "even facility facilities." Another example: "Money is never mentioned, as such. Resources is the prime substitute, although expenditures (allocations, appropriations and funds) are also popular." Additionally, planners call those who move from the city "gross out-migrants" and if a planner drives through a neighborhood to look around he is making "a field windshield survey."

R.A.F. Slang. One byproduct of modern warfare is slang, but for reasons that are not clear, those serving in the R.A.F. during World War II produced a remarkably broad and rich slang vocabulary. In 1942 an example of R.A.F. talk along with its translation appeared in *The New York Times:*

Three ropey types, all sprogs, pranged a cheeseye on bumps and circuits. One bought it; the other two went for a Burton. The station-master took a dim view and tore them off a strip. They'd taken along a shagbag wofficer, who was browned off. The queen bee was hopping mad.

Translation:

Three unpopular individuals, all brand new pilots, crashed a wornout airplane while practicing circuits and landings. One was killed; the other two were reprimanded severely. The station commander disapproved strongly and roundly berated them. They had taken along with them a somewhat plain WAAF officer, who was bored. The station's WAAF commander was very angry.

   While the only place this slang can still be heard in full bloom is in the old World War II movies, some of its words and phrases have become part of the language—"good show," "in the drink," "get cracking," "to tick off."

Reverse gobbledygook. A banquet-table form of English that revels in its terse directness. It is the exact opposite of written gobbledygook. It was first discussed in an unsigned article in *Fortune* in 1950, which further explained:

> Thanks to reverse gobbledygook, the less you have to say, the more emphatically you can say it. All one has to do is use certain hard-hitting expressions, and refer as frequently as possible to the fact that these expressions are being used. A sure forewarning of its on-rush, accordingly, is a prefatory announcement by the speaker that he is not going to beat around the bush, pull any punches, pussyfoot, use two-dollar words, or the like. The rest is inevitable; so standardized are the expressions of reverse gobbledygook that an audience would be stunned to attention were a single one of them altered by so much as a word. (One of these days a clever speaker is going to capitalize on this. "Gentlemen," he will say, "I offer a panacea.")

Slurvian. An American dialect without geographic limitations, which was discovered, named, and reported on by John Davenport in an article in *The New Yorker* in 1949. A few examples of phonetically spelled Slurvian:

   Bean. *n.* A living creature, as in *human bean.*

Cactus. *n.* The people in a play or story.
Murca. *n.* Nation to which Slurvians return after Yerpeen trips.
Plight. *adj.* Courteous.

Sociologese. The bloated, awkward language of sociologists. Russell Baker may have had the last word on it when he wrote, "There are many dead languages, but the sociologists' is the only language that was dead at birth."

Strine. Australian way of running words together, often practiced by those who can speak distinct proper English:

> **Emenyjiwant?:** How many do you want?
> **Hammachizit?:** How much is it?

Texlexical. Manner of speaking in Texas, whether it be in a big city like *Yewst'un* or in the *rule* areas of the state. Chase Untermeyer, state legislator, has been involved in the *whored bidness* of collecting fine examples for his Tex-lexicon, which is now in preparation. Several of his best finds were revealed in a recent column by George Will and included:

> **Lowered Barn:** An English poet (1788–1824).
> **Forced:** A large group of trees, as "Lemme showya mah pine forced."
> **Hard:** Employed, as "I hard him to do the job." Also a man's name, as "Mah wife's a cousin of Hard Hughes."

Texlish. Another name for Texlexical. This is the term used by Jim Everhart in his *Illustrated Texas Dictionary of the English Language.* Some examples from Everhart's collection:

> **All crisis:** That embargo which began with the oil embargo.
> **Bob wahr:** Fencing material.
> **Mihyon:** $1,000,000.
> **Tarred:** Exhausted.

Vietlish. Term created by Richard Lingeman for the particular jargon created by official Washington to explain the war in Southeast Asia. It was well described by the late Peter Lisagore: "A whole language was created to minimize that we were in war, and didn't know how to fight it." Although this archly euphemistic language has fallen into disuse since the end of the war, it stands as an example of how lies, ruses, dodges, and distortions can be wrapped in words and simple phrases. Among many, were:

Strategic hamlet: Refugee camp, or as a *New York Times* reporter explained, "A few people are driven together, a roll of barbed wire was thrown over their heads and the strategic hamlet was finished."

Search and destroy: Destroy and then search.

Positive response: One of Lyndon Johnson's terms for bombing.

Incursion: Invasion.

Returnee: Defector.

Structure: A hut, once destroyed. One of a number of "before and after" terms. A bomber pilot explained these in a 1966 letter to the editors of *Aviation Week & Space Technology,* pointing out that once destroyed, a "straw-thatched hut" officially became a "structure," a dead pig or goat, a "pack animal," a splintered set of logs felled across a stream, a "bridge," and a sunken one-man dugout a "boat." This process was called "target verification."

Windyfoggery. The linguistic condition that embraces the gobbledygook of government and business with such afflictions from other fields as pseudoscientific jargon and unintelligible art criticism. This broad term is the creation of Theodore M. Bernstein, who explained that wind and fog do not normally exist in nature, but do in language, where "the greater the wind the more impenetrable the fog."

TRAVEL WORDS

—Terms in Transit—

Aclinic-line. The imaginary location near the equator where the magnetic needle has no dip.

Afterbody. Something (debris, another craft) that follows a spacecraft in orbit.

Apolune. The point in lunar orbit that is farthest from the moon. *Perilune,* on the other hand, is the point in the orbit closest to the center of the moon.

Bollard. The traditional name for the large posts to which ships are tied, bollard is increasingly being used to describe those inverted rubber cones used to mark traffic lanes and detours. The word is also used to describe the posts that are strategically placed near supermarkets to keep you from walking off with a shopping cart.

Break-off phenomenon. The feeling that occasionally occurs during high-altitude flight when one feels totally separated from the earth and human society.

Bumping post. The upright device at the end of a railroad track to keep the train from rolling too far.

Afterbody

Calash. The upper, collapsible portion of a baby carriage.

Cat's paw. A slight breeze that shows itself on the surface of the sea as a slight ripple.

Cisatlantic. On this side of the Atlantic. The opposite of transatlantic.

314/WORDS

Bollard

Paul Dickson/315

Davit. Crane used to hold a lifeboat that is used to swing it out over the water and lower it.

Deadlight. Metal covering clamped over portholes in storms.
Diaphragm. The flexible corridors between railroad passenger cars.
Eyre. The circuit taken by itinerant judges.
Fiddles. Rails or battens placed across shelves on boats and ships to keep objects in place when the vessel rolls and pitches at sea.

Fishybacking. Transporting loaded trailers by ship, akin to piggyback-ing, which is moving trailers by railroad flatcars.

Fluke. One of the points of an anchor; designed to catch on the bottom.

Frog. An X-shaped railroad track crossing where one line intersects another. Some-times called a diamond.

FTL. Faster-Than-Light travel. Modern physics shows that it is impossible, but science fiction writers have found a number of imaginative ways around the objection of im-possibility.

Gnotobiotics. The use of germ-free animals for use in space probes.

Gobbles. To say that a car gobbles is to say that it runs fast, presumably gobbling up gasoline.

Gurry. An old New England sailor's term for a combination of sewage, decayed fish, or whale meat, rancid oil, and brackish seawater. Gurry gave off a powerful smell that tended to stay with a ship even when it washed down.

Guzzle. Cape Cod talk for a channel between two sandbars.

Howdah. The seat on the back of an elephant. (Howdah is also New Yorkese for "How to," as in "Jatellum howdah get dere?")

Impact attenuation devices. Back in the 1960s Representative H. R. Gross of Iowa issued periodic Gobbledygook Awards for overblown terms for simple objects. One award went to the Bureau of Public Roads for calling the old oil drums used to block off construction areas "impact attenuation devices." Gross also honored the Air Force for calling a parachute an "aerodynamic personnel decelerator" and the Army for calling a shovel a "combat emplacement evacuator."

Intermodal transportation facility. The name given to a bike rack in a train station by the Department of Health, Education and Welfare in the 1970s.

Jiggle-bar. Noisy rough-spot intentionally put on a road or highway to keep drivers awake or alert them to a toll area or something equally important. They are also known as *rumble strips.*

Lagan. Goods that have been sunk but that are marked with an attached buoy. Not to be confused with *flotsam* (floating debris) and *jetsam* (cargo thrown from a ship to lighten it).

Lanai. Hotel term for a private terrace or balcony that comes with a room. Pronounced lan-eye.

Lightening holes. Holes found in bridge elements to make them lighter. Lightening holes are also found on ships.

Lingtow. A rope for pulling contraband ashore.

Mobility aid. What the Space Agency calls a handrail or footrail in a spacecraft. Used in NASA descriptions of Skylab and the Shuttle.

Oilberg. Alternate name for the new Very Large Crude Carriers (VLCC). These gargantuan ships are the largest moving things ever built by man, with decks as long as a quarter of a mile. These ships employ the iceberg principle, in that 80 percent of their great size is underwater.

Paul Dickson/319

Ornithopter. A flying machine with wings that flap.

Pantograph. The upward-pushing apparatus that extends between a streetcar or electric train and the overhead electric wires from which it gets its power.

Pirogue. A canoe fashioned from the hollowed trunk of a single tree. Pronounced pier-ogg.

Pillowed. Stewardess term, as in "Would you like to be pillowed?"

Plimsoll mark. A circular mark prominently displayed on a ship's hull. It is used as a safe-load line to indicate how heavily the ship can be loaded. Named for Samuel Plimsoll (1824–1898), British statesman and maritime reformer.

Rack rate. Hotel equivalent of "list price"—the officially stated price of a room from which discounts are sometimes made.

Scud. Aviator's term for small masses of cloud moving below a solid deck of higher clouds.

Sinistrodextral. Moving from left to right.
Snubbing post. The post around which a ship's line is thrown.

Taffrail. The rail around the stern of a ship.

Thwart. The seat in a small boat.

Viaggiatory. Traveling frequently.

Waveson. Goods floating on the water after a shipwreck.

Waywise. Skilled or talented at not getting lost.

Wheel guards. The small cement or asphalt bars that you park your car wheels against in parking lots.

Xenodocheionology. A love of hotels and inns. Pronounced zeno-deckion-ology.

WORD WORDS

—A Glossary of Terms for Things We Say and Write—

Abecedarius. An acrostic in which the initial letters appear in alphabetical order. This is one of several acrostic words. Another is *mesostich,* which refers to an acrostic composition in which the middle letters form a word or phrase. The garden-variety acrostic is a composition in which the first letter of each line forms a word or message. An acrostic in which the final letters form a word or phrase is called a *telestich.*

Ablaut. The changing of a vowel in the root of a word to modify use or meaning, as the change from get to got.

Acromonogrammatic. Applied to a passage or verse in which each line begins with the letter with which the preceding line ended.

Addisonian termination. The scholarly name for the habitual practice of using prepositions to end sentences with. Named for Joseph Addison, who was addicted to the terminal preposition. Among others, Winston Churchill sided with Addison when he termed the rule against sentences ending in prepositions "nonsense up with which I will not put."

Adoxography. Writing cleverly on a trivial subject.

After-wit. The wisdom or cleverness that comes too late. Clifton Fadiman's term was *staircase wit,* or "what you would have said if you had happened to think of it at the time."

Amphigory. Writing that sounds good but lacks sense.

Anacolouthon. A sudden switch from one grammatical construction to another in the same sentence: a sudden shift of direction in the middle of an utterance. "I can't believe that you—Oh! forget it!" Pronounced anna-co-luthon.

Ananym. A name written backward.

Aphaeresis. Omitting the initial letter or letters of a word—'neath for beneath or 'gainst for against. Pronounced afar-ee-sis.

Aphthong. A letter or letters not sounded in a word.

Apocope. Omitting some of the final letters of a word—for instance, tho' for though.

Aposiopesis. Breaking off in the middle of a statement, as if suddenly realizing that someone's feelings are being hurt or about to be hurt: "The reason that people find you so hard to get along with, Fred, is that . . . well, I'd better not say it."

Battology. Excessive repetition in speech or writing.

Boustrophedon. A system of writing in which the words proceed from right to left for a line and then head back in the other direction as in:

> The quick brown fox jumped
> .head dog's lazy the over

The early Greeks experimented with this system and gave it a name that means, literally, "as the ox turns." It refers to the way in which an ox moves when ploughing a field.

Cacography. Bad spelling; cramped or indistinct writing.

Catagraph. First draft.

Chiasmus. A change in word order in two parallel phrases or lines: Chess is the game of kings and the king of games.

Clerihew. A short biographical verse-form created by E. Clerihew Bentley. A typical example:

> *Sir Humphry Davy.*
> *Abominated gravy.*
> *He lived in the odium*
> *Of having discovered Sodium—*

Paul Dickson/323

Cheville. An unnecessary word. In poetry, a word used to extend the length of a line.

Chiastic. Inverting words in otherwise similar phrases or sentences: "He went to the door, to the door went he."

Cledonism. Using circumlocution to avoid using words believed to be unlucky; for example, counting "twelve, twelve plus one, fourteen . . ."

Counterword. A word that has been used so much it has lost its original meaning: *darling, great,* and *cool,* for example.

Dialect geography. The proper name for the branch of linguistics concerned with the regional differences in vocabulary, accent, and usage. Dialect geographers are, for example, fascinated by the fact that a *hero* in New York City is a *grinder* or *torpedo* elsewhere in New York State, an *Italian* in northern New England, a *hoagy* in Philadelphia, a *sub* in Washington, D.C., and so forth.

Diasyrm. Damning with faint praise.

Digraph. A single sound expressed by writing two letters—*th, ph,* etc.

Dithyramb. A wild, emotional outpouring, whether it take the form of a poem, speech, hymn, song, or writing.

Doublet. An unwanted repetition of letters, words, or passages. The newsletter *Editorial Eye* has commented on them:

> Doublets most often occur within wordds and figures (1,50000), between tween words, and at the end of a line and the beginning beginning of the next.

Elide. To slur or cut off, as a final vowel.

Emblem poetry. A poem arranged typographically into a recognizable shape that suggests the subject of the poem. Pyramids, butterflies, crosses, wineglasses, and columns are among the most common forms. Sometimes called *shaped verse.* Here is an example, an old prohibitionists' poem:

TURNING THE WINE-CUP.

BY JOHN P. TROWBRIDGE.

Hail! all ye children of this land!
A cheerful, mirthful, numerous band,
With your eager faces
And your graces,
Come,
Come,
Come,
Every one,
And let us
Take
Hold
Upon
This
WINE CUP,
Yes,
This
Great
WINE CUP,
This red wine cup,
This CRUEL wine cup,
This accursed wine cup,
This all-intoxicating cup,
That from the ancient times
Has been filling up with crimes,
And with anguish and with tears,
And with sin, and hate, and fears,
And with bitter pains and dread,
And with cursings strongly said;
While it slowly swelleth higher,
Higher, with an all-consuming fire
That from out the lustrous wine
Darts its forked flame, to twine
Round its victims, like a breath
Mixed with want, or woe, or death.
Ah! dear children, come and stand,
One great Home Guard in the land;
Take this treacherous, gilded cup,
Take and place it right side up;
Right side up, in glebe and town,
Which always should be upside down.
And let
The fears,
And wine,
And tears
Escape
Forevermore.
From the Home Guard.

Embolalia. Hesitation forms in speech—*you know*'s, *um*'s, *uh*'s, extra *okay*'s, and, like, other things said when we aren't sure what to say. Right? Okay?

Epibole. Beginning consecutive clauses or statements with the same word, for rhetorical effect.

Epizeuxis. The repetition of a word, for emphasis.

Eponym. A real or mythical person whose name is given to an invention, attribute, institution, nation, etc. The earl of Sandwich, Lord

Cardigan, and the earl of Davenport are among the most famous examples in English.

Escape words. Words used in place of those which might be considered sacrilegious or obscene. *Golly, gosh,* and *gad* are all escape words for God. It has also been referred to as "Deconic swearing."

Grammatolatry. The worship of words.

Grues. Term coined by Robert Louis Stevenson to describe the morbid rhymes popular in Victorian times. Many featured "Little Willie" and a few are still recalled from time to time, such as this high school mnemonic for chemical formulae:

> *Little Willie is no more,*
> *For what Little Willie thought was H_2O*
> Was H_2SO_4.

Hendiadys. The figure of speech in which one idea is stated by the use of two words joined by "and"—e.g., "Look and see if anyone is coming."

Holophrase. A single word that expresses a complex idea.

Homonym slip. The use of one homonym for its counterpart—*too* instead of *two, there* instead of *their,* and so forth.

Hyperbaton. The transposition of words, usually to create a different effect. Example, "He wandered earth around."

Hyperurbanism. A usage that comes from the overcorrection of "bad" English; giving an overly elegant pronunciation to a word. Examples: using "she and I" excessively; pronouncing the *t* in *often.*

Idioglossia. The invented speech of children who are closely related, used for private communication.

Klang association. Hearing one word in the sound of another and being influenced in our use or understanding of it. *Fakir* suggests *fake,* but has nothing to do with that word. *Dastardly* has the klang of *bastard* in it, and *noisome* is offensive but generally quiet. It can be assumed that certain words and meanings die out because the klang is too great, such as may have been the case with the old plural form of penny, *penis,* and the all-but-forgotten word of "thrush-like, looking like a thrush," which was *turdiform.*

Lethologica. The temporary inability to recall a word or a name: that which is on the tip of your tongue.

Lipogram. A piece of writing that lacks a certain letter or letters. E. V.

Wright's novel *Gadsby* is a 50,000-word lipogram without any *e*'s. Wright, whose book was published in 1939, wrote the whole thing with the *e*-typebar of his typewriter tied down. Cedric Adams once pointed out that a natural lipogram takes place in counting. One can count to a thousand before using an *a* in spelling a number.

Logodaedaly. The capricious coining of words.

Logogogue. Person who lays down the law concerning words and their use.

Logomachy. A dispute about words and their meanings.

Meiosis. The opposite of *hyperbole*—making less of something rather than more of it. For instance, saying that winning the Nobel prize was "not bad." Columnist Sydney J. Harris has pointed out that the British have a passion for meiosis. "They say 'not half bad' about something we would call terrific, call a World War 'the late unpleasantness,' and the Atlantic Ocean a 'pond.'"

Merism. A figure of speech in which a whole is expressed by two contrasting parts: young and old, head to foot, and ins and outs are all merisms.

Metanalysis. Word misdivision that sometimes leads to amusing results; e.g., Londonderry Air becoming London derriere.

Metotymy. Replacing the name of one thing for the name of another, such as saying "today the White House announced . . ." when it is understood that you mean the President or his administration.

Misguggle. A sentence or passage that is worked over by so many hands that it is no longer intelligible; any form of mishandling. This old Scottish term for bad handling has found new users in recent years, including some in computers who talk of misguggled data and misguggled programs.

Mnemonic device. Something, often a sentence or series of words, that helps one to remember something else; an aid to memory. "Did Mary Ever Visit Bill?" can be used to recall the order of English peerage (duke, marquess, earl, viscount, baron).

Orthoëpy. The study of pronunciation. The fascinating thing is that some orthoëpists pronounce with an emphasis on the *or* while others stress the *tho*.

Palindrome. Word or passage that reads the same forward and backward. "Sex at noon taxes" and "Dennis and Edna sinned" are two sentence-palindromes.

Palinode. A poem that retracts something the poet said earlier. One of the most famous palinodes was written by Gelett Burgess, who wrote "The Purple Cow":

> I never saw a Purple Cow,
> I never hope to see one;
> But I can tell you anyhow,
> I'd rather see than be one.

It became so popular that five years later, in 1900, he wrote:

> Ah, yes, I wrote "The Purple Cow"—
> I'm sorry now I wrote it!
> But I can tell you anyhow,
> I'll kill you if you quote it.

Panagram. A sentence or verse containing all of the letters of the alphabet. Often used to test typewriters, i.e., "The quick brown fox . . ." Here are several fine examples for people tired of the quick brown fox:

> Pack my box with five dozen liquor jugs.
> Waltz, nymph, for quick jigs vex Bud.
> Jackdaws love my big sphinx of quartz.
> The five boxing wizards jump quickly.

Paragoge. The addition of a meaningless sound to the end of a word such as the New England *r* sound heard at the end of law*r* and umbrella*r*.

Paralipsis. A statement that pretends to conceal what is really said. For example, "I will not call him a mean-spirited lout, because this is neither the time nor the place for character assessment."

Paronomasia. Punning, a playing on words.

Pasimology. The art of speaking through gestures.

Pathetic fallacy. Ascribing human passions to nature: cruel snows, caressing clouds, and the like.

Phatic. Pertaining to speech that is meant to express friendship or sociability rather than convey information. The conversation in a receiving line is invariably phatic.

Pleonasm. The introduction of superfluous words: the use of more words than are required for the expression of an idea; excessive verbiage; over-explanation in which too many words are used.

Portmanteau word. A word formed by the blending of two or more other words. Smog, for instance, is a portmanteau of the words *smoke* and *fog*. The term comes from *Alice in Wonderland* and appears as Alice asks Humpty-Dumpty to explain the word *slithy* from the opening line of *Jabberwocky:* "Twas brillig and the slithy toves . . ." He tells Alice, "Well 'slithy' means lithe and slimy . . . You see there are two meanings packed into one word." A small collection of examples:

Bash. Bat + Mash.

Bit. Binary + Digit. (Computerese.)

Blot. Black + Spot.

Blotch. Blot + Blotch.

Bonk. Bank + Conk.

Brunch. Breakfast + Lunch.

Chortle. Chuckle + Snort. Lewis Carroll's most famous portmanteau word.

Clump. Chunk + Lump.

Clash. Clap + Crash.

Contrails. Condensation + Trails.

Convair. Conveyed by Air.

Doff. As "to doff one's clothes," from *do off.*

Don. As "to don a garment," from *do on.*

Flare. Flame + Glare.

Flurry. Flutter + Hurry.

Flush. Flash + Blush.

Frumious. Fuming + Furious, from Lewis Carroll's *Jabberwocky.*

Gidget. Girl + Midget (1959).

Knoll. Knell + Toll.

Liger. Lion + Tiger. The offspring of a male lion and a female tiger. The opposite mating produces a *tigon.*

Mimsy. Miserable + Flimsy. A Lewis Carroll creation from the *Jabberwocky.*

Mingy. Mean + Stingy.

Mixaphor. Mixed + Metaphor, a short form created by Theodore M. Bernstein.

Motel. Motor + Hotel.

Napalm. Naphthene + Palmitate.

Noxema. Nox (for knocks) + Eczema, commercial skin preparation.

Pixel. Picture + Element.

Porridge. Pottage + Porrets.

Quasar. *Qua*si-*S*tellar radio resource.

Slang. It has been guessed that this originally came from Slovenly + Language.

Slithy. Slimy + Lithe. From Lewis Carroll's *Jabberwocky.*

Slosh. Slop + Slush.

Smaze. Smoke + Haze.

Smice. Smoke + Ice. A fog containing ice crystals.

Smist. Smoke + Mist.

Smog. Smoke + Fog. The *Oxford English Dictionary* says that this word was created in 1905 by a Dr. Des Voeux.

Smust. Smoke + Dust.

Socialite. Social + Light. (This blend, which first appeared in *Time,* January 7, 1929, may be that magazine's most successful coinage.)

Sparcity. Sparseness + Scarcity.

Splatter. Splash + Spatter.

Splutter. Splash + Sputter.

Telethon. Television + Marathon.

Transistor. Transmitter + Resistor.

Twirl. Twist + Whirl.

Prolepsis. In a narrative or drama, a hint of coming events.

Psellism. Defective pronunciation.

Retronym. A noun that has been forced to take on an adjective to stay up-to-date. For instance, *real cream* and *live performance* are retronyms for cream and performance that have been brought about with the advent of nondairy creamers and prerecorded performance. The term was created by Frank Mankiewicz, president of National Public Radio.

Rhopalic. A line or passage in which each word has one more letter or syllable than the one before it.

Rumbelow. A combination of meaningless syllables, such as the "yo-ho-ho's" of rowing sailors.

Sandwich words. Words of two or more syllables that have been split open and spread with spicy filling. *indegoddampendent, obligoddamgation,* and *irrefuckingsponsible* are classic examples. In *Anat-*

omy of Dirty Words, author Edward Sagarin tells of several British soldiers who were playing cards with the radio on during World War II. One of the cardplayers realized that he was hearing the infamous Axis Sally and yelled to one of his buddies sitting nearer the radio, "Turn off the propafuckinganda!"

The term *sandwich word* was coined by linguist Harold Wentworth. The number of sandwich words that have been created over the years is tredamnendous and they exist in fandamntastic variety.

Schizoverbia. The phenomenon that occurs when one takes a compound word, splits it, and turns it into a descriptive phrase. For instance, calling income tax forms the most "rigged up marole" imaginable or calling children "ragged little muffins." The term was coined by Frederick Packard in a 1946 *New Yorker* article entitled *"Schizoverbia."*

Semantic infiltration. Term created by Fred C. Ikle to describe the process by which we come to use the language of our adversaries in describing political or military situations. For instance, calling invading forces "peacekeeping forces," or "liberation forces."

Syncope Omitting some of the middle letters of a word, usually for the sake of brevity—med'cine for medicine or o'er for over.

Tacenda. Those things that should not be mentioned.

Tapinosis. Use of degrading diction when talking of someone.

Thunk. A light verse that plays with syntax. An example that appeared in an article on thunking in the magazine *Country Journal* goes like this:

> *The peeping Tom designed to peep*
> *At Miss Godiva when she's sleep,*
> *Wherefore on hands and knees he crept*
> *And underneath her curtain pept.*
>
> *Behind him, though, a watchman crope,*
> *Pursuing peepers while she stope,*
> *and pounced on Tom because he pope.*

Tmesis. The separation of a compound word by an intervening word or words.

Univocalic. A piece of writing containing only one vowel. "Eve's Legend," a short story written by Lord Holland in 1824, omits all the vowels except *e*. The first paragraphs of "Eve's Legend":

> Men were never perfect; yet the three brethren, Verses, were ever esteemed, respected, revered, even when the rest, whether the select few, whether the mere here, were left neglected.
>
> Peter wedded Hester Green—the slender, stern, severe, erect Hester Green. The next, clever Ned, wedded sweet Ellen Heber.
>
> Steven, ere he met the gentle Eve, never felt tenderness; he kept kennels, bred steeds, rested where the deer fed, went where green trees, where fresh breezes, greeted sleep.

Xenoglossia. Understanding a language one has never learned.

WORDS AT WORK

—A Mix of Terms from the Salesroom, Law Office, and Other Places Where People Make a Living—

Additur. The power of the court to increase the amount of money awarded to a plaintiff by a jury.

Asporation. The act of illegally taking things and carrying them away.

Barratry. The stirring up of lawsuits or quarrels. Often applied to lawyers who inspire suits they benefit from.

Beback. Pejorative name used by salesmen to describe prospective customers who leave saying they will be back but are never seen again. The word sounds especially good in context: "If you are going to stereotype all salesmen as dishonest, then all customers might be stereotyped as chiselers, squirrels, flakes, pipe smokers, bebacks." (An article in *The Washington Post* by salesman Bill Adams.)

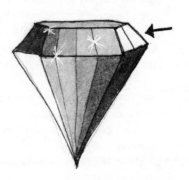

Bezel. An upper facet of a cut gem. It is above the *girdle* but beneath the *table*.

Bulletproof. Said of a contract or other document that has no loop-holes.

Byte. Computerese for a groups of bits, often eight, that are convenient to work with. A bit is an abbreviation for *bi*nary digi*t*.

Cartnapping. Retail food industry term for the theft of shopping carts.

Chad. The droppings of a computer card when it has been punched up with information.

Champerty. Taking over a lawsuit being brought by another, either by buying the other person's claim or sharing the winnings. Champerty is illegal.

Congeneration. Generation of electricity from a source that would be normally wasted—wood chips, steam that escapes into the air, trash, etc.

Escheat. The state acquiring money or property because the proper owner cannot be found.

Estoppel. In court, being stopped from proving something because something said before shows the opposite. For instance, if one signs a deed, he can be *estopped* later from going to court to prove that it is wrong.

Firmware. Data-storage devices and other elements of a computer system that are neither hardware nor software.

Fungible. Things which are easily replaced with other things. A pound of coffee, for instance, is fungible, while a Monet is not.

Gazump. In real estate, raising the price of a property after a deal has been struck.

Gentrification. The process by which the well-off swarm into an old neighborhood, rehabilitate the houses, escalate property values, and attract new businesses. It forces out the poor, who cannot afford to live in the area anymore.

Issue. Lawyer's word for children. When the will of John B. Kelly, millionaire contractor and father of Princess Grace, was read, it contained this small lecture on legalese: "Kids will be called 'kids' and not 'issue,' and it will not be cluttered up with 'parties of the first part,' 'per stirpes,' 'perpetuities' . . . and a lot of other terms that I am sure are only used to confuse those for whose benefit it was written."

Liveware. Computer scientists, technicians, and other humans found around computers; what is left when you eliminate hardware and software.

Mingling. Current real estate term for one or more unrelated single people, couples, or families sharing a house or apartment for the purpose of saving money and coping with inflation.

Modesty panel. The name of an extra panel on a secretary's desk that makes it difficult to look at her legs.

Mooch. Term used in the automobile trade for a customer who thinks he can outsmart the salesman. Mooches often carry calculators into the showroom.

Multure. The miller's fee for grinding grain.

Nibble. Half a byte.

Novation. The substitution, by agreement, of an old contract for a new one with all of the rights under the old now ended.

Ranchplex. Two-story houses with no basement, current realtor's term.

Remittitur. The power of a judge to decrease the amount of money awarded to a plaintiff by a jury.

Replevin. A lawsuit to get back personal property in the hands of another.

Seisin. Full and complete ownership and possession of land.

Sharpshooter. Current legal slang for the lawyer who aims at loopholes.

Trover. An old type of lawsuit involving property in which you claimed a piece was lost and showed that it was now in the hands of another. It got around the difficult business of actually showing that the property was taken.

Twitching. Northwoods term for dragging a log along the ground with the help of a *scoot,* a short, stubby sled.

Usufruct. Old legal term for the right to use something as long as it is not broken, used up, or changed.

Waldo. Mechanical hands used to extend human hands, such as are used in handling nuclear material. The name comes from a science fiction story, "Waldo," by Robert A. Heinlein, in which such hands were envisioned.

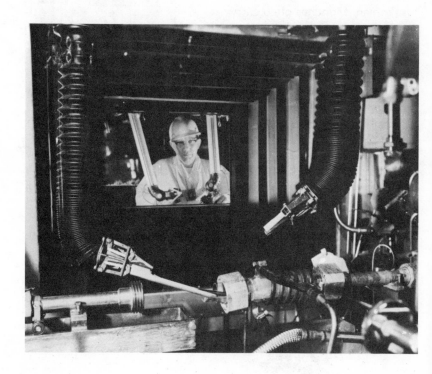

Wall-breaking. Variation on the theme of a ceremonial groundbreaking; for instance, a bank that is about to install an electronic teller or a drive-up window may choose to hold such an event, replete with a ceremonial sledgehammer.

WRITTEN WORDS

—A Font of Printer's, Writer's, and Editor's Terms—

Ascender. That part of a letter which rises above the main body, as in *b*.

Bastard title. The title of a book printed by itself on the odd page preceding the full title page. Also called *half-title* and *bas-title*.

Below the fold. A reference to a page-one newspaper story that is important but not important enough to appear above the fold.

Best food day. The day of the week on which a newspaper places heavy emphasis on food or carries a special food section. The "best food day" is therefore the best day to advertise food.

Biblioclast. A destroyer of books.

Bildungsroman. A novel that specifically deals with a young man's road to maturity. Created from the German word *bildung,* for growth, and the French *roman,* for novel.

Blow-in card. The name of the piece of paper that falls out of a magazine and falls into your lap. These cards, usually appeals to subscribers, are also known as *lap cards.*

Breaker. A biblioclast who rips illustrated books apart to sell the plates individually.

Card plate. Book page that contains a list of books by the same author. The card plate traditionally backs the bastard title page.

Catchword. Word at the head of a page, such as those found at the tops of pages in dictionaries.

Ceremonial opening. Beginning a chapter of a book with a large ornamental letter.

Circus makeup. The use of many different typefaces on one page to create attention.

Descender. That part of a letter which falls below the main body, as in *p* and *q*.

Doublet Doublet. Matter that is set by mistake a second time.

Ear. A small box of information to the right or left of the title line of the front page of a newspaper. Ears commonly contain weather synopses, the edition (Late City Edition), or the paper's slogan.

Elhi. Publishing jargon for the elementary through high school book market. Also, known more widely as *K-12* (that is, Kindergarten through twelfth grade).

Etaoin shrdlu. Two words produced when one runs his fingers down the two vertical left-hand rows of a linotype machine. Traditionally, if a mistake was made, the operator would run his finger down one or both of these lines to fill in the line, which would be discarded later. Since they were sometimes left in by accident, newspapers have been known to inform us that, "The Revolutionaries were running short of ammunition, medical supplies, fund and etaoin shrdlu."

French fold. Arrangement by which all the printing is done on one side of a page and then the page is folded so that the blank side does not show, such as is done with most greeting cards.

Furniture. Pieces of wood or metal that are used to create margins or white spaces in printing.

Grangerize. To illustrate a book by adding your own prints, photographs, and clippings. The term comes from James Granger, who published his *Biographical History of England* with pages left blank for just this purpose.

Gutter. The space created by the inner margins at the fold of a book.

Incavo. The hollowed-out portion of an intaglio or engraved work.

Index. In addition to the one appearing in the back of a book, an index is a hand that the reader should take special notice of.

Lobster trick. The newspaper shift that comes on after the last edition has gone to press. It is usually a reduced shift that comes on in the early morning hours.

Off its feet. Term for type that is not standing straight and is making an incomplete impression.

Opisthosgraphy. Writing on the back of a piece of paper.

Palimpsest. Parchment that has been written on, erased, and then written on again.

Paste-down. The half of the endpaper that lines the inside front cover of a hardback book. The other half is called the *free endpaper*.

Peçuliars. Infrequently used characters in a type font. Like § ¿ £

Pell. Parchment in a roll.

Pi. Printer's term for mixed type; jumbled, unusable type.

Piling. Typing term for those times when letters pile on top of one another. Like *o*.

Recto. The front side of a book leaf; the right-hand page of a book, which always bears an odd page number.

River. Undesired band of white space that runs through a number of lines of type because one word in each line ends at a given point.

Second Coming type. The largest, boldest headline type available to a newspaper.

Sinkage. The lowered position of type matter on a page that starts a chapter or special section.

Slug. Very brief identifying headline used at the top of the continued portion of a newspaper or magazine article. The slug for an article headlined "Administration Plans Massive Budget Cuts" might simply say "Budget."

Tail. The margin at the bottom of a book page. The upper margin is called the *head.*

Topstain. Color applied to the top edge of book pages. It is usually a darker color, as the purpose of topstain is to prevent fingerprints from soiling the top of the book.

Verso. The left-hand page of a book, bearing an even page number; the reverse side on the leaf.

Where list. A list accompanying a graph or diagram that gives the values of symbols and letters.

Widow. A line containing an awkwardly small amount of type, such as part of a word.

Wrongfont. In printing, a piece of type of a face different from the other letters around it.

THE LAST WORD

A passion for words is not something that can be turned on and off like a faucet. So it follows that just because this collection has been exhibited, there is no reason to stop collecting. In fact, the urge gets stronger.

At present I am just beginning a new set of things to collect, including these:

—*A CB Atlas of America. Cow Town* (Fort Worth), *Circle City* (Indianapolis), *Lucy Anna* (Louisiana), *Cigar City* (Tampa), and others.

—*Gudgeons.* This is one of those remarkable words with dozens of meanings. In this case gudgeons tend to be obscure and diverse pieces of hardware. A few of the gudgeons I have already collected: (1) A pin holding two pieces of stone together, (2) a ring that fits over a gate hook to keep it in place, (3) the socket for the rudder of a boat, (4) either of the two supporting knobs that keep a cannon in its carriage.

—*A Dieter's List of Fat Names.* A word list for the refrigerator door.

—*A Dutch Dictionary.* For reasons I have yet to figure out, there are dozens of Dutch terms in English (*Dutch rub, Dutch uncle, Dutch oven, Dutch door,* etc.). I hope to establish the definitive Dutch collection. I am also looking for other national names (*German silver, Irish twin, French kiss,* etc.).

—*Klangers.* Words that give the wrong impression—*aprosexia, inspissed, ideotropic,* and so forth.

—*Mibtionary.* The definitive collection of marbles terms.

—*Food Slang.* A rich American tradition including *Cincinnati oysters* (pork products, to short-order cooks), *pep tires* (GI term for doughnuts during World War II), *burnt offerings* (roast beef in the Navy), and the *5B's* (a meal of Boston baked beans and brown bread).

The most important collection I am working on is a collection of *family words.* These are words that Allen Walker Read once described as those which "have had their currency within family units." They are always amusing and sometimes fill important gaps in the language. Here are the first examples I have collected. A few come from friends, the rest were gathered from people who called-in to Norman Mark's radio show in Chicago. I mentioned my interest in family words to Mark and he invited listeners to call them in while I was a guest on his show.

Chizzly. Chilly + Drizzly. A particular kind of day.

FHB. Family Hold Back, a family expression that has gained wide acceptance as a way of telling the family that food is in short supply but that guests are not supposed to know it. Eric Partridge wrote that it dates from the mid-nineteenth century.

GMPOT. One family's response to FHB. It stands for Guests Making Pigs Of Themselves.

Goobies. Collective term for all the things that a teen-ager should not do. It is used in one family as shorthand before the kids go out in the evening: "Beware of the goobies."

Melvin. The rubbery crust that forms on the top of pudding. A third-generation family word believed to go back to a neighborhood kid named Melvin who loved to scrape the "melvin" off pudding.

Mizzled. Being misled in the extreme. From a family that believes there are times when the word misled sounds too tame.

Nephrotyte. A person who "looks good but does nothing."

Phlug. Pocket lint.

Ploop. The roll of fat that commonly appears after the holidays and ploops down over the belt.

Prutt. Sediment at the bottom of a cup of coffee.

Pukele cord. Name created by a 5-year-old for the dried remnant of the umbilical cord that came home from the hospital with his new baby brother. Pronounced puke-il.

Rowley. The knob on the back of an alarm clock that is pulled out to set the alarm. One family sought a name for this knob for years, and then, when driving through Rowley, Massachusetts, it dawned on them that the name fit perfectly.

Show towel. One family's term for a guest towel. Show towel is a more accurate name since guest towels are never used, even by guests.

Snack pockets. Side fat; "love handles."

Sowie. The dark area under the porch.

Yulke. The little grains of dried secretion found in the corner of one's eyes in the morning; dried duck butter. It is pronounced yule-key.

I would love to hear from readers with family words to pass along as well as from those of you with ideas for new collections and additions to those collections in this book. With any luck there will be a *Words II* that will contain, among other things, the world's finest collection of family words. This collector can be reached at Box 80, Garrett Park, MD 20896.

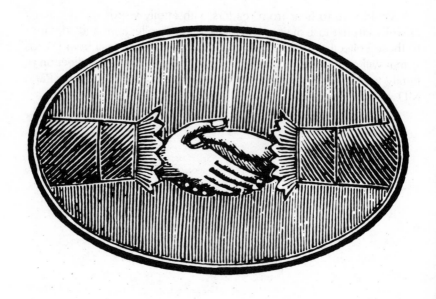

ACKNOWLEDGMENTS & BIBLIOGRAPHY

A number of people have helped me find words for this book. In addition to those I have already acknowledged for their efforts in helping me compile the list of synonyms for *drunk,* I would like to thank the following people for their particular help: Ernest Hildner, Fitzhugh Mullan, Tracy Connors, Bob Skole, Norman Mark, Joe Goulden, Bill O'Neill, Ellen T. Crowley, Bill and Virginia Cressey, and, as always, Nancy Dickson. I would also like to thank Andrew Dickson for his help with the illustrations.

In preparing this book, I have used hundreds of books, pamphlets, magazine and newspaper articles. Here is a listing of the most important sources I used. To conserve space I have not listed the major general-purpose dictionaries which, of course, were invaluable.

Adams, Charles C. *Boontling: An American Lingo.* Austin: University of Texas, 1971.
Adams, J. Donald. *The Magic and Mystery of Words.* New York: Holt, Rinehart and Winston, 1963.

Adams, Ramon F. *Western Words*. Norman, Okla.: University of Oklahoma Press, 1948.

Allison, Norman and Sonia. *Drink's Dictionary*. Glasgow: Collins, 1978.

Bacon, Kenneth H. "When the Navy Says ABRACADABRA It Isn't Really Magic." *The Wall Street Journal* (August 31, 1977), pp. 1, 33.

Barber, Richard and Anne Riches. *A Dictionary of Fabulous Beasts*. Ipswich, England: Boydell Press, 1971.

Barlough, J.E. *The Archaicon*. Metuchen, N.J.: Scarecrow Press, 1974.

Barnhart, Clarence L., Sol Steinmetz, and Robert K. Barnhart, *The Barnhart Dictionary of New English since 1963*. New York: Harper & Row, 1973.

_____. *The Second Barnhart Dictionary of New English*. New York: Harper & Row, 1980.

Barron, John N. *The Language of Painting*. Cleveland: World Publishing, 1967.

Bender, James F. "Ourway Ecretsay Anguageslay." *The New York Times Magazine* (December 31, 1944), pp. 14–15.

Bendick, Jeanne. *How Much and How Many*. New York: Whittlesey House, 1947.

Berg, Paul C. *A Dictionary of New Words in English*. New York: Crowell, 1953.

Bernstein, Theodore M. *Dos, Don'ts & Maybes of English Usage*. New York: Quadrangle, 1977.

_____. *More Language That Needs Watching*. New York: Atheneum, 1962.

_____. *The Careful Writer*. New York: Atheneum, 1978.

Berrey, Lester V. and Melvin Van Den Bark. *The American Thesaurus of Slang*. New York: Crowell, 1952.

Bombaugh, C.C. *Oddities and Curiosities of Words and Literature,* ed. and annot. by Martin Gardner. New York: Dover, 1961.

Borgman, Dmitri A. *Beyond Language: Adventures in Word and Thought*. New York: Scribner's, 1967.

Bowler, Peter, *The Superior Person's Little Book of Words*. The Hawthorne Press (Melbourne, 1979).

British Broadcasting Corp., *More Words*. BBC Publishing (London, 1977).

Brown, Ivor. *A Rhapsody of Words*. London: Bodley Head, 1969.

_____. *A Ring of Words*. London: Bodley Head, 1967.

_____. *A Word in Your Ear*. London: J. Cape, 1942.

_____. *Having the Last Word*. New York: Dutton, 1951.

_____. *I Break My Word*. London: J. Cape, 1951.

_____. *I Give You My Word*. New York: Dutton, 1948.

_____. *Just Another Word*. London: J. Cape, 1943.

_____. *Mind Your Language*. New York: Capricorn, 1962.

_____. *No Idle Words*. New York: Dutton, 1951.

_____. *Say the Word*. New York: Dutton, 1948.

_____. *Words in Our Time*. London: J. Cape, 1958.

Bruton, Eric. *Dictionary of Clocks and Watches*. New York: Bonanza, 1963.

Burgess, Gelett. *Burgess Unabridged.* New York: F.A. Stokes, 1914.

Byrne, Josefa Heifetz. *Mrs. Byrne's Dictionary.* Secaucus, N.J.: Citadel, 1974.

Carling, T.E. *The Complete Book of Drink.* New York: Philosophical Library, 1952.

Carter, John. *ABC for Book Collectors.* New York: Knopf, 1966.

Ciardi, John. *A Browser's Dictionary.* New York: Harper & Row, 1980.

Colby, Elbridge. *Army Talk.* Princeton, N.J.: Princeton University Press, 1943.

Copperud, Roy H. *American Usage and Style: The Consensus.* New York: Van Nostrand Reinhold, 1980.

Crowley, Ellen, ed. *Acronyms, Initialisms and Abbreviations Dictionary.* Detroit: Gale Research, various dates and editions.

Dalrymple, Denis. *Pub Talk.* Henley-on-Thames, England: Gothard House, 1975.

Darling, Charles H. *The Jargon Book.* Aurora, Ill.: Aurora, 1919.

Day, Harvey. *Occult Illustrated Dictionary.* New York: Oxford, 1976.

De Funiak, William Q. *The American-British, British-American Dictionary.* Cranbury, N.J.: A.S. Barnes, 1978.

De Sola, Ralph and Dorothy. *A Dictionary of Cooking.* New York: Meredith Press, 1969.

Dickson, Roy Ward. *The Greatest Quiz Book Ever.* London: Wolfe Publishing, 1974.

Doty, Robert C. "Parlez-Vous NATO?" *The New York Times* (October 18, 1959).

Doxat, John. *International Distillation of Drinks and Drinking.* London: Ward Lock, 1971.

Drepperd, Carl W. *Primer of American Antiques.* Garden City, N.Y.: Doubleday, 1944.

Durant, Mary. *The American Heritage Guide to Antiques.* New York: American Heritage Press, 1970.

Eckler, A. Ross. *Word Recreations.* New York: Dover, 1979.

Ellyson, Louise. *A Dictionary of Homonyms.* Mattituck, N.Y.: Banner Books, 1977.

Espy, Willard R. *An Almanac of Words at Play.* New York: Potter, 1975.

————. *Say It My Way.* Garden City, N.Y.: Doubleday, 1980.

Evans, Bergen. *Comfortable Words.* New York: Random House, 1962.

Ferm, Vergilius. *A Brief Dictionary of American Superstitions.* New York: Philosophical Library, 1965.

Flexner, Stuart Berg. *I Hear America Talking.* New York: Van Nostrand, 1976.

Frazier, George. "Doubletalk." *Life* (July 5, 1943).

Frommer, Harvey. *Sports Lingo.* New York: Atheneum, 1979.

Garber, Aubrey. *Mountainese.* Radford, Va.: Commonwealth Press, 1976.

Gaynor, Frank. *Dictionary of Mysticism.* New York: Philosophical Library, 1953.

Goliad, Ray. *Scholar's Glossary of Sex*. New York: Heinemann, 1968.

Gould, John. *Maine Lingo: Boiled Owls, Billdads, and Wazzats*. Camden, Maine: Down East Magazine Press, 1975.

Hall, Robert A., Jr. *Melanesian Pidgin Phrase-Book and Vocabulary*. Baltimore, Md.: Linguistic Society of America, 1943.

Hayakawa, S.I. *Language in Thought and Action*. New York: Harcourt Brace, 1941.

Haywood, Charles F. *Yankee Dictionary*. Lynn, Mass.: Jackson and Phillips, 1963.

Henke, James T. *Courtesans and Cuckolds: A Glossary of Renaissance Dramatic Bawdy*. New York: Garland, 1979.

Hinch, Derryn. *The Scrabble Book*. New York: Mason/Charter, 1976.

Hinsie, Leland E. and Robert Jean Campbell. *Psychiatric Dictionary*. New York: Oxford University Press, 1960.

Hofford, Tony and Martha Wright. *What's That Word*. Wakefield, R.I.: Times Press, 1954.

Hollander, Zander, ed. *The Encyclopedia of Sports Talk*. New York: Corwin Books, 1976.

Homer, Joel. *Jargon*. New York: Times Books, 1979.

Hook, J.N. *The Grand Panjandrum*. New York: Macmillan, 1980.

Hughes, Spike. *The Art of Coarse Language*. London: Hutchinson, 1974.

Hunsberger, I. Moyer. *The Quintessential Dictionary*. New York: Hart Publishing, 1978.

Hunt, Bernice Kohn. *The Whatchamacallit Book*. New York: Putnam's, 1976.

Jacobs, Jonathan Noah. *Naming-Day in Eden*. New York: Macmillan, 1969.

Jennings, Charles B. *Weigh the Word*. New York: Harper & Brothers, 1957.

Johnson, Burges. *The Lost Art of Profanity*. New York: Bobbs-Merrill, 1948.

Johnstone, William D. *For Good Measure*. New York: Avon, 1977.

Jordanoff, Assen. *Jordanoff's Illustrated Aviation Dictionary*. New York: Harper & Brothers, 1942.

Kimball, Warren Y. *A Selection of Fire Terminology*. Boston: National Fire Protection Association, 1961.

King, Aileen. *Dictionary of Cooking Terms*. London: Forbes Publishing, 1976.

Kurzban, Stan and Mel Rosen. *The Compleat Cruciverbalist*. New York: Van Nostrand, 1980.

Lambdin, William. *Doublespeak Dictionary*. New York: Pinnacle Books, 1979.

Leider, Morris and Morris Rosenblum. *A Dictionary of Dermatological Words, Terms and Phrases*. New York: McGraw-Hill, 1968.

Levinson, Leonard Louis. *Webster's Unafraid Dictionary*. New York: Macmillan, 1967.

Loane, George G. *1,001 Notes on "A New English Dictionary."* Privately published, 1920.

Lucas, Alan. *The Illustrated Encyclopedia of Boating.* New York: Scribner's, 1977.

Maleska, Eugene T. *A Pleasure in Words.* New York: Simon and Schuster, 1981.

Markus, John. *Electronics Dictionary.* New York: McGraw-Hill, 1978.

Mathews, Mitford M. *Americanisms.* Chicago: University of Chicago Press, 1966.

Matthews, C.M. *Words, Words, Words.* New York: Scribner's, 1979.

Mawson, C.O. Sylvester. *The Dictionary Companion.* Garden City, N.Y.: Halcyon House, 1932.

McAdam, E.L. and George Milne. *Johnson's Dictionary: A Modern Selection.* New York: Pantheon, 1963.

McCulloch, Dean Walter F. *Woods Words.* Portland: Oregon Historical Society, 1958.

Mencken, H.L. *The American Language.* New York: Knopf, 1937.

———. *Supplement One: The American Language.* New York: Knopf, 1945.

Mendelsohn, Oscar A., *The Earnest Drinker.* New York: MacMillan, 1950.

Merriam-Webster, *6,000 Words: A Supplement to Webster's Third New International Dictionary.* Springfield, Mass.: G. & C. Merriam Co., 1976.

Michaels, Leonard and Christopher Ricks. *The State of the Language.* Berkeley: University of California Press, 1980.

Milberg, Alan. *Street Games.* New York: McGraw-Hill, 1976.

Mitchell, G. Duncan. *A Dictionary of Sociology.* Chicago: Aldine, 1968.

Morgan, Paul and Sue Scott. *The D.C. Dialect.* New York: The Washington Mews Press, 1975.

Morris, William and Mary. *Morris Dictionary of Word and Phrase Origins,* Vols. I–III. New York: Harper & Row, various dates.

Moss, Norman. *What's the Difference?* New York: Harper & Row, 1973.

Muir, Frank and Patrick Campbell. *Call My Bluff.* London: Methuen, 1972.

Murphy, John J. *The Book of Pidgin English.* Brisbane: W.R. Smith and Paterson, 1962.

Opie, Iona and Peter. *The Lore and Language of Schoolchildren.* London: Oxford University Press, 1959.

Oran, Daniel. *Law Dictionary.* St. Paul, Minn.: West, 1975.

Partridge, Eric. *A Dictionary of Slang and Unconventional English: Two Volumes in One.* New York: Macmillan, 1961.

———. *A Dictionary of the Underworld.* New York: Bonanza, 1961.

———. *The Gentle Art of Lexicography.* New York: Macmillan, 1963.

Pei, Mario and Frank Gaynor. *Dictionary of Linguistics.* New York: Philosophical Library, 1954.

Pei, Mario. *Language of the Specialists.* New York: Funk & Wagnalls, 1966.

———. *The Many Hues of English.* New York: Knopf, 1967.

———. *Words in Sheep's Clothing.* New York: Hawthorne, 1969.

Pflug, Raymond J. *The Ways of Language: A Reader.* New York: Odyssey Press, 1967.

Picken, Mary Brooks. *The Fashion Dictionary.* New York: Funk & Wagnalls, 1973.

Plunkett, E.R. *Folk Names and Trade Diseases.* Stamford, Conn.: Barrett, 1978.

Pollock, Alben J. *The Underworld Speaks.* San Francisco: The Prevent Crime Bureau, 1935.

Quinn, Jim. "A Nose by any Other Name—Would It Still Smell?" *The Washington Post* (October 14, 1977).

Randolph, Vance and George P. Wilson. *Down in the Holler: A Gallery of Ozark Folk Speech.* Norman, Okla.: University of Oklahoma Press, 1953.

Ream, Rev. S. *Curiosities of the English Language.* Central Cleveland, Ohio: Central Publishing House, 1925.

Reid, Alastair. *Ounce, Dice Trice.* Boston: Little, Brown, 1958.

———. *Passwords.* Boston: Atlantic Monthly Press, 1963.

Reifer, Mary. *Dictionary of New Words.* New York: Philosophical Library, 1955.

Rocke, Russell. *The Grandiloquent Dictionary.* Englewood Cliffs, N.J.: Prentice-Hall, 1972.

Safire, William. *On Language.* New York: Times Books, 1980.

Sagarin, Edward. *Anatomy of Dirty Words.* New York: Lyle Stuart, 1962.

Salak, John S. *Dictionary of American Sports.* New York: Philosophical Library, 1961.

———. *Dictionary of Gambling.* New York: Philosophical Library, 1963.

Sayer, Edgar Sheappard. *Pidgin English.* Toronto: Privately published, 1943.

Schaun, George and Virginia. *Words and Phrases of Early America.* Annapolis, Md.: Greenbury Publishing, 1963.

Schur, Norman W. *British Self-Taught: With Comments in American.* New York: Macmillan 1973.

Schwartz, Alvin. *Chin Music: Tall Talk and Other Talk.* New York: Lippincott, 1979.

Severn, Bill. *Place Names.* New York: Ives Washburn, 1969.

Sherk, Bill. *Brave New Words.* Garden City, N.Y.: Doubleday 1979.

Shipley, Joseph T. *Dictionary of Early English.* New York: Philosophical Library, 1955.

———. *Playing With Words.* Englewood Cliffs, N.J.: Prentice-Hall, 1960.

———. *Word Play.* New York: Hawthorne, 1972.

Simon, André L. and Robin Howe. *Dictionary of Gastronomy.* New York: McGraw-Hill, 1970.

Spears, Richard A. *Slang and Euphemism.* Middle Village, N.Y.: Jonathan David, 1981.

Sperling, Susan Kelz. *Poplollies and Bellibones.* New York: Potter, 1977.

Steible, Daniel J. *Concise Handbook of Linguistics*. New York: Philosophical Library, 1967.

Stonebone, Brig. Gen. Cyclops. *A Pamphlet on the Four Basic Dialects of Pig Latin*. Los Angeles: William Murray Cheny, 1953.

Stoutenburgh, John, Jr. *Dictionary of the American Indian*. New York: Philosophical Library, 1955.

Syatt, Dick. *Country Talk*. Secaucus, N.J.: Citadel Press, 1980.

Taylor, A. Marjorie. *The Language of World War II*. New York: Wilson, 1944.

Tyron, Henry H. *Fearsome Critters*. Cornwall, N.Y.: Idlewild Press, 1939.

U.S. Army. *Dictionary of United States Army Terms*. Washington, D.C.: Department of the Army, 1975.

U.S. Department of Labor. *Dictionary of Occupational Titles*. Washington, D.C.: Department of Labor, various dates and editions.

U.S. Nuclear Regulatory Commission. *A Handbook of Acronyms and Initialisms*. Washington, D.C.: NRC, 1979.

VERBIA with Miriam Berg. *A Play on Words*. New York: Macmillan, 1969.

Versand, Kenneth. *Polyglot's Lexicon: 1943–1966*. New York: Links Books, 1973.

Vogt, Arno R. *Can You Classify Sciences?* New London, Conn.: Privately printed, 1958.

Wedeck, Harry E. *Classical Word Origins*. New York: Philosophical Library, 1957.

———. *Dictionary of Aphrodisiacs*. New York: Philosophical Library, 1961.

———. *Dictionary of Magic*. New York: Philosophical Library, 1956.

Weekley, Ernest. *The Romance of Words*. London: John Murray, 1913.

Wentworth, Harold. *American Dialect Dictionary*. New York: Crowell, 1944.

Wentworth, Harold, Flexner Wentworth, and Stuart Berg. *Dictionary of American Slang*. New York: Crowell, 1960.

Weseen, Maurice H. *Dictionary of American Slang*. New York: Crowell, 1938.

Whitbread and Co. *Word for Word: An Encyclopedia of Beer*. London: Whitbread and Co., Ltd., no date.

Whittaker, Otto. *Such Language*. New York: Grosset & Dunlap, 1969.

Wilson, Everett B. *Early America at Work*. New York: A.S. Barnes, 1963.

Winick, Charles. *Dictionary of Anthropology*. New York: Philosophical Library, 1956.

Woods, Ralph L. *How to Torture Your Mind*. New York: Funk & Wagnalls, 1969.

Wright, Joseph. *English Dialect Dictionary*. Oxford, England: Oxford University Press, 1923.

Wyman, Walker D. *Mythical Creatures of the North Country*. River Falls, Wis.: River Falls State University Press, 1969.

It should be mentioned that there are three periodicals that all word collectors and fanciers should consider subscribing to: *Word Ways* (*the* journal of recreational linguistics—Spring Valley Rd., Morristown, N.J. 07960), *Verbatim* (its purpose "to inform, amuse, and entertain" lovers of the English language—Essex, Conn. 06426), and *Maledicta* ("The International Journal of Verbal Aggression"—331 South Greenfield Ave., Waukesha, Wisc. 53186).

INDEX

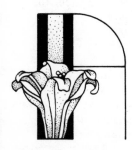

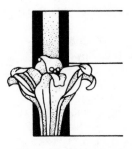

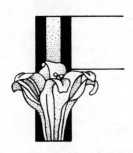

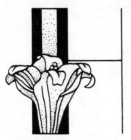

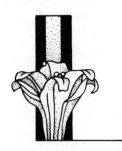

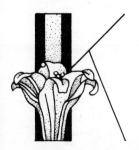

Paul Dickson/359

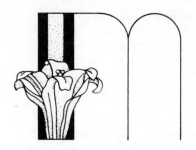

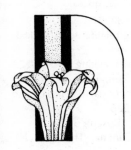

Packard, David, 112
Packard, Frederick, 331
palindrome, longest, 195
Pamphlet on the Four Basic Dialects of Pig Latin, A (Cheny), 98
"Parlez-Vous NATO?" (Doty), 303
parochial school football victories, 3
Parslow, Robert, 308
Partridge, Eric, 142, 228, 231, 234, 342
Pasell, Peter, 196
Peavey, Joseph, 130
Pei, Mario, 213
Peia, Ernest, 73
Pelagius, 137
Pelmore, Bruce, 179
people, words descriptive of, 203–205
People magazine, 233
People's Almanac, The, 224
Personnel Administration, 180, 185
Pettiward, Daniel, 169
pharmacists' notations, 99
Philadelphia Inquirer, The, 232
Philip, Prince, of England, 181
phobia words, 1, 224–227
Picken, Mary Brooks, 83
pidgin, 213–216
Pidgin English (Sayer), 215
Piercy, Marge, 114
Piggy, Miss, 72
Play on Words, A (VERBIA), 245
Pleasure in Words, A (Maleska), 305
pliers, words for, 1–2

Plimpton, George, 184
Plunkett, E. R., 167–168
Polk, James K., 40
Porter, Temple G., 179
portmanteau word, 5–6, 329–330
prescription terms, 99
Price, Roger, 180, 183
printing, words relating to, 160–163, 337–340
prophecy, words relating to, 217–223
Proxmire, William, 184
Psychiatric Dictionary (Hinsie and Campbell), 226
Psychobabble (Rosen), 307
"Punks Are Coming, The" (article), 231
punk words, 228–235
"Purple Cow, The" (Burgess), 327–328

"Que Paso" column, 107
Quintessential Dictionary (Hunsberger), 182

radar, 5, 7
Random House Dictionary of the English Language, 17, 196–197, 231

Paul Dickson/363

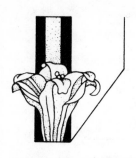

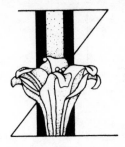